er

A

...oted
to u..   Cormier.
Written   ..perts, the
volume oft.   ...pproaches to the
range of Corn.   ...novels.

The newly-comm.   ...plore the author's earlier best-
known writings for ...   ...as well as his later less critically
examined texts, focusing on key issues such as adolescence, identity,
bullying and child corruption. Recognising Cormier's achievement,
this long-overdue critical resource is essential reading for anyone with
an interest in his influential work and lasting impact on young adult
fiction.

Introduction by Adrienne E. Gavin. Essays by: Holly Blackford,
Stefania Ciocia, Susan Clancy, Amy Cummins, Karyn Huenemann,
Andrew F. Humphries, Pat Pinsent, Dimitrios Politis, Clare Walsh.

Adrienne E. Gavin is Professor of English Literature at Canterbury
Christ Church University, UK.

This latest series of *New Casebooks* consists of brand new critical essays
specially commissioned to provide students with fresh thinking about
key texts and writers. Like the original series, the volumes embrace
a range of approaches designed to illuminate the rich interchange
between critical theory and critical practice.

New Casebooks
Collections of all new critical essays

CHILDREN'S LITERATURE

ROBERT CORMIER
Edited by Adrienne E. Gavin

ROALD DAHL
Edited by Ann Alston & Catherine Butler

C. S. LEWIS: *THE CHRONICLES OF NARNIA*
Edited by Michelle Ann Abate & Lance Weldy

J. K. ROWLING: *HARRY POTTER*
Edited by Cynthia J. Hallett & Peggy J. Huey

FURTHER TITLES ARE CURRENTLY IN PREPARATION

For a full list of published titles in the past format of the New Casebooks series, visit the series page at www.palgrave.com

---

New Casebooks Series

Series Standing Order
ISBN 978–0–333–71702–8 hardcover
ISBN 978–0–333–69345–2 paperback
(Outside North America only)

You can receive future titles in this series as they are published by placing a standing order. Please contact your bookseller or, in case of difficulty, write to us at the address below with your name and address, the title of the series and the ISBN quoted above.

Customer Services Department, Macmillan Distribution Ltd, Houndmills, Basingstoke, Hampshire RG21 6XS, England

---

New Casebooks

ROBERT CORMIER

Edited by

ADRIENNE E. GAVIN

First published 2012 by
PALGRAVE MACMILLAN

Palgrave Macmillan in the UK is an imprint of Macmillan Publishers Limited, registered in England, company number 785998, of Houndmills, Basingstoke, Hampshire RG21 6XS.

Palgrave Macmillan in the US is a division of St Martin's Press LLC, 175 Fifth Avenue, New York, NY 10010.

Palgrave Macmillan is the global academic imprint of the above companies and has companies and representatives throughout the world.

Palgrave® and Macmillan® are registered trademarks in the United States, the United Kingdom, Europe and other countries.

ISBN 978–0–230–31331–6   hardback
ISBN 978–0–230–31332–3   paperback

This book is printed on paper suitable for recycling and made from fully managed and sustained forest sources. Logging, pulping and manufacturing processes are expected to conform to the environmental regulations of the country of origin.

A catalogue record for this book is available from the British Library.

A catalog record for this book is available from the Library of Congress.

Contents

Series Editor's Preface

Welcome to the latest series of New Casebooks. Each volume now presents brand new essays specially written for university and other students. Like the original series, the new-look New Casebooks embrace a range of recent critical approaches to the debates and issues that characterize the current discussion of literature. Each editor has been asked to commission a sequence of original essays which will introduce the reader to the innovative critical approaches to the text or texts being discussed in the collection. The intention is to illuminate the rich interchange between critical theory and critical practice that today underpins so much writing about literature.

Editors have also been asked to supply an introduction to each volume that sets the scene for the essays that follow, together with a list of further reading which will enable readers to follow up issues raised by the essays in the collection.

The purpose of this new-look series, then, is to provide students with fresh thinking about key texts and writers while encouraging them to extend their own ideas and responses to the texts they are studying.

Martin Coyle

Notes on Contributors

Holly Blackford (PhD, University of California, Berkeley) is an Associate Professor of English at Rutgers University-Camden, USA where she teaches and publishes literary criticism on American, children's and adolescent literature. She has published books and articles on Susanna Rowson, Harriet Jacobs, Edith Wharton, Louisa May Alcott, Emily Brontë, Henry James, Mark Twain, L. M. Montgomery, J. M. Barrie, Laura Ingalls Wilder, Frances Hodgson Burnett, Carlo Collodi, E. B. White, Carson McCullers, Harper Lee, Truman Capote, Jamaica Kincaid, Anita Diamont, Julia Alvarez, Shirley Jackson, Margaret Atwood, J. K. Rowling, Stephenie Meyer and Neil Gaiman. Her books include *Out of This World: Why Literature Matters to Girls, 100 Years of Anne with an "e": The Centennial Study of* Anne of Green Gables (ed.), *Mockingbird Passing: Closeted Traditions and Sexual Curiosities* and *The Myth of Persephone in Girls' Fantasy Literature.* She chairs the International Children's Literature Association Article Award Committee and is currently researching queer adult male characters in children's literature as well as the influence of late Victorian developmental psychology on child consciousness in the novel.

Stefania Ciocia is a Senior Lecturer in English at Canterbury Christ Church University, UK where she works primarily on twentieth- and twenty-first-century American and post-colonial writing. Within the field of Children's Literature, her publications reflect her interest in young adult and crossover fiction, as well as in issues of canonicity and in the study of rewritings, sequels and adaptations of classic texts.

Susan Clancy has been an educator all her life, working with young people, adults, parents and fellow educators. After wide experience in schools she moved to the tertiary sector, where she initiated and ran a number of successful subjects and courses relating to children's literature. Her life passion is children's literature and the multiple multimodal texts that have evolved from it. Presently she holds a position as an Adjunct Education Lecturer at Charles Sturt University in Wagga Wagga, Australia, working in research, education, and writing and conducting workshops and seminars in the areas of literature, literacy, multiliteracies and teaching practice. She has worked and written extensively in these areas.

Amy Cummins is Assistant Professor of English at the University of Texas Pan American, USA. She earned a PhD in English at the University of Kansas. She teaches and writes about young adult literature, English education and multiethnic literature. Her work has been published in scholarly journals and in books such as *We Wear the Mask: Paul Laurence Dunbar and the Politics of Representative Reality* (Kent State University Press, 2010). She has recently had articles published in the *ALAN Review* and in *SIGNAL Journal*.

Adrienne E. Gavin is a Professor of English Literature at Canterbury Christ Church University, UK, where she convenes the MA and PhD programmes in English. Her research interests lie in Victorian and Edwardian Literature, Childhood in Fiction, Children's Literature, Crime Fiction, Biography, Textual Editing and Women's Writing. She is author of *Dark Horse: A Life of Anna Sewell* (2004), the proposal for which won the Biographer's Club Prize 2000. She has also produced critical editions of Caroline Clive's *Paul Ferroll* (2008), Henry de Vere Stacpoole's *The Blue Lagoon* (2010), C. L. Pirkis's *The Experiences of Loveday Brooke, Lady Detective* (2010) and Anna Sewell's *Black Beauty* (2012). She is editor of *The Child in British Literature: Literary Constructions of Childhood, Medieval to Contemporary* (2012) and co-editor with Christopher Routledge of *Mystery in Children's Literature* (2001), with Andrew F. Humphries of *Childhood in Edwardian Fiction* (2009; winner of the Children's Literature Association Edited Book Award), and with Carolyn W. de la L. Oulton of *Writing Women of the Fin de Siècle: Authors of Change* (2012). She is currently co-editing with Andrew F. Humphries the essay collection *Transport in British Fiction: Technologies of Movement, 1840–1940*.

Karyn Huenemann (BA, University of British Columbia; MA, University of Toronto; MPhil, Goldsmiths' College, University of London) is an instructor in English Literature at Simon Fraser University in Burnaby, British Columbia, Canada. Her specialties are Children's and Young Adult Literature, Canadian Literature before 1920 and Literature of the South Asian Diaspora. She has also taught issues of post-humanism and fantasy, and is fascinated by the intersection of the post-modern as a literary style with the post-human as a cultural phenomenon; Robert Cormier's *Fade* (1988) is thus a favourite among young adult texts. She has published book chapters on Flora Annie Steel and James De Mille, and a number of articles on Sara Jeannette Duncan and Rudyard Kipling. She is currently working on a critical edition of Sara Jeannette Duncan's *The Path of a Star* for Ronsdale Press in Vancouver.

Andrew F. Humphries has a PhD in English from the University of Kent and an MA from Cambridge University and is a Senior Lecturer in Education at Canterbury Christ Church University, UK. At the University he is mainly engaged as a tutor on the PGCE English Secondary course but also lectures on twentieth-century literature in the Department of English and Language Studies. He is co-editor with Adrienne E. Gavin of the awarding-winning *Childhood in Edwardian Fiction: Worlds Enough and Time* (Basingstoke: Palgrave 2009). His recently completed PhD dissertation is entitled '"A Great Sense of Journeying":Transport and Cultural Transition in the Novels of D. H. Lawrence'. He has also recently presented conference papers on Edwardian fiction, D. H. Lawrence, Rudyard Kipling and H.G. Wells. With Adrienne Gavin he is currently editing *Transport in British Fiction:Technologies of Movement, 1840–1940*.

Pat Pinsent is a Senior Research Fellow in the National Centre for Research in Children's Literature at Roehampton University, London, UK. Children's Literature is the subject matter of most of her 15 books. Since her retirement in 1998, her teaching has mostly been confined to the supervision of MA and PhD students. Among her areas of research interest is the relationship between children's literature and spirituality/religion. She also edits *The Journal of Children's Literature Studies; Ibbylink* (the journal of the British Section of the International Board on Books for Young People) and *Network* (a Christian feminist journal for those interested in spirituality, theology, ministry and liturgy).

Dimitrios Politis (BA, School of Philosophy, University of Athens; MA in 'Children's Literature Studies', University of Warwick, UK; PhD, University of Athens) lectures on Children's Literature and Neohellenic Literature at the University of Patras, Greece. He also lectures on the Theory of Literature (Postgraduate Programme) at the universities of Patras and Athens. As well as an anthologiser of a literary *Anthology* intended for Greek primary school students (2006) and a co-author of the book *Children's Ideas about Children's Literature* (2010) (in Greek) he has also has edited books on Literature for Children and Adolescents, including: *Literary Book and School* (2008) and *Modern Adolescent Literature* (2011) (both in Greek). He is a member of numerous Children's Literature associations and is active in Greek and European (research) projects. His research interests are focused on children's literature as well as on the theory and teaching of literature, and he has published several articles on various aspects of these topics.

Clare Walsh is Senior Lecturer in English at the University of Bedfordshire, UK and Course Leader for the MA in Children's Literature and Culture, which has been taught at the University since 2001. In order to complement her teaching on the MA, she has published a number of journal articles and chapters in books on the work of young adult and crossover writers, including Philip Pullman, John Christopher, Melvin Burgess and Mark Haddon. She is currently co-editing with Pat Pinsent a collection of essays on the representation of class in children's literature.

Introduction

Adrienne E. Gavin

Robert Cormier has been termed 'the founding father of [young adult] dark realism',[1] 'the single most important writer in the whole history of young adult literature',[2] and 'in the top ten writers who are essential reading for an understanding of the development of children's literature in the twentieth century'.[3] Translated into over a dozen languages,[4] Cormier's novels are popular, influential, critically acclaimed, and controversial. Characterised by cinematic style, clear diction, and innovative narrative techniques, his texts feature adolescent protagonists who are pitted mercilessly against corrupt power structures or manipulated by iniquitous individuals. Infused with crime, violence, betrayal, fear, failure, psychological coercion and alienation, his work depicts the loss or corruption of innocence, elicits moral questioning, and features pessimistic or open endings.

As his first and most famous young adult novel, *The Chocolate War* (1974), made so ironically clear, Cormier did not write chocolate box fiction. Instead his harsh, gritty realism annihilates the classic hero story so that the 'little guy', the lone hero, the teen protagonist, does not succeed against all odds, does not win out in the end, does not make good despite setbacks, and ends instead in disillusionment, defeat, or death. However hard his protagonists strive, higher corruption is more powerful, and the individual becomes an expendable nobody – or body. Being a nobody, of course, reflects the universalising yet alienating concept not only of the solitary figure in the face of mass corruption but also the feeling of aloneness, 'me-against-the-worldness', that is integral to adolescence itself. Coming of age in Cormier's novels is not an ultimately glorious transition into an adulthood full of potential, but the crushing realisation for his young characters that they have already in some way failed and that dreams of future success or of being the person they thought they could be are often futile in a corrupt world. Less overtly, however, his fiction also suggests that individual acts of goodness or of taking a moral stance in the face of insuperable odds have an intrinsic worth, however stark their outcomes.

1

That this is the first collection of critical essays devoted to Cormier's work reflects the fact that while his fiction is widely admired, reviewed, studied, and taught it has been, surprisingly, less often the subject of sustained academic research, particularly from a literary critical rather than a pedagogical perspective. This collection aims to address that lack by offering essays that discuss the range of Cormier's young adult fiction. Written by children's literature scholars in Britain, North America, Europe, and Australia, the volume's nine essays take a variety of critical and theoretical approaches to Cormier's work, offering diverse ways of reading his contribution to young adult fiction.

The volume is structured so that its earlier essays (Chapters 1–4) criti-cally analyse themes and aspects central to Cormier's writing – adolescent invisibility, questions of disguise and identity, Cormier's Catholic-inflected sense of evil, and aspects of child corruption – while its later essays (Chapters 5–9) read his work through various theoretical lenses including educational, historicist, and queer theory as well as a range of reader response approaches. Several of the discussions highlight ways in which Cormier's work engages readers. This critical emphasis is apt for young adult fiction as those concerned with teenage texts often have an interest in how and what teenagers read – as censorship challenges to Cormier's work attests. The discussions here, however, are concerned not with content-suitability judgements but with the ways in which Cormier's works themselves strongly elicit readers' responses. If Cormier, as he frequently stated, was inspired to write many of his stories by a 'what if' scenario, his texts equally provoke readers to ask 'what if': What if I were in that position? Having to make that decision? To act or not act? How would I cope? Could I live up to my own, or heroic ideals? And what does it mean if I can't? 'I'm very conscious of my reader,' Cormier stated, 'I write to upset the reader, and to provoke the reader, and I feel I can go to my full capacity for th[e] intelligent reader, who often turns out to be 14 years old'.[5] The 'interactivity' of Cormier's work is, as Patty Campbell notes, one of its 'striking characteristics'.[6] His books do not offer a passive read; readers must engage actively with Cormier's texts: filling in gaps, guessing outcomes, following clues, pondering ambiguities, while also reassessing their own preconceptions about good and evil, trust and betrayal, the right thing to do and the wrong.

Overall, the discussions in this volume highlight the complexity of Cormier's writing in its stylistic innovations, narrative ambitiousness, and moral questioning. They emphasise the humanity of Cormier's work and argue that even his darkest characters display human qualities and engage in behaviour that, if not forgivable, is explicable. Cormier's novels challenge preconceptions about good and evil and ask what it is to be human in the face of seeming inhumanity. Just as his heroes are flawed, imperfect, and subject to temptations, so, too, his 'monsters' (a favourite Cormier term) – killers, manipulators, terrorists – are not dehumanised. They reflect the dark side of everyone, as his best known monster Archie Costello tells Obie in *Beyond the Chocolate War* (1985): "'I'm you. I'm all the things you hide inside you'".[7]

The following essays also examine Cormier's postmodernist and metafictive techniques, showing that his novels reveal that there is no one truth. His fiction raises issues, too, about what characters – and implicitly readers – should do with perceived truths and secrets when discovered. Showing how extreme events alter people and how teenage uncertainties are magnified by shocking events, Cormier's work encourages questioning: Who am I? Who are you? What is evil? How can I remain uncorrupted? Who can be trusted? How can I deal with guilt and failure? How do I do the right thing? Analysing issues of adolescent identity and foregrounding the challenging nature of Cormier's work, the essays in this volume explore some of the special qualities of and particular questions raised by Cormier's work.

Robert Cormier's life and works

Some biographical knowledge of Cormier is useful in considering his work, as some of his texts, including *Fade* (1988) and *Frenchtown Summer* (1999), bear clear autobiographical traces. His settings, too, were inspired by his love for his home town, Leominster, a small city in Massachusetts. Although he travelled widely to speaking engagements and writers events, Cormier lived his entire life in Leominster, within three miles of the house in which he was born on 17 January 1925.[8] He set most of his fiction in Monument, a fictionalised Leominster featuring many renamed landmarks: library, church, schools. Cormier grew up in French Hill (which he fictionalised as Frenchtown), an area of Leominster settled by French Canadian immigrants, including his paternal grandfather. His mother was Irish and he was the second of eight children, including a younger brother who died aged three when Cormier was five. Raised a Roman Catholic during the Depression years in a close-knit working-class community where the adults worked in the comb and plastics factories, he began his education taught by nuns at a parochial school and developed an early love of movies and literature. A bookish, unathletic boy, whose literary leanings made him feel 'always ... like an outsider',[9] he experienced bullying, but several high school teachers encouraged his writing. When he graduated in 1942, after being rejected for military service in World War II because of short-sightedness, light weight, and ill health,[10] he worked nights at the local factory, taking courses at Fitchburg State College during the day. In 1944 a college instructor sent his story 'The Little Things that Count' to a magazine which published and paid for it, encouraging Cormier's aim to write for a living. Initially writing commercials for radio station WTAG from 1944–6, he spent over 30 years working for newspapers, including the *Worcester Telegram* and *Fitchburg Sentinel*, as a reporter, then associate editor and, using the pseudonym John Fitch IV, as a columnist. In 1948 he married Constance Senay, also from Leominster, with whom he had three daughters and a son. In 1959, 1973 and 1974 he won journalism awards for his human interest stories.[11]

Alongside his newspaper career Cormier developed his credentials as a fiction writer, publishing short stories in popular magazines such as *Redbook*, *McCall's* and the *Saturday Evening Post*. On the basis of an unpublished novel, he secured a literary agent and produced three novels for adults: the critically praised *Now and At the Hour* (1960) about a man facing death from cancer; *A Little Raw on Monday Mornings* (1963) which centres on a woman whose daughter is murdered and who then becomes pregnant to a fellow factory worker; and *Take Me Where the Good Times Are* (1965) recounting a 70-year-old man's 'escape' from an infirmary. Continuing to publish stories and writing unpublished novels while his children were teenagers,[12] Cormier's next novel did not appear until 1974, but it was to be his most famous and launched his career as a young-adult author.

Inspired by his son's decision not to sell chocolates for a school fundraising campaign, the plot of *The Chocolate War* was provoked by Cormier thinking 'what if?' What if his son's decision had not been accepted by the headmaster? What if his schoolmates had ostracised him? Cormier states that he wrote this novel about brutality and corruption in a Catholic boys' school '"entirely innocent that there were such things as young adult novels. I thought I was just writing a novel"'.[13] His agent pitched it for the young adult market and seven publishers rejected it, some urging Cormier to change its bleak ending, which he refused to do.[14] Both acclaimed and attacked on its publication, it is now a classic of young adult fiction but remains a controversial novel, one of the most regularly censorship challenged in America.

Cormier went on to produce two further books for adults: *Eight Plus One* (1980), a collection of previously published short stories featuring several young characters, and *I Have Words to Spend: Reflections of a Small-Town Editor* (1991), a collection of his newspaper columns. The other 13 books that followed *The Chocolate War* were all for young adults, although Cormier often stated that he did not regard himself as a young-adult author.[15] As his novels attest, Cormier did not let the young-adult label restrict how or what he wrote.[16] His second teen novel was the psychologically and narratively complex *I Am the Cheese* (1977), which centres on Adam Farmer whose family has been placed in the witness protection programme and who is himself controlled by unnamed – ostensibly governmental – authorities in an institution. His next, *After the First Death* (1979), again structurally intricate, focalises through three teenagers a terrorist attack on a busload of children.

The Chocolate War, *I Am the Cheese* and *After the First Death* entrenched Cormier's standing as a leading writer for teenagers. Each won multiple awards – including *New York Times* Outstanding Book of the Year awards – and, as a body of work, earned Cormier the Margaret A. Edwards Award for significant and lasting contribution to young adult literature from the American Library Association in 1991. Like these three novels, most of his future work also won Best Book for Young Adults Awards from the American Library Association, and in 1992 he was given the ALAN award for outstanding contribution to adolescent literature.[17]

In 1978, following *I Am the Cheese*, Cormier had left journalism to pursue fiction full-time. He continued writing about teen protagonists within secretive, powerful, corrupt institutions in *The Bumblebee Flies Anyway* (1983), which tells of terminally ill teenagers in an experimental medical facility, and *Beyond the Chocolate War*, his sequel to *The Chocolate War*. Introducing an element of fantasy into his otherwise realist plots, in 1988 he published *Fade*, a metafictional, postmodernist text involving a series of narratives that tell of uncles and nephews who have – or are cursed with – the power of becoming invisible. *Other Bells for Us to Ring* (1990; published in Britain in 1991 under Cormier's original title *Darcy*[18]), set in 1943, tells of 11-year-old protestant Darcy Webster's friendship with a Catholic friend.

In his sixties and early seventies Cormier turned more towards crime fiction and slimmer novels. *We All Fall Down* (1991) involves the perpetrators, the victim's sister, and the mysterious, murderous 'Avenger' of a house trashing and attempted rape. *Tunes for Bears to Dance to* (1992), tells of 11-year old Henry Cassavant's relationship with a Holocaust survivor and of Henry's manipulation by an anti-Semitic shopkeeper. *In the Middle of the Night* (1995) is a psychological thriller centred on 16-year-old Denny Colbert who becomes involved in a dangerous relationship with a mysterious phone caller connected to his father's past. *Tenderness* (1997) focuses on 18-year-old serial killer Eric Poole, teen runaway Lori Cranston, and weathered detective Jake Proctor who is tracking Eric. Exploring concepts of heroism, *Heroes* (1998) recounts injured World War II hero Francis Cassavant's[19] return to Frenchtown to extract vengeance for past betrayal by another war – and personal – hero, Larry LaSalle. *Frenchtown Summer*, inspired by Cormier's own 1930s childhood, is a verse narrative about the relationship of a boy and his father.

After breaking his back in a fall in 1997, Cormier's health began to fail and following a stroke in 2000 he was discovered to have inoperable cancer and died on 2 November that year.[20] Published posthumously in 2001, his final novel, *The Rag and Bone Shop* (2001), is the unremitting interrogation of 12-year-old Jason by detective Trent who is determined to extract from him a confession that he has murdered a seven-year-old girl.

Although he wrote about the dark side of life, Cormier was, his biographer Patty Campbell records, a genial family man very much involved in his local environment, visiting local libraries daily and 'a kindly, cheerful, decent sort of person' who 'cared profoundly about goodness'.[21] An obituary described him as an 'American novelist whose work was a hotline to the hearts and minds of teenagers all over the world'.[22] Famously, he opened a literal hotline in *I Am the Cheese* by using as Amy Hertz's phone number his own number, allowing readers to call him up to talk about his work.[23] That he did so seems a response to Holden Caulfield's wish in J. D. Salinger's *The Catcher in the Rye* (1951): 'What really knocks me out is a book that, when you're all done reading it, you wish the author that wrote it was a terrific friend of yours and you could call him up on the phone whenever you felt like it'.[24] Cormier stated that Salinger's novel made him see 'that adolescence could be something very dramatic to write about ... it had a definite influence on me'.[25] Cormier was also influenced by Thomas Wolfe's fiction, 'the clear simplicity of Hemingway's language',[26] and, as Pat Pinsent in Chapter 3 explores, Graham Greene was Cormier's 'great mentor'.[27] 'The novels of Graham Greene are like textbooks to me', he wrote.[28] His work reveals, too, as Stefania Ciocia highlights in Chapter 4, the influence of crime fiction: '"I love detective stories"' Cormier wrote '""they always deliver a beginning, middle and end, a satisfying climax or epiphany"'.[29]

He was also undoubtedly influenced by the period in which he began writing his teen fiction: a time of terrorist attacks and hijackings, the Watergate scandal, the Vietnam War, questioning of political authority and systems, and the collapse of old cultural norms.

Critical responses to Cormier's fiction

Cormier's novels are often seen as part of the New Realism in young adult fiction that emerged in the 1970s. As Anne Scott MacLeod writes, the 'social revolutions of [that decade] transformed children's literature. Old taboos fell, subjects excluded from children's books for years appeared everywhere. Death, divorce, alcohol and drugs, racism and sexism as identified social evils, and, eventually sexuality became commonplace in literature for the young'.[30] Jennifer Keeley observes, however, that New Realist novels tend to have positive or at least instructive endings.[31] Cormier's young adult texts, by contrast, favour bleak or ambiguous endings. '"I really love ambiguity"',[32] Cormier explained, 'it's ... possible to add something beyond the climax, something unresolved perhaps or a provocative after-thought – thus the book never really ends in the reader's mind and lingers after the last page has been turned'.[33] Intrepid texts which rarely flinch from revealing – or, as Susan Clancy in Chapter 8 discusses, from examining – truths, his fiction opened new possibilities in teenage fiction, as young adult writer Chris Lynch notes: '*I Am the Cheese* was without question the most important YA title in my development as a writer. It was the book that made me say, "Hot Damn, you can DO that? You can write a story that raw and real without translating it for the reader?" I cannot tell you how liberating that was for me.'[34]

Apart 'from being strikingly vigorous stylistically and conceptually original,' as Mitzi Myers comments, Cormier's work 'made it possible to see what had formerly been considered a narrow, narcissistic genre as capacious enough to handle an intellectual novel of ideas'.[35] Cormier's work expresses clear interests in ideas such as heroism, patriotism, power, guilt, evil, and complicity with evil, but is also concerned with psychological power-play – intimidation, coercion, brain washing, and manipulation – and with very physical aspects of life – lust, crime, violence, and death.

Protagonists' negotiation of human relationships is also central to Cormier's work, especially the masculine relationships of teen males with fathers, male peers, and male authority figures. Such relationships are an inherent part of the predominantly male world of Cormier's young adult fiction. In Cormier's work mothers tend to be absent,

8 Introduction

emotionally sad, or insular, while younger women feature as the objects of teen male sexual desire or as victims of crime, with comparatively few – Kate Forrester in *After the First Death*, Darcy Webster in *Other Bells for us to Ring / Darcy*, Lori Cranston in *Tenderness*, Lulu O'Hearn in *In the Middle of the Night*, and Jane Jerome in *We All Fall Down* – becoming major characters.

The critical and popular success of Cormier's work is partially due to the fact that, for all its narrative complexity and challenging content, it is written cleanly, readably, with tension-filled, pacey plots that go beyond the norms. Honed by his journalistic skills in tight, direct writing, Cormier's prose is taut and lean, the pared down language accentuating the starkness of his subject matter. Characterised by sinewed diction, poetic nuance, and literary allusions, his style is studded with clear, vivid images: 'the wind like a snake slithering up my sleeves';[36] 'a sigh escaped me, like a ghost abandoning my body';[37] 'his fingers like pale spiders with a victim in their clutch'.[38] Cormier claimed that 'the movies and cinema have had more of an effect on my books than books themselves',[39] and his cinematic techniques – short scenes, changing perspectives, economical dialogue – have often been noted. Film adaptations have been made of some of Cormier's novels,[40] but he himself admitted that they are hard to film because 'there are so many interior things going on in' them: psychological aspects and interior monologues.[41] Expression of such 'interior things', including Cormier's goal to capture the 'universal and timeless' feelings of adolescence,[42] is enhanced through his polyphonic use of multiple narrators, interchanging narrative perspectives, and shifting time frames. As Perry Nodelman notes, *The Chocolate War* provides 'the perspectives of thirteen different people'.[43] Manifold viewpoints heighten the postmodern qualities of Cormier's work, revealing that there is no single truth and that things are not always as they seem.

How Cormier writes has been widely lauded, but what Cormier writes *about* has been questioned by those concerned with what teenagers read. Patty Campbell records that when *The Chocolate War* was published a review in the American Library Association's *Booklist* was printed with a black border, attacking it as '"a book that looks with adult bitterness at the inherent evil of human nature and the way young people can be dehumanised into power-hungry and bloodthirsty adults"'.[44] Particularly in the United States, there have been cases seeking to remove Cormier's books from high school curricula and libraries on the grounds of their nihilistic, bleak, and cynical vision; use of offensive language; depiction of violence and sexuality; picturing of authority figures and institutions in a bad light; and controversial subject matter, including the killing of children, psychological coercion, rape, brutality, and death. As Wendy Hart Beckman outlines, 'The Chocolate War was the fourth most challenged book of the 1990s and was the most-challenged book of 1998 and 2004'.[45] I Am the Cheese, too, was central in what began as an 1985 protest by a student's grandmother against the book on the grounds that it 'contained vulgar language and advocated humanism and behaviourism',[46] through death threats and fire bombings directed at teachers who wanted to teach it, to become a Federal law suit against a Florida high school's banning of it and other texts.[47]

Cormier's view was that '"There are no taboos. Every topic is open, however shocking. It is the way that the topics are handled that's important, and that applies whether it is a 15-year-old who is reading your book or someone who is 55"'.[48] His teen readers, he maintained are '"not upset about the world I portray because they're in that world every day, and they know it's war, psychological war"'.[49] 'You seldom get a censorship attempt from a 14 y[ea]r old boy', he stated in an interview shortly before his death. 'It's the adults who get upset. The letters I get are letters of support and the line that runs through them all is[:] You tell it like it is'.[50]

Literary criticism of Cormier's work almost universally draws attention to its darker elements. His use of irony[51] and the postmodernity of his work are also regularly noted,[52] and there has been a sustained interest in reader response especially, as Nodelman noted in 1983, in the ways in which Cormier's fiction 'does a number' (plays tricks) on readers.[53] The morality of Cormier's work is also often discussed by critics. Sylvia Patterson Iskander, for instance, argues that 'The climactic structure of his novels with their shocking, unhappy, but quite realistic endings reinforces not the temporary defeats or a bleak pessimism, but rather a longing for justice' and an argument for moral responsibility.[54] C. Anita Tarr, however, argues that Cormier's work lacks moral agency, that his characters do not act morally, and that in The Chocolate War this is reflected in the unchallenged misogyny of its characters.[55] The predominately 'male-gaze', masculine world of Cormier's novels has provoked charges such as Tarr's of misogyny, while Yoshida Junko argues that The Chocolate War is itself 'a powerful indictment of conventional manhood'.[56] Critics also express disparate views on whether Cormier's protagonists are heroic. Nancy Veglahn, for example, suggests yes[57] while Tarr argues no,[58] and some propose that Cormier's work resembles traditional tragedy.[59]

Writing in 1981 Anne Scott MacLeod suggested that, with their interest in society's systems, Cormier's early young adult fictions

were 'at bottom, political novels'.[60] Viewing them as 'important' but
not '"great books"' MacLeod predicted that they would not 'outlast
their topical relevance'.[61] Their topicality has, however, if anything,
increased – particularly in regard to such issues as terrorism, youth
crime, and political and institutional corruption, and their position in
the canon of young adult fiction is now secure.

New insights into Cormier's writing

The following essays revisit some of the common areas of critical
interest in Cormier's work, extending these to consider his later and
lesser examined fiction, while also offering new ways of reading his
work. The volume opens with Karyn Huenemann's 'Fade to Black'
(Chapter 1), which examines the theme of adolescent invisibility
across a range of Cormier's fiction, with a particular focus on *The
Chocolate War, Beyond the Chocolate War, Heroes* and *Fade*. She shows
that in cases where teen invisibility is central, Cormier's threatened
teenage protagonists either stand up to threats from the adult world,
become invisible in order to wage 'guerilla warfare' against adult
corruption, or intentionally fade into the margins to escape harm. For
Cormier's adolescent characters, being socially invisible aids psychosocial transformation from dependent child to independent adult, but
for this to be fully successful, Huenemann argues, the adolescent also
needs to return to visibility with his or her moral integrity intact.

In '"So many disguises"' Andrew F. Humphries (Chapter 2) draws
attention to concepts allied with invisibility – transparency, surveillance, disguise and exposure – in considering questions of identity
in *After the First Death* and *Heroes*. Cormier's young adult characters,
Humphries shows, have identities that develop and shift as they
struggle for the self-realisation that is central to teenage development
and self-consciousness. Their identities emerge and change through
the often extreme crises and trials they face. Cormier's novels foreground identity as something not fixed but evolutionary, with his teen
protagonists attempting both to understand themselves and to disguise
their identities from the surveillance of hostile adult society.

Turning from questions identity to consider religious concepts
of wrong, Pat Pinsent's 'Fascinated by Evil' (Chapter 3) discusses
Cormier as a Catholic novelist. She explores ways in which his pre-
Vatican Two Catholic upbringing coloured Cormier's work and
influenced his fascination with evil. Highlighting affinities between
Cormier's fiction and that of fellow Catholic Graham Greene, Pinsent
shows how a sense of the church adds textual richness and operates

as a formative agent on Cormier's protagonists. Focusing on *The Chocolate War, Beyond the Chocolate War, After the First Death, Fade,* and *Darcy* (*Other Bells for Us to Ring*), and commenting on *Frenchtown Summer*, Pinsent reveals that while his work frequently portrays evil, it also contains the possibility of redeeming grace.

Often connected to concepts of evil is the idea of child corruption, representations of which Stefania Ciocia examines in '"Nobody out of context"' (Chapter 4). Her essay analyses how far *We All Fall Down, Tenderness* and *The Rag and Bone Shop* contribute to contemporary literature's debunking of the myth of childhood innocence. Featuring young criminals who commit brutal crimes against equally young victims, Cormier's crime novels for teenagers nevertheless perpetuate traditional ideas of childhood innocence, Ciocia argues, rather than reflecting his reputation for pessimism and stark portrayals of evil. His texts reveal child criminals who are made, not born, she suggests, whose behaviour, no matter how brutal or destructive, is explicable and ameliorated by extenuating circumstances.

Brutal behaviour is also discussed in Amy Cummins's '"You have to outlast them"' (Chapter 5) which analyses Cormier's depiction of bullying in *The Chocolate War* and *Beyond the Chocolate War*. Using educational research on peer harassment and administrator intimidation practices in educational institutions, Cummins shows that the novels' Trinity high school reflects real-life patterns that perpetuate a bullying culture. Examining the roles of characters including Brother Leon, Archie Costello, Jerry Renault, Emile Janza, Obie, and The Vigils secret society, she discusses the bullying triad of bully, victim, and bystander. Although Archie is often regarded as the most despicable character in these novels, Cummins argues that Brother Leon's manipulation of power and betrayal of his educational and religious leadership duties is worse. Higher authorities such as the Bishop and school governors are also culpable, Cummins suggests, for allowing a bullying environment to exist.

Also examining *The Chocolate War* and *Beyond The Chocolate War*, Holly Blackford in '*Männerbund* and *Hitler-Jugend*' (Chapter 6) discusses ways in which these novels reflect the 'queer perceptions' of Nazis that, together with the closeting of homosexuality, studies of 'obedience perils', and the rise of the 'organisation man', were common in America in the 1960s. The essay reads Trinity high school as analogous to the *Hitler-Jugend* (Hitler Youth), set within a *Männerbund*: the all-male society glorified by Nazis. The novels foreground male characters who take pleasure in brutalising others, connecting this with repressed homosexuality, Blackford shows.

Yet Cormier's portrayal is paradoxical, suggesting that 'the shaming of the queer is precariously Nazi-like' while at the same time its own 'thinly veiled gay-coded Nazi perpetrators reinforce stereotypes'.

In the first of three essays in the volume which focus on Cormier's fiction in relation to reader response, Clare Walsh in 'Inducing Despair?' (Chapter 7) discusses *The Chocolate War*, *I Am the Cheese*, and *After the First Death* as anti-*Bildungsromans* that thwart their protagonists' transition to adulthood and end darkly. Walsh asks what subject positions these novels provide for young adult readers, and whether these encourage them to be 'compliant' or 'interrogative' readers. Using critical discourse analysis, she argues that while *The Chocolate War* challenges the moral certainties of traditional boys' school stories, it replaces these with morally confusing messages delivered via a pseudo-dialogic address, endorsing the view that resistance to the powers of corrupt institutions is futile. Similarly, despite offering a complex narrative structure, *I Am the Cheese* is ultimately disempowering for teen readers. By contrast, the 'genuinely polyphonic' *After the First Death* invites young readers to question their assumptions about patriotism, terrorism and heroism.

Susan Clancy in 'Framing the Truth' (Chapter 8) considers ways in which Cormier frames the concept of truth. Drawing on the 'reader-oriented theories' of Umberto Eco, Wolfgang Iser, and particularly Louise Rosenblatt to set out theoretical underpinnings for the wide range of reader responses Cormier's work elicits, she also discusses Cormier's own views about truth and its roles in his writing and society. Through analysis of truth in *Tunes For Bears To Dance to*, *We All Fall Down* and *Tenderness*, Clancy examines Cormier's use of irony and shows how his characters are forced to face often unpalatable truths and realise, too, that relationships built on lies and fantasy cannot succeed.

Like Walsh and Clancy, Dimitrios Politis is interested in reader response approaches to Cormier's fiction, and in 'Interactive Texts and Active Readers' (Chapter 9) he explores Cormier's 'Adolescent Poetics' in the light of Wolfgang Iser's theory of Aesthetic Response. Outlining Iser's theory and discussing a range of Cormier's works, Politis demonstrates that, rather than presenting a 'schematic view' of fictional worlds for readers, Cormier offers them challenging reading procedures, necessitating their concentrated participation in 'actualising his writing'. Cormier's protagonists, he argues, strive hard to understand the situations in which they are placed but are dominated by power structures. In the same way, his readers are 'both potentially active in the making of meaning and passive in the imposition of textual signs that direct their reading activity'.

In many ways critical work on Cormier is just beginning: we have the corpus of his work, time has elapsed since his death, and criticism of his work that reaches beyond value judgements is needed. The essays in this volume seek to contribute to this task.

Notes

1. Mitzi Myers, '"No Safe Place to Run To": An Interview with Robert Cormier', *The Lion and the Unicorn*, 24 (2000): 445–64, at 445.
2. Michael Cart, quoted in Marilyn E. Marlow et al., 'Robert Cormier Remembered', *Publisher's Weekly*, 1 January 2001: 39.
3. Peter Hunt, 'Robert Cormier', *Children's Literature* (Oxford: Blackwell, 2001): 51–3, at 51.
4. Cormier in Mitzi Myers: 452.
5. 'Robert Cormier Meets Melvin Burgess: Part 1', chaired by Jonathan Douglas, London, 11 July 2000: www.achuka.co.uk/special/cormburg. htm (accessed 3 May 2012).
6. Patty Campbell, *Robert Cormier: Daring to Disturb the Universe* (New York: Delacorte, 2006): 40.
7. Robert Cormier, *Beyond the Chocolate War* [1985] (New York: Dell Laurel-Leaf, 1986): 264.
8. 'Robert Cormier Meets Melvin Burgess: Part 1'.
9. 'Robert Cormier Meets Melvin Burgess: Part 2', chaired by Jonathan Douglas, London, 11 July 2000: www.achuka.co.uk/special/cormburg2. htm (accessed 3 May 2012).
10. Ibid.
11. Campbell: 11–33.
12. Campbell: 26–7.
13. Cormier quoted in Lyn Gardner, 'Dead Bodies in Suburbia', *Guardian Review* 19 August 2000: www.guardian.co.uk/books/2000/aug/19/ booksforchildrenandteenagers (accessed 3 May 2012).
14. Campbell: 28.
15. Campbell: 48.
16. 'Robert Cormier Meets Melvin Burgess: Part 1'.
17. For a listing of Cormier's awards see Campbell: 273–7.
18. Campbell: 170.
19. As Campbell states, the shared surname Cassavant used for the protagonists of *Tunes for Bears to Dance to* and *Heroes* does not seem to be obviously linked (192 n. 15).
20. Campbell: 30.
21. Forward to Campbell: n.p.
22. Gardner: n.p.
23. Campbell: 13.
24. J. D. Salinger, *The Catcher in the Rye* [1951] (London: Penguin, 1958): 22.

25. Cormier quoted in Jennifer Keeley, *Understanding I Am the Cheese* (San Diego, CA: Lucent, 2001): 23.
26. Campbell: 19.
27. 'Robert Cormier Meets Melvin Burgess: Part 2'.
28. Robert Cormier, 'A Character by Any Other Name…', *English Journal*, 90(3) (2001): 31–2, at 31.
29. Cormier, quoted in 'Robert Cormier', Internet Public Library (1996): www.ipl.org/div/askauthor/Cormier.html (accessed 3 May 2012).
30. Anne Scott MacLeod, *American Childhood: Essays on Children's Literature of the Nineteenth and Twentieth Centuries* (Athens, GA: University of Georgia Press, 1994): 210. Essay originally published in *Children's Literature in Education*, 12.2 (Summer 1981): 74–81.
31. Keeley: 30.
32. Cormier quoted in Campbell: 191.
33. Cormier in Mitzi Myers: 454.
34. Quoted in Lisa Rowe Fraustino, 'The Age of Cheese: Readers Respond to Cormier', in Alethea Helbig and Agnes Perkins (eds), *The Phoenix Award of the Children's Literature Association, 1995–1999* (Lanham, MD: Scarecrow Press, 2001): 111–17, at 115.
35. Myers: 458.
36. Robert Cormier, *I Am the Cheese* [1977] (New York: Dell Laurel-Leaf, 1991): 12.
37. Robert Cormier, *In the Middle of the Night* [1995] (New York: Dell Laurel-Leaf, 1997): 17.
38. Robert Cormier, *The Chocolate War* [1974] (London: Puffin, 2001): 86.
39. 'Robert Cormier Meets Melvin Burgess: Part 2'.
40. *I Am the Cheese*, Almi Pictures, directed by Robert Jiras. Perf. Robert MacNaughton, Hope Lange, Don Murray, Robert Wagner, Cynthia Nixon, 1983; *The Chocolate War*, MCEG, directed by Keith Gordon. Perf. Ilan Mitchell Smith, John Glover, Wally Ward, 1988; *Lapse of Memory* (adapted from *I Am the Cheese*), Gerard Mital and Max Films co-production, directed by Patrick Dewolf. Perf. John Hurt, Marthe Keller, Matthew Mackay, 1992; *The Bumblebee Flies Anyway*, USA Entertainment, direct by Martin Duffy. Perf. Elijah Wood, Rachel Leigh Cook, Janeane Garofalo, Joe Perrino, 1999; *Tenderness*, Lionsgate, directed by John Polsen. Perf. Russell Crowe, Sophie Taub, Jon Forster, Laura Dern, 2009.
41. 'Robert Cormier Meets Melvin Burgess: Part 2'.
42. 'Robert Cormier Meets Melvin Burgess: Part 1'.
43. Perry Nodelman, 'Robert Cormier's *The Chocolate War*: Paranoia and Paradox' in Dennis Butts (ed.) *Stories and Society: Children's Literature in its Social Context* (Basingstoke: Macmillan, 1992): 22–36, at 24.
44. Betsy Hearne, 'Whammo, You Lose', *Booklist* 1 July 1974, 1199, quoted in Campbell: 67.
45. Wendy Hart Beckman, *Robert Cormier: Banned, Challenged, and Censored* (Berkeley Heights, NJ: Enslow, 2008): 81. Also see Herbert N. Foerstel,

'Voices of Banned Authors', in *Banned in the USA: A Reference Guide to Book Censorship in Schools and Public Libraries*, revised and expanded edition (Westport, CT: Greenwood, 2002): 201–4.

46. Foerstel: 40.
47. See Foerstal: 39–50, 152–4; Beckman: 90–5; ReLeah Lent and Gloria Pipkin, 'We Keep Pedaling', *ALAN Review* (Winter 2001): 9–11.
48. Cormier quoted in Gardner: n.p.
49. Foerstel: 148–9.
50. 'Robert Cormier Meets Melvin Burgess: Part 1'.
51. Millicent Lenz, 'A Romantic Ironist's Vision of Evil: Robert Cormier's *After the First Death*', in Priscilla A. Ord (ed.) *Proceedings of the Eighth Annual Conference of the Children's Literature Association, University of Minnesota, March, 1981*, (Boston: Children's Literature Assoc, 1982): 50–6.
52. See Patricia Head, 'Robert Cormier and the Postmodernist Possibilities of Young Adult Fiction', *Children's Literature Association Quarterly*, 21(1) (1996): 28–33; Robert LeBlanc, *Postmodernist Elements in the Work of Robert Cormier* (Saarbrücken, Germany: VDM Verlag, 2009).
53. Perry Nodelman, 'Robert Cormier Does a Number', *Children's Literature in Education*, 14(2) (1983): 94–103.
54. Sylvia Patterson Iskander, 'Readers, Realism, and Robert Cormier', *Children's Literature*, 15 (1987): 7–18.
55. C. Anita Tarr, 'The Absence of Moral Agency in Robert Cormier's *The Chocolate War*', *Children's Literature* 30 (2002): 96–124.
56. Yoshida Junko, 'The Quest for Masculinity in *The Chocolate War*: Changing Conceptions of Masculinity in the 1970s', *Children's Literature* 26 (1998): 105–22, at 113.
57. Nancy Veglahn, 'The Bland Face of Evil in the Novels of Robert Cormier', *The Lion and the Unicorn*, 12(1) (1988): 12–18.
58. Tarr: 96–124.
59. Kenneth L. Donelson and Alleen Pace Nilsen, *Literature for Today's Young Adults*, 7th edn (Boston: Pearson, 2005): 119; Kara Keeling, '"The Misfortune of a Man Like Ourselves": Robert Cormier's *The Chocolate War* as Aristotelian Tragedy', *ALAN Review* 26(2) (Winter 1999): 9–12.
60. MacLeod: 189–97, at 190, 194.
61. Ibid.: 195.

1

Fade to Black: Adolescent Invisibility in the Works of Robert Cormier

Karyn Huenemann

The underlying theme of much of Cormier's work is, in the words of Patricia J. Campbell, 'the eternal question ... How can we confront the utterly Implacable and still remain human?'[1] Cormier approaches this question from many angles, with each of his adolescent protagonists facing difficult but different instances of the seeming ruthlessness of the adult world. In each case, too, his central teen characters find themselves facing the daunting world alone. They are invisible – emotionally, spiritually, and physically – to those more powerful in the world, yet they need to negotiate that world successfully in order to transform from children into adults. Discussing the theme of adolescent invisibility across a range of Cormier's work, but paying particular attention to four of Cormier's novels in which invisibility is central – *The Chocolate War* (1974), *Beyond the Chocolate War* (1985), *Heroes* (1998) and *Fade* (1988) – this essay explores what happens when adolescent characters respond differently to the 'Implacable' situations Cormier constructs for them.

Through his metaphorical explication of the liminal nature of adolescence, and the various ways in which his protagonists manifest their invisibility, Cormier presents his young adult readers with '"writing [that] portrays realistic situations, realistic language, and realistic outcomes – not necessarily happy ones"'.[2] The efficacy of this approach renders Cormier's writing powerful yet accessible. His intent was to provide his readers with honest information, to help make their own transition to adulthood as smooth and effective as possible. He knew that his novels '"found their way to classrooms"',[3] and as he states: 'Spurred on by hundreds of letters . . . ignited by the knowledge that my work would be studied, dissected, and probed in classrooms - these facts demanded that I seek the best within myself. One cannot write casually or carelessly for that readership'.[4]

Consideration of Cormier's corpus uncovers how, in particular, the adolescent sense of invisibility is transformed by his characters into action, thereby illuminating some of the darkest possibilities of adolescent experience. Cormier's texts assert that being socially invisible can be an effective agent in psychosocial transformation, but that the adolescent needs to return to visibility, with his or her moral integrity intact, in order to develop successfully from dependent child to independent adult. This transition is not easy, and Cormier's texts are generally neither pleasant nor uplifting. They are, perhaps as a result, immensely popular with young adult readers (although not always with parents and other authority figures).

Cormier creates what Peter Hollindale calls 'the adolescent novel of ideas':[5]

a highly intelligent and demanding literature ... which speaks with particular directness to the young adult mind – the mind which is freshly mature and intellectually confident, mentally supple and relatively free of ideological harness ... The adolescent novel of ideas is marked at its best by the logic, spaciousness, and lack of compromise of its 'what if's?'[6]

Cormier's position as arguably 'the single most important writer in the whole history of young adult literature'[7] results from his 'deeply honest and moral refusal' to provide a panacea for the 'hard questions' his texts pose[8] or to write down to his audience. As Zibby Oneal observes, 'Cormier dares to tell them something else and we gasp at his daring. Take a look at the world, he says. Failure happens. Despair ensues. This is also part of what is true.'[9]

While a number of authors for young adults today successfully emulate Cormier's technique, at their several moments of production Cormier's works were ground-breakingly honest in the starkness of their messages. Cormier respected his young audience, considering them worthy of the most complex narrative structures, the most troubling sociopolitical issues and situations, and his readers respond to his belief in them. In an interview with Herbert Foerstel, Cormier explained that his adolescent readers are 'not upset about the world I portray because they're in that world every day, and they know it's war, psychological war. ... they say I tell it like it is. This is the way life is, and they are tired of books where everyone walks off into the sunset together.'[10]

Cormier's texts are fundamentally *honest*. The rules of the adult world are different from those of childhood, more complex and with greater consequences, and adolescents have to figure the game out for themselves. Cormier felt – or hoped – that his texts would support his adolescent readers in this journey. They obviously feel that he has succeeded; as Cormier told an interviewer at *Writing* magazine, "'letter after letter from students tell me that, ... [t]hey identify with and derive comfort from characters who reflect their own doubts and feelings'".[11] As his friend and colleague George Nicholson notes, Cormier 'came to recognize that in those brief teen years came the pattern for adulthood. And he was determined that his readers have that swift shock of recognition even when adults missed his goal.'[12]

Before he published his first controversial young adult novel, *The Chocolate War*, Robert Cormier was an author of adult novels, with a 'critical reputation as the novelist of the "little people"'[13] and a 'rare sense of artistic integrity'.[14] Yet, even then, he conceptualised adolescence as a time of invisibility, a time when the child transforming into the adult faded from sight. *A Little Raw on Monday Mornings* (1963) tells the story of a single mother's hardships; her adolescent daughter, Dorrie, however, reveals Cormier's preoccupation with the complexities of the transition from childhood to adulthood. Dealing with the trauma of her sister's death, Dorrie feels as if she has disappeared: "'Everybody looked at me funny, like they couldn't see me, like I was invisible. I had the feeling nobody could hear me or see me, as if I wasn't even there'".[15] This feeling persists, both for Dorrie and for Cormier; it haunts adolescent characters throughout his work.

This is not to say that the premise of all of Robert Cormier's work is the invisibility of adolescence; his novels present a significant range of messages and styles, but even where this theme is not central it does manifest itself. In *Frenchtown Summer* (1999), Cormier's novel-length prose poem, Eugene's sense of invisibility is real, but fleeting: he 'felt like a ghost/on Mechanic Street/transparent as rain'.[16] Later, having disturbed his father's late night contemplation, he 'glides like a ghost/to the bedroom'.[17] In *Tunes for Bears to Dance to* (1992), the abused Doris Hairston 'came and went like a ghost, appearing suddenly and then fading away',[18] while the actions of the protagonist, Henry Cassavant, that precipitate the crisis of the novel, are performed at night, significantly hidden from the watchful morality of the adult world. At the beginning of *Tenderness* (1997), Eric Poole tantalisingly disappears from sight the first time Lori Cranston sees him – "'I stopped and looked back but he was gone and the spot where he had been standing was a lonesome place'"[19] – just as Lori later appears 'out of the past like a ghost'.[20] In *We All Fall Down* (1991), Abby and Buddy Walker feel abandoned by their parents. Abby equates their neglect with child abuse: "'You know what we are, Buddy? ... Victims. Victims of child abuse. ... Not sexual abuse or even physical abuse. But just as bad in its own way. ... Mothers and fathers too selfish about themselves and ignoring their children. ... I mean, ignoring the hurt, the invisible stuff that happens to kids. What's happening to us.'"[21]

Buddy's invisibility to his parents – and their resulting failure to help him successfully through this troubling period of his life – lead him to alcoholism and the dissolution of a promising relationship.

In *I Am the Cheese* (1977), adolescent invisibility is most obviously reflected in the need for secrecy in Adam Farmer's girlfriend Amy Hertz's 'numbers', youthful pranks played on adult society. A deeper sense of invisibility, however, lies in Adam's family having to 'disappear' into the witness protection programme: a wiping out of their identity that results in the taking of Adam's parents' lives and ultimately the erasure of Adam's formal identity, his sense of self, and his very sanity. His true identity, like his history, remains invisible: to the reader until the end of the novel, and seemingly to Adam until the inevitable, imminent end of his life. Like the cheese in the childhood song 'The Farmer in the Dell', Adam 'stands alone'; the individual is rendered invisible by the inhuman machinations of the state apparatus, the power of patriotism, and an unthinking adherence to regulations and regimes. This theme surfaces more strongly in *After the First Death* (1979).

In *After the First Death*, three adolescent characters similarly 'stand alone': Kate Forrester who is the driver of a school bus hijacked by terrorists; Miro Shantas, the youngest terrorist and the last left alive, who is deserted by the deaths of his comrades and Artkin, the leader who might be his father; and Ben Marchand who is betrayed by his Army commander father when he sends Ben willingly into a life-threatening situation. Kate longs to disappear, to melt out of herself and the situation she is trapped in through no fault of her own. Miro believes himself to be a man, assuming an 'adult' role when he wears his terrorist ski-mask, hiding his youth behind the woollen fabric; yet he also feels 'like a prisoner' in the mask, as if he were 'looking out at the world but not part of it' even though 'the mask gave him a sense of power and authority'.[22] Ben, on the other hand, recognises the vulnerability of his adolescence, and strives to succeed in the very adult role his father foists upon him: that of messenger to the terrorists. His father has counted on Ben's inability to sustain the adult role, his inevitable cracking under torture; when Ben discovers this, he feels that he no longer exists – to his father, his classmates, himself – 'I felt invisible again and looked to see if I actually left footprints behind me in the snow'.[23]

In *I Am the Cheese* and *After the First Death*, the protagonists' sense of invisibility is ultimately connected with their failure to integrate into adult society and to survive adolescence: in both cases, the result of explicitly ruthless behaviour by adults around them. In *Other Bells for Us to Ring* (1990; published as *Darcy* in Britain [1991]), invisibility works as a more positive force in the life of young Darcy Webster. The pivotal emotional moment in the novel is when Darcy's best friend, Kathleen O'Hara, disappears. Kathleen is restored to Darcy only when John Francis, Kathleen's brother, tells Darcy of Kathleen's death, his breath in the cold December air appearing as 'puffs of steam … as if the terrible words were made visible'.[24] Kathleen is similarly 'made visible' when Darcy realises that her promise – 'I will not desert you'[25] – has been kept by her spirit. Darcy alone hears the bells of St Jude's ring on Christmas Eve, and remembers Kathleen's assertion that there would be 'other bells for us to ring' as adults. Darcy has passed the portals of adulthood, aided by the strength of the invisible Kathleen, absent in death, but present nonetheless: 'I stood there in the bedroom holding my childhood in my hands. When my father called to me, I said good-bye to that lost childhood and went into the living room to open my Christmas gifts.'[26]

In the Middle of the Night (1995) presents the theme of invisibility more negatively. The antagonist, Lulu O'Hearn, remains invisible to all, so much so that the reader is initially convinced she is a figment of her brother's psychotic imagination. She is a Lazarus figure, dead and brought back to life, haunting the story from beginning to end, as the young girl who was denied the opportunity to transform into a stable, well-adjusted adult. Her terror-inducing calls are made to Denny Colbert's home 'in the middle of the night' until Denny, asserting his independence and maturity, picks up the phone instead of his father. Once this connection is made, the phantom Lulu orchestrates his demise as payment for his father's fatal mistake 20 years earlier. Denny conceals his involvement with Lulu from his already troubled parents; once again, the adolescent protagonist remains alone, hiding his situation from the adults who could possibly help him. His self-induced invisibility ultimately endangers his life.

In *The Bumblebee Flies Anyway* (1983), Barney Snow is a patient in an experimental hospital, where terminally ill patients allow themselves to be experimental subjects for the advancement of medical science. Because he is not in pain, Barney thinks he is not dying, and assumes that is why 'the nurses passed him by as if he did not exist';[27] yet because he is a patient there, Cassie Mazzofono, whom he admires, equally discounts his existence. Barney is thus doubly invisible: in being a patient, and, he assumes, not of the terminally ill population. In reality, the staff have built an invisible wall between themselves and all the patients in their care, giving attention when needed, but no comforts, as '"most of the patients here are past the need for luxuries"';[28] both their physical and their emotional needs are ignored. Within the nightmare space Cormier has created, where the adolescent patients suffer unseen, Barney manages to exert his growing sense of self and is determined to provide for his companions what the adult world denies them: their dreams. He and his fellow inmates dismantle 'The Bumblebee', a bright-red mock-up of an MG from the junkyard next to the hospital, and reconstruct it in the attic in order to aid one of their number, the dying Mazzo, '"to have that last ride. Go out in a blaze of glory"'.[29] In this case, being unseen is an advantage that facilitates their surreptitious night time activities.

Cormier's final novel, *The Rag and Bone Shop* (2001) contains little reference to the metaphor of invisibility, except in protagonist Jason Dorrant's active desire to avoid his schoolmates and in his being happy that 'mostly they ignored him'.[30] What does provide thematic continuity is the conclusion, in which the previously childish protagonist leaves detention, and makes the decision to exercise his adolescent propensity for deception. He severs his connection with the adult world that he depended upon – that failed him – and embarks on a path of violence.

Despite the peripherality of invisibility in some of Cormier's fiction, its continuity as theme persists, providing an insight into the adolescent world that many authors do not explore in quite the same way. Cormier's attention to 'invisible' teen characters highlights the difficulties adolescents face and the fact that sometimes those adolescents fail. His novels reveal that, in Cormier's own words, '"all is not right with the world and the good guys don't always win"'.[31]

Most critical discussion of Cormier's work focuses on his early novels – *The Chocolate War*, *I Am the Cheese* and *After the First Death* – and ignores his later, equally powerful works. Focus on his early novels supports Anne Scott MacLeod's claim that Cormier writes 'what are, at bottom, political novels' rather than 'taking for [his] model adolescents themselves, with their paramount interest in self, individual morality, interior change, and personality',[32] whereas his later novels present more strongly his characteristic balance between the socio-political and adolescent psychology, especially issues of self-definition and identity. In considering later works, Kathy Latrobe and Trisha Hutcherson note that '[a]mong the topics and issues Cormier has explored are hidden or concealed identity in *Fade* ... , *Heroes* ... and *The Bumblebee Flies Anyway*'.[33] While a few critics such as Latrobe and Hutcherson have mentioned Cormier's use of invisibility as a theme, none has investigated it in any detail. The closest to a thematic consideration of invisibility in Cormier's work is Joyce Sweeney's 'The Invisible Adolescent: Robert Cormier's *Fade*', a chapter in Nicholas Karolides' *Censored Books II*, which considers *Fade* from a specifically anti-censorship perspective.[34] The novel's title itself suggests the centrality of invisibility as a theme in *Fade*, and Latrobe and Hutchinson are right in adding *Heroes* to their list.

In those texts in which the theme of adolescent invisibility *is* central – *The Chocolate War*, *Beyond the Chocolate War*, *Heroes* and *Fade* – Cormier presents three approaches adolescents take to threatening situations: they stand up against the adult world; they disappear or hide in order to carry out guerrilla warfare against often corrupt powers in the adult world; or they fade intentionally into the background to hide from harm.

The Chocolate War and *Beyond the Chocolate War*

Cormier is probably best known for *The Chocolate War* and the controversy it has caused since its publication, yet *The Chocolate War* is in some ways the least representative of Cormier's works. Its protagonist, Jerry Renault, asserts his independence against the abusive powers of authority: significantly, he stands out rather than 'fades'. Yet the progression of Jerry's response to the tyranny The Vigils and Brother Leon present over him, reveals Jerry as a prime – if counter – example of Cormier's metaphor of adolescent invisibility.

The 'what if' which inspired *The Chocolate War* was a sale of chocolates at Cormier's teenage son's school. His son chose not to sell the chocolates, which, while almost unprecedented, was accepted by the administration without demur.[35] In *The Chocolate War*, the success of the chocolate sale at Trinity high school assumes serious significance for Brother Leon, the acting Headmaster, who has pilfered school funds, which he must now repay. He recruits a secret student society – The Vigils, who manipulate the student body with 'assignments' – to assist him in raising chocolate sales. Jerry's 'assignment' is to refuse to sell chocolates for ten days, then to begin selling them again. Jerry, however, for reasons unknown even to himself, continues to refuse to sell them even after the ten days have expired: He defies not only Brother Leon, but also The Vigils. Both reap their revenge. Initially, Jerry is a hero to his schoolmates, who begin to follow his lead, but Brother Leon and Archie Costello, the leader of The Vigils, position Jerry's actions as dangerously unsupportive of school morale. When Jerry still refuses, pressure from The Vigils causes the student body to ostracise him; he has lost the battle, and the war: 'Suddenly, he was invisible, without body, without structure, a ghost … It was as if he were the carrier of a strange disease and nobody wanted to become contaminated. And so they rendered him invisible, eliminating him from their presence.'[36]

In a final violent scene, Archie arranges for Jerry to be beaten severely in a boxing match; Jerry is left broken, almost dead. As Jerry's friend Goober helps to carry him towards the waiting ambulance, Jerry tries to articulate what he has learned: '"They tell you to do your own thing, but they don't mean it. They don't want you to do your own thing, not unless it happens to be their thing too. … Don't disturb the universe, Goober"'.[37]

MacLeod notes that Jerry's stand against the 'Implacable', 'has not only failed, it is repudiated … In one brief paragraph, Cormier has abandoned an enduring American myth to confront his teenaged readers with life as it more often is – with the dangers of dissent, the ferocity of systems as they protect themselves, the power of the pressure to conform.'[38]

This is what happens when the socio-politically naïve adolescent stands up against the evil powers that exist in the world. Rendered invisible by his schoolmates' fear of The Vigils, Jerry is vulnerable. By the end of The Chocolate War, Jerry has not successfully returned to visibility. As the sequel reveals, he instead retreats to the wilds of Canada to heal himself, beaten in his solitary stance against a powerful system.

Cormier did not intend to write a sequel to The Chocolate War. Indeed, he followed this novel with three others before succumbing to reader pressure and publishing Beyond the Chocolate War in 1985. What is significant about Beyond the Chocolate War in terms of invisibility is Jerry's decision – despite the fact that he will again be beaten by Emile Janza, his boxing opponent from The Chocolate War – to return to Trinity. In making this decision, Jerry is once more standing up for what he believes in – now more strongly. He again intends to stand alone, but this text – and his passive nonresistance to Janza's aggression – show that his contemplative period of recovery has made him a man. Alone, The Chocolate War argues against a solitary heroic stance, but Beyond the Chocolate War supports and mediates that message, suggesting that Jerry has learned a valuable lesson, and that the message is not, ultimately, 'Don't disturb the universe', but rather, in Cormier's own words, '"we all lose when the good guys don't do anything"'.[39] The underlying message of Beyond the Chocolate War is that '[e]vil must be resisted collectively'.[40] Jerry, who now stands visibly against the corruption he perceives, nonetheless does not stand out aggressively:"'They want you to fight, Goober. And you can really lose only if you fight them. ... You have to outlast them, that's all'".[41]

Standing out against corrupt authority is dangerous, but Jerry's 'triumphant nonresistance',[42] in the words of Campbell, reveals inner strength and comparative social invisibility to be powerful tools of self-defence.

Heroes

In *Heroes*, Francis Cassavant's story is told from two temporal positions: his return from World War II, during which a grenade has blown away most of his face; and his memories of life before his enlistment, as an adolescent in Monument, Massachusetts. Francis returns without a face; he is not corporally invisible, but he is unrecognisable even to his childhood friends. He covers his face with a scarf, and when he engages a room in his old neighbour's tenement she does not recognise him:'This was proof that the scarf and the bandage were working in two ways: not only to hide the ugliness of what used to be my face, but to hide my identity.'[43]

It is slowly revealed that Francis hides his identity in order to murder his childhood Recreation Supervisor, Larry LaSalle. Both he and Larry had gone to war; both had received the Silver Star for bravery; both were heralded as heroes of their small Massachusetts town. We learn that on his first leave from the army, the hero 'Larry LaSalle, the best of the best'[44] had raped Nicole, the girl Francis loves. Francis, blaming himself for not protecting Nicole, forges a birth certificate to enlist, and attempts suicide by falling on a grenade that threatens his battalion. Thus, in trying to commit an unpardonable sin (for he, like his creator, Cormier, is Catholic), he is made a hero, and returns home filled with anger and self-loathing.

Francis waits for Larry to return as well – 'they all come back to Frenchtown sooner or later'[45] – to murder him for what he did to Nicole, to Francis's life, and to Francis's naïve adolescent understanding of heroism and honour. For that is what lies at the bottom of Francis's angst: his inability to live up to his own vision of the heroic:

'I have been a fake all along. ...

I went to the war because I wanted to die. ... I was too much of a coward to kill myself. In the war, in a battle, I figured it would be easy to get killed. And I wouldn't be disgracing my father and mother's name. I looked for chances to die and instead killed others, and two of them kids like me...'.[46]

He ultimately confronts a broken, leg-less, yet unrepentant LaSalle, who eventually admits his own emotional trauma, and tells Francis that 'one gun is enough for what has to be done. ... Whether you know it or not, you've accomplished your mission here. And you couldn't have killed me anyway, in cold blood.[47]

As Francis leaves, Larry's final words are significant; even as he contemplates his own self-destruction, Larry is heroic enough to try to heal Francis's pain, telling him, '"You would have fallen on that grenade anyway. All your instincts would have made you sacrifice yourself for your comrades"'.[48] With these words, Francis is redeemed; he seeks out Nicole, with whom he settles the past but learns there is no future, and he contemplates heroism:

'I remember what I said to Nicole about not knowing who the real heroes are and I think of my old platoon ... Scared kids, not born to fight and kill. Who were not only there but who stayed, did not run away, fought the good war. And never talk about it. And didn't receive a Silver Star. But heroes anyway. The real heroes.'[49]

Thinking himself a man, Frances used his invisibility to find and destroy Larry LaSalle; ultimately, however, he recognises that maturity — and true heroism — also involves a humility, a type of self-imposed invisibility for those who 'never talk about' their heroic actions.

In the end, LaSalle's heroism, complicated by his unquestionable sins, forces Francis to reassess his own identity, to leave behind adolescence and resume the transformation towards adulthood that has been arrested by his anger — both at LaSalle and at himself. LaSalle's final sin — suicide — frees Francis to grow towards manhood, if he so chooses, but, typical of Cormier's style, we are left to infer what Francis's choice will be.

Fade

Fade not only contains Cormier's strongest example of invisibility as a metaphor for adolescent experience, but is also the most artfully constructed of Cormier's novels. Hollindale makes a comment regarding *I Am the Cheese* that is equally true of *Fade*: 'The book is technically demanding, requiring a sophisticated reader. However, *sophisticated* is not synonymous with *adult*'.[50] This sophistication is yet another way in which Cormier shows his respect for his reading audience. As he commented in an interview with Campbell, 'I've aimed for the intelligent reader and have often found that that reader is fourteen years old'.[51] The complex structure of *Fade* is a mystery that unfolds as the five sections – 'Paul', 'Susan', 'Paul', 'Ozzie', and 'Susan' – reveal the relationship between their eponymous characters and between the two texts: the manuscript Susan is reading (Paul Moreaux's story) and the novel the reader is holding (Paul Roget's story). This postmodern metafictive structure becomes an additional challenge for the reader, one that holds as much interest as the plot it unfolds.

Joyce Sweeney's passing comment, that the fade 'was meant to be seen as part of what happens to every teenager, as the blinders of childhood wear off',[52] encapsulates a significant part of what Cormier was doing with this novel, but is left tantalisingly unexplored in her defence of *Fade* against censorship. Paul Moreaux learns – significantly as he reaches puberty –that he can become invisible at will, a characteristic passed from uncle to nephew, as his Uncle Adelard informs him. Adelard 'was always disappearing',[53] coming and going from their lives with no warning, a hobo, a traveller, a vagrant with a purpose, running from the effect of the fade on his life, as he tells Paul:

> 'In the old days, the fade made me crazy. Took command of my body, my senses. Made me do things that were opposite to my nature. ... One night I robbed ten stores, in a town in Ohio. Broke into them in a frenzy, crazy. ... but the next morning, like a hangover, I looked at the money in a panic. And gave it away. Mailed some of it back to a few of the stores. The sin, Paul, is that I *wanted* that money, wanted to go on a big spree. But could not. Had to give it back. Maybe that is the real curse of the fade. That I couldn't use it for pleasure. ...
> I saw what I had become. A something, a monster. This is what the fade made me. A monster.
> But I already knew that.
> And I knew that I, too, was a monster.'[54]

Paul learns early that the fade is not 'a gift' as he had first supposed, but a curse. As soon as he can command the fade, he uses it to spy on people he knows in town: 'I could go anywhere I thought. Into any of those tenements. Spy on whomever I chose'.[55] However, when he does, he sees Mr. Dondier, the grocer, pay his classmate Therese for oral sex, and witnesses his twin friends Page and Emerson in an incestuous affair. In the first instance, he vomits and runs from the shop; after the second, he remembers a conversation with his uncle:

> 'If the fade is a gift, why are you so sad all the time?'
> 'Did I ever say it was a gift?' he replied. ... 'What's the opposite of a gift, Paul?'
> 'I don't know.'
> But now I knew. Or thought I knew.[56]

The learning process is painful, and ultimately Paul vows never to summon the fade again. Nevertheless, as with Adelard, Paul finds that the fade is itself a power:

'I … refused to consider what nightmares would be unleashed if I invited the fade. The fade invited itself, however, depleting me, coming again and again, and I was helpless to prevent its assault.'[57]

The fade speaks to Paul, as it must have to Adelard; it serves as an evil conscience telling him how much he wants to do ill. Paul, however, resists its force, living as a recluse, invisible to the world, just as Adelard ran from town to town. It is here that the fade as metaphor for the adolescent experience of invisibility and biological transformation becomes strongest. As Roberta Seelinger Trites suggested in a 2006 presentation to the Children's Literature Association, neurologists have determined that adolescents' emotional brain activity takes place in a completely different place from adult emotional activity, and the area of the brain adolescents use to process emotions is not as effective or well controlled as that the adult brain uses.[58] Compounded with other biological changes occurring in the adolescent body, this might account for the commonly expressed adolescent sense of being out of control of their emotions, or even controlled by their emotions, just as Paul is initially controlled by the fade. Neither of the other two faders in the story – Adelard or Paul's illegitimate nephew Ozzie Slater – are as successful as Paul in controlling the fade. The narrative suggestion is that inner, moral strength can aid in learning the self-control necessary during the adolescent period of heightened emotional responses to the world.

The onus is upon Paul to find the next fader before he reaches puberty. When he finally locates his sister's illegitimate son, Ozzie, we are plummeted into a horror story worthy of Cormier's friend, Stephen King. When the fade comes to Ozzie, he quickly realises its evil potential, and uses it to kill his drunken, abusive stepfather. The fade, not controlled by any moral certitude, possesses Ozzie completely, and he goes on a rampage of violence. Paul arrives in the middle of this, and is forced by Ozzie to summon the fade to defend himself. In breaking his promise never to summon the fade, he ends up killing Ozzie, leaving himself even more emotionally broken than before.

Robert Unsworth sees the fade as representing 'a potentially evil force within us all'.[59] The fade is also a metaphor for the anger and desires that spring unbidden from the psyche at inopportune moments. Adelard tried to run from the responsibility of learning the nature of the fade and how to deal with it; Ozzie lets the negative emotions

grow within him, and truly does become the monster Adelard and
Paul feared they were. Paul, on the other hand, presents an example
of the strength of will necessary to control the well of emotions
within; only when he runs up against the uncontrolled evil of Ozzie
does his moral strength fail him. Once again, Cormier is revealing
moral strength as a necessary but not sufficient component of survival
within a complex and often malevolent world. His novels reveal a
level of evil in the world that Perry Nodelman sees as fundamentally
reassuring, in that 'the distance between [the protagonist's] plight and
our own lives ought to make us realise how comparatively illegitimate
our own self-pity might be'.[60]

Cormier's fiction suggests that while adolescents have the obligation
to educate themselves politically and socially, in some circumstances
that education will not be sufficient. By constructing challenging
'what if' situations, by illustrating hypothetical dangers – both physical
and emotional – for his adolescent protagonists, Cormier enables the
young adult reader to experience vicariously the heightened emotions
such traumatic situations might elicit. This in turn parallels the heightened emotional responses of teenagers to events in their own lives.
Adolescents are said to feel more deeply, to respond more strongly, to
social and emotional stimuli than either children or adults. Cormier
uses this knowledge to force his readers to look beyond their own
lives to bigger social issues, but he never loses sight of the fact that the
individual reader will be most concerned with the individual reader.
Sweeney astutely assesses where Cormier's power ultimately lies:

> It is clear he cares about his young readers enough to never lie to them,
> never sugar-coat the things they need to know. He has the courage to
> warn them, in *Fade* and elsewhere, that life will not always be fair, that
> sometimes they will suffer, and that they have to be brave and stick to
> their principles – not because life will shower them with rewards, but
> because, in the end, their own sense of honor and integrity is all they
> have.[61]

Through the different approaches Cormier's adolescents take in their
confrontations with the adult world – standing out, acting from a
position of invisibility, or using their social invisibility as protective
cover – Cormier reveals his understanding of the adolescent situation.
As one reader writes, "'I always felt that Robert Cormier could see
me when he wrote. Maybe he didn't know *me* – but he knew kids like
me'".[62] Cormier's novels express his belief that "'Happy endings are not
our birthright. You have to do something to make them happen'",[63]
but they also importantly 'see' and reveal the invisible adolescent.

Notes

1. Patricia J. Campbell, *Presenting Robert Cormier* (Boston, MA: Twayne, 1989): 37.
2. '"I Have Led a Thousand Lives": An Interview with Robert Cormier', *Writing* 23(3) (2000): http://proxy.lib.sfu.ca/login?url=http://search.ebscohost.com/login.aspx?direct=true&db=aph&AN=3796970&site=ehost-live (accessed on 2 June 2006).
3. Quoted in Patty Campbell, *Robert Cormier: Daring to Disturb the Universe* (New York: Delacourt, 2006): 49.
4. Ibid.: 49.
5. Peter Hollindale, 'The Adolescent Novel of Ideas', *Children's Literature in Education*, 26(1) (1995): 83–95, at 85.
6. Ibid.: 86–7.
7. Michael Cart, in Marilyn E. Marlow et al., 'Robert Cormier Remembered', *Publisher's Weekly*, 1 January 2001: 39.
8. Zibby Oneal, '"They Tell You to Do Your Own Thing, but They Don't Mean It": Censorship and *The Chocolate War*', in Nicholas J. Karolides (ed.) *Censored Books II: Critical Viewpoints 1985–2000* (Lanham, MD: Scarecrow, 2002): 179–84, at 180.
9. Ibid.: 182.
10. Herbert N. Foerstel, 'Voices of Banned Authors', *Banned in the USA: A Reference Guide to Book Censorship in Schools and Public Libraries* (Westport, CN: Greenwood, 2002): 131–78, at 148, 150.
11. 'I Have Led a Thousand Lives', n.p.
12. Marlow et al.: 39.
13. Campbell (1989): 117.
14. S. J. Grady quoted in Campbell (1989): 188.
15. Robert Cormier, *A Little Raw on Monday Mornings* [1963] (New York: Avon, 1980): 36.
16. Robert Cormier, *Frenchtown Summer* [1999] (New York: Laurel Leaf, 2001): 2.
17. *Frenchtown Summer*, 1999: 17.
18. Robert Cormier, *Tunes for Bears to Dance to* [1992] (New York: Laurel Leaf, 1994): 15.
19. Robert Cormier, *Tenderness* [1997] (New York: Delacorte, 2004): 94.
20. *Frenchtown Summer*: 124.
21. Robert Cormier, *We All Fall Down* [1991] (New York: Laurel Leaf, 1993): 83.
22. Robert Cormier, *After the First Death* [1979] (New York: Laurel Leaf, 1991): 40.
23. *After the First Death*: 10.
24. Robert Cormier, *Other Bells for Us to Ring* [1990] (New York: Laurel Leaf, 2000): 142.
25. Ibid.: 152.
26. Ibid.

27. Robert Cormier, *The Bumblebee Flies Anyway* [1983] (New York: Laurel Leaf, 1993): 43.
28. Ibid.: 43.
29. Ibid.: 137.
30. Robert Cormier, *The Rag and Bone Shop* [2001] (New York: Laurel Leaf, 2003): 12.
31. Quoted in Campbell (1989): 62.
32. Anne Scott MacLeod, 'Robert Cormier and the Adolescent Novel', *Children's Literature in Education*, 12.2 (1981): 74–81, at 74.
33. Kathy Latrobe and Trisha Hutcherson, 'An Introduction to Ten Outstanding Young-Adult Authors in the United States', *World Literature Today*, (2002): 68–73, at 69.
34. Joyce Sweeney, 'The Invisible Adolescent: Robert Cormier's *Fade*', in Nicholas J. Karolides (ed.) *Censored Books II: Critical Viewpoints 1985–2000* (Lanham, MD: Scarecrow, 2002): 163–66.
35. Campbell (2006): 27.
36. Robert Cormier, *The Chocolate War* [1974] (New York: Laurel Leaf, 2000): 223.
37. Ibid.: 259.
38. MacLeod: 76.
39. Roger Sutton, '"A Kind of Funny Dichotomy": A Conversation with Robert Cormier', *School Library Journal*, 37(6) (1991): 28–33, at 29.
40. Campbell (2006): 85.
41. Robert Cormier, *Beyond the Chocolate War* [1985] (New York: Laurel Leaf, 1986): 224.
42. Campbell (2006): 42.
43. Robert Cormier, *Heroes* [1998] (New York: Laurel Leaf, 2000): 4–5.
44. Ibid.: 52.
45. Ibid.: 53.
46. Ibid.: 112–13.
47. Ibid.: 117.
48. Ibid.
49. Ibid.: 134.
50. Hollindale: 87.
51. Campbell, 'A Loving Farewell to Robert Cormier', *Horn Book Magazine*, 77(2) (2001): 245–8, at 248.
52. Sweeney: 164.
53. Robert Cormier, *Fade* [1988] (New York: Delacorte, 2004): 4.
54. Ibid.: 209–10.
55. Ibid.: 81.
56. Ibid.: 130.
57. Ibid.: 223.
58. Roberta Seelinger Trites, Mike Cadden, and Karen Coats, 'Forum: Examining the Critical Pedagogy of Young Adult Literature.' *Children's Literature Association Annual Conference*. Manhattan Beach, CA. 9 June 2006.

59. Robert E. Unsworth, 'Rev. of *Fade*, by Robert Cormier', *School Library Journal*, (Oct. 1988): 160.

60. Perry Nodelman, 'Robert Cormier Does a Number', *Children's Literature in Education*, 14(2) (1983): 94–103, at 102.

61. Sweeney: 166.

62. Kerry Halls, quoted in Campbell (2006): 6.

63. Quoted in Campbell (2006): 44.

2

'So many disguises': Questions of Identity in Robert Cormier's *After the First Death* and *Heroes*

Andrew F. Humphries

Questions of identity are important to Robert Cormier's young adult protagonists as part of their engagement with the unstable and shifting postmodern world that they must negotiate. Cormier's teenagers are emergent adults who share a quest, ultimately, to discover, as the doomed Ben Marchand in *After the First Death* (1979) expresses it, 'Who I am'.[1] It is the way in which identity emerges through crisis, however, that Cormier foregrounds. His teenage characters are not fixed: they are works in progress that shift with the uncertainties of the trials they encounter. Identity becomes more the focus of an ongoing inner dialogue than a defining character statement. Characters like Kate Forrester, the teenage bus-driver and heroine of *After the First Death*, challenge the notion of identity as something identifiable. Identity shifts. One never knows how one is going to be or act. She acknowledges that 'there were other Kate Forresters, and she wondered about them sometimes'[2] as if identity is more about multiple selves than about a defining personality that determines one's fate. Kate's own identity becomes of pivotal importance in the novel at the moment the hijackers enter the school bus and realise that the driver 'turned out not to be a man'.[3] Kate's gender – she has replaced the regular driver, her uncle, for the day – shifts the whole dynamic of the terrorist plans and unsettles the focus of their narrative. As the hijack intensifies, Kate challenges more and more the idea that identity is recognisable or sustainable in any material sense: 'She often wondered where her disguises left off and the real Kate Forrester began. So many disguises. There was the most obvious one, the disguise provided by nature: she was blond, fair-skinned, slender, no weight problems, had managed to avoid adolescent acne. A healthy body with one exception: a weak bladder.'[4]

Cormier's characters are not to be taken at face value. One's apparent identity, Kate's thoughts seem to suggest, might be a cover for something quite different or quite other. Like many of Cormier's young adult characters, Kate unsettles the picture of herself and questions its authenticity. It is the 'so many disguises' in Cormier's stories that present a truth about his young adult characters as they attempt, on the one hand, to understand themselves, and, on the other hand, to adopt disguises to hide their identities from a watching and hostile adult society.

After the First Death the main focus of this essay, exposes these questions surrounding identity through the intensity of its plot. It tells of the hijacking of a bus load of kindergarten children. The bus is driven to what becomes known as 'the Bridge' where the hijacker-terrorists position themselves to negotiate with the US army base known as Delta, threatening to kill the children unless their demands are met. The key narrative voices of the story are those of three teenagers brought together by the hijack: Kate Forrester, the day's temporary bus driver; Ben Marchand, the army General's 16-year-old son who is sent to the Bridge as a go-between and negotiator; and Miro Shantas, a teenage terrorist schooled in refugee camp poverty who is devoted to his terrorist mentor and leader of the hijack, Artkin. For Artkin and Miro America is the implacable enemy which has taken away their 'homeland'.[5]

Mitzi Myers has praised Cormier's 'unflinching portrayals of adolescents who must somehow achieve selfhood in an intimidating and manipulative universe'.[6] For Cormier, teenage identity is a volatile agent that must negotiate a world of apparently fixed adult values and structures that one cannot trust. The identity of his young adult heroes and heroines is expressed, it seems, as much by the bravery and honesty of their thoughts as by the bravery and honesty of their actions. We are rarely allowed to forget that as adolescents they are 'other' to the adult world they negotiate.

Cormier takes the question of identity seriously and also expects his readers to so do. As he states, it is important for him that the reader engages with the process of identity as it emerges in his characters:

[y]ou can have a clever plot and fine writing but if the reader doesn't believe in the characters, doesn't love them or hate them or doesn't identify with them, then the story won't work. ... Until I 'hear' the voice of a character I can't proceed.... And what happens eventually to that character, as well as others, affects me greatly.[7]

Identity in Cormier's narratives, as this statement reveals, is about establishing the 'voice of a character' but it becomes more complex than this. Identity becomes a term that incorporates the sense of 'disguise' that young adult characters must adopt to cope with exposure to the adult world but it also refers to the inner voices Cormier's teenage characters must acknowledge in their attempt to understand themselves better. In Cormier's narratives, identity emerges in a world of intense watchfulness and exposure. His novels privilege a sense of surveillance that puts his characters under an intense scrutiny that they must learn to accommodate, deflect, or deceive.

Surveillance and secrecy: the watching world

A novel about identity, *After the First Death* becomes a story, also, about surveillance because survival in the novel hinges upon knowledge of others and how they might behave. Characters scrutinise each other for evidence of who they are and what they might be hiding. Surveillance is also internalised. Cormier's teenage characters continually question the truths about themselves that the narrative exposes. Such surveillance or questioning is often precarious in Cormier's stories. It can be dangerous for characters to read situations too well. In *After the First Death*, for example, both Kate and the five-year-old child Raymond – who is later shot by Artkin in reprisal for a sniper's killing of the terrorist, Antibbe – read early on their own deaths in the masks of the hijackers and it is largely their heightened perceptiveness that brings about their deaths.

Secrets, therefore – the withholding of identity and knowledge – are part of Cormier's world of masks and surveillance in which trust becomes precarious. In *Heroes* (1998), Sister Mathilde tells disfigured teenage soldier Francis Cassavant that Nicole Renard is '"a secretive girl ... But, then, we all have secrets, eh, Francis?"'[8] In other words, one can never trust that the identity people intend us to see is the whole story. In *After the First Death*, as negotiations with Delta over the 'Bridge' become tense and uncertain, Artkin tells Miro that the problem with the world is that '"there is no trust on either side"'.[9] Later, in justification of his torture of young Ben Marchand and in his ruthless plan to kill as many children on the bus as it takes, Artkin argues that '"No one could be trusted in these times ... Even children could be what they seemed not to be"'[10] A place without trust is always watching for signs of betrayal. Miro has been taught by Artkin that 'you must carry nothing with you that may betray you'.[11] In this sense there is a correlation here between betrayal and the exposure of identity, and yet often the ambivalence of such an exposure for young adults is at the forefront of Cormier's treatment. While Miro worries he might give away too much of his inner self, Kate worries that Miro's failure to see her for who she really is will enable him more easily to kill her.

At one point on the bus, for example, when Miro points his gun at Kate as she sits in the driving seat, she interprets this exposure as both releasing and threatening. Kate feels 'mildly claustrophobic and also transparent, as if the boy could see right into her mind'.[12] There is something both intimate and dangerous about such transparency. To be transparent in Cormier is to be understood but also to be caught out or revealed. To be transparent in the revelation of emotional truth is part of Kate's hope of breaking through Miro's closed terrorist identity: his literal and metaphorical mask. As their relationship intensifies through close proximity and danger, Kate articulates this 'transparency' more overtly as a sexual sign. For her to survive, Miro 'had to look upon her as a human being. More than that: as a desirable young woman, and not a victim'.[13]

Given Kate's mistrust of the distinction between truth and disguise, this attempt at transparency becomes dangerously close to a lie. The sexual woman is a part she must act that might genuinely represent her attraction to Miro but might equally be interpreted by him as a deception or diversion. At the end of the novel, just before he kills Kate, Miro reveals the dangers of misreading signals about identity when he tells her, as he drags her into the woods to escape the battle, '"No more words, Kate, no more games"'.[14] Her openness and attempts to be 'transparent' have been dangerously misinterpreted by Miro as simply an act or a disguise.

Like Kate, Ben Marchand also conveys the claustrophobia and transparency of young adult exposure. A suicidal recluse as a result of his near-death experience at the Bridge, he watches the world from his schoolroom where he sits at a typewriter, imprisoned by his own sense of isolation and loss of identity. The world of Ben's childhood, when appearances and identities could be believed, had been secure, but he now knows that his father is not the father he had thought him to be. General Marcus Marchand has a secret Inner Delta identity as General Rufus Briggs.[15] His father's true identity, for Ben, 'has always been too shadowy to pin down'.[16] Like the other key adult figure in the story, Artkin, whom Miro considers a 'superb actor',[17] General Marchand's identity is a cover: he acts a part and studies his role carefully just as he studies others like Ben for roles they might play. While Ben tries to search behind his father's professional mask, he is aware, also, of himself being watched. Ben's failure at the Bridge to become the young man he thought his father and Delta had trained him to be – in fact the General had calculated on such a failure – has triggered a crisis of identity from which he cannot escape. He is caught between the childhood view of himself seen through his father's eyes, and the adult he has failed to become.

This wounded and suicidal Ben – very different from the patriotic and trusting boy sent out by his father a year before to save the kidnapped children on the bus – is psychologically damaged beyond repair. In this sense there are two Bens in the novel: the one before and the one after 'the Bus and the Bridge'.[18] The novel's complex use of time and structure, however, complicates this simple divide. The Ben after the 'Bus and the Bridge' is no longer the Ben who had identified with his father's military codes as a student of the Delta academy. The bridge experience – being tortured by Artkin and taking a terrorist's bullet in the chest during his attempted escape – has exposed Ben too soon to a reality he was unprepared for: the trauma of his insignificance and anonymity and the fact that his identity does not matter.

During Ben's torture by Artkin on the Bridge readers see him through Miro's eyes as 'hollow and empty' with the 'look of the betrayer'.[19] Ben has, in his own eyes, betrayed the Inner Delta culture and community he was born to defend. The belief system he has lived by, based on heroism and military self-sacrifice for the nation, has been destroyed in him by the realisation of his powerlessness – the powerlessness of a child – against Artkin. The terrorist has forced him to reveal, not simply information about the timing of his father's intended attack, but also his own emptiness. The attack information is false. It has been deliberately revealed to Ben by his father based on his assumption that his son will crack under interrogation. Both Ben and Miro see this moment on the bridge as an initiation: a point at which they expect to achieve adult identity based upon their fulfilment of promised manhood.

After the bridge attack, Ben is like the walking dead. He is a 'skeleton rattling [his] bones'[20] as if the bullet in his chest has actually killed him and only his consciousness lives on. He is isolated from life and feels 'invisible' to the extent that he looks behind him as he walks to see if he actually leaves footprints in the snow.[21] Ben's 'first death', as he calls it[22] – the bullet on the bridge that should have killed him – prevents him from returning to life or to the identity he has grown up believing in: the identity he had seen as a child reflected in his father's gaze. Ben experiences an extreme version of teenage displacement; he lives a twilight life between childhood and adulthood but belongs to neither. When his father comes to visit him in his solitary room at the school after the attack, Ben is aware that his father's scrutiny searches for this lost 'child' identity: 'Finally, he swiveled and looked at me. Really looked. As if he were studying me. I wondered what he hoped to see – the kid I'd been a long time ago when a child is innocent, without blemishes? ... Or was he seeing me as I was last summer before the Bus and the Bridge? Before the Betrayal'.[23]

For Ben after the 'Bridge' his father becomes 'the phantom', who, even when absent, is 'already in the room with me, watching and waiting'.[24] Ben's eventual suicide – his second death – at Brimmler's bridge is his despairing attempt to escape not only the surveillance of his father but the tortured scrutiny of his own conscience.

In Cormier's fiction, surveillance is a relentless search for identity: the truth about 'who I am'. Ben extends this sense of exposure to 'watching and waiting' in a metafictive way when he moves momentarily out of his own narrative to invite the reader to step from the shadows and be identified: 'Who the hell are you anyway, out there looking over my shoulder as I write this? I feel you there, watching, waiting to get in. Or is anybody there?'[25] The reader becomes a momentary intruder. It is also, perhaps more significantly, a wider statement about teenage exposure to scrutiny that Cormier gives voice to in his narratives in a way that makes the reader feel complicit in the teenager's agony. The reader is forced by Ben's challenge to ask the question who is watching whom.

The reader, it seems, is being propositioned by Ben in the context of what Patricia Head has called Cormier's 'books written for the adult-within the child'.[26] While aimed at teenagers, Cormier's stories, Head suggests, ask us to acknowledge the adult identity emerging through a child's shifting vulnerability. Characters like Ben, broken children as they might appear, ask to be taken seriously as adults. Ben's sharing of a sophisticated and dark irony in his narratives is a testimony to this aspiration. Cormier's young adults like Ben and Kate, or like Francis in *Heroes* or Jerry Renault in *The Chocolate War* (1974), seem to resist definition by stereotype, and their narratives challenge the sense that they can be too conventionally or conveniently judged. Until the very end of *Tenderness* (1997), for example, the teenage murderer Eric Poole refuses to accept the label 'monster' given to him by his adult nemesis, the ageing Lieutenant Proctor. Proctor's surveillance of Eric throughout the novel is an attempt to prove his criminal identity by catching him in the act of murdering another young woman. Eric tells Proctor that '"names mean nothing to me"'.[27] He refuses to be tagged and identified by a name and, in so protesting, invites readers to look beyond 'names' to understand why he is what he is.

This call upon the reader to wrestle with identities and see them as unfixed or undetermined, is part of what Head calls the 'postmodernist features of Cormier's writing', which 'bring new possibilities to reader and critic, because the relationship between author and reader is fore-grounded'. She adds that 'the security of the text is often destabilised further by the narrative form'.[28] It seems part of Cormier's intention, therefore, that the reader, like his teenage protagonists, should be exposed to uncertainty: an uncertainty that has at its heart the crisis of identity.

Ben Marchand epitomises adolescent fear of exposure. Identifying one's deeper self to the world is fraught with danger and uncertainty. This fragility is acknowledged by the damaged Ben whose voice can only emerge falteringly through his typewriter while he remains vocally silent, as he states:'keeping my lips sealed, my mouth clenched tight so that the scream I keep inside does not escape and fill the room with its anguish'.[29]

What emerges through Cormier's young adult protagonists, there-fore, is their truthfulness: a truthfulness that is liable to compromise their own safety or contradict the identity they present to others. Truthfulness is central to Cormier's exposure of shifting adolescent identity. It may not always, as in the case of Eric Poole, represent a truthfulness that fits established moral codes. Often Cormier's teenage characters challenge established views, placing them with those young adult fiction narratives that Caroline Hunt believes 'speak directly to the adolescent experience' and 'use language that some adults do not like, mention experiences ... that make some adults uncomfortable, and examine the possibility ... of serious challenges to authority'.[30] Cormier states that he is '"not in the business of providing good role models or models of any kind, old or young"',[31] and figures of adult authority in his novels, like General Marchand in *After the First Death*, Larry LaSalle in *Heroes*, or Brother Leon in *The Chocolate War*, do not set a moral standard for their teenage charges to follow. Because adults or adult structures prove to be cynical or untrustworthy, Cormier's teenagers must often develop their own moral codes and their own sense of redemption to stay true in an adult world of deception and expediency. Cormier's ability to unsettle the reader as he represents this world through his young adult characters' consciousness of desta-bilisation and displacement is what makes his novels so uncomfortable and thought-provoking.

Shocks are part of Cormier's realism. He shows things as they are without apology, and his novels refuse to lie. In this sense, lies become a distortion of identity and require his characters to re-evaluate themselves, their allegiances, and their perception of events. Attacking Holocaust deniers in 2000, Cormier stated that he was "'afraid of big lies ... because they're so big that they tend to be believed after a while'".[32] In *The Chocolate War*, for example, the 'big lie' is not about the corruption of staff and pupils in Catholic private schools. That would be too easily evaded by readers eager to distance themselves from the moral dilemma the novel proposes. The lie is more about the ways a society – late twentieth-century American society in particular – uses the mechanisms of democracy and liberty to betray the very principals it designed to guard individual rights. Readers cannot hide from Cormier's moral challenge to the big lies, even if those lies are seen materially to succeed within the narrative itself, as they do in *The Chocolate War*. 'Big lies' in Cormier, require his characters to declare or identify themselves as individuals: to show where they stand in a world of no escape.

The 'stranger slowly taking shape'

In *Heroes*, too, there is nowhere to hide. At the end of the novel, Francis, the returning soldier, his face disfigured beyond recognition by a grenade in the war, tracks down to a hotel room the now physically damaged fallen hero, Larry LaSalle, in order to shoot him. For Francis, it is not simply murder or revenge. The shooting will avenge LaSalle's rape of Nicole Renard but, more significantly, it will force expiation of LaSalle's betrayal of a generation of youth who believed in his lie – the lie that he is a hero and a role model – and became tainted by it. Truth, for Francis, is to acknowledge the distortion of identity that his broken face symbolises. That same disfigured face, however, reveals an inner truth about Francis's identity: it is not fixed by events and can be released from its past. He realises this when, on his return to Frenchtown, he looks in a mirror and sees not himself but 'a stranger slowly taking shape'.[33] This mistrust of surface appearance characterises Cormier's foregrounding of identity as something not fixed or binding but evolutionary.

Francis's identity has been as much shattered by LaSalle's treachery as by the grenade that injured him, and LaSalle seems curiously accepting of Francis's disfigurement, advising his would-be killer that he should not be afraid to show his damaged face to the world as "'a symbol of how brave you were, the Silver Star you earned'".[34] LaSalle accepts the disguise as truth. His seemingly generous words are betrayed, however, by the falsity of his own tarnished image. He has shown a false face to the world for years, behind which he hid his

'"evil"' corruption of the '" 'sweet young things"' he was employed
as a youth leader to protect.[35] Faces like Francis's might be disfigured
but true while beautiful faces like LaSalle's can hide irredeemable
corruption. Francis's disgust at LaSalle's cynicism becomes a wider
disgust at himself and at the world that has condoned such a lie.
LaSalle's war hero image is as big a deception, it seems, as the big lie
of the 1941 Japanese attack without warning on Pearl Harbor, which
overshadows the novel and its trust in the innocence of appearances.
Shooting LaSalle might restore the truth. 'I had always wanted to be a
hero', Francis states, 'but had been a fake all along. And now I am tired
of the deception and have to rid myself of the fakery'.[36]

The phrase that prevents Francis pulling the trigger, finally, is
typical of Cormier's questioning of identity at a moment of truth.
LaSalle asks him '"Does that one sin of mine wipe out all the good
things?"'[37] Human identity is more complex, the novel suggests,
than a single bullet can decide. Cormier's young adult heroes, like his
readers, are challenged to respond to such complexities by searching
beyond stereotypes of good and evil.

To return to *After the First Death*, Kate's complexity lies in her
reluctance to accept her own identity as stable or fixed. The extremity of the situation on the bus makes Kate begin to question her
true identity. An articulate observer of herself, Kate thinks about her
personality often during the story. The sophistication of her interior
monologue achieves that Bakhtinian 'double-voicedness' that Mike
Cadden detects as a key feature of Cormier's young adult fiction, which
shows 'adolescent readers equal and multiple narrative viewpoints that
equip them to identify the irony in the text'.[38] While this can be seen
in the multiple perspectives on the same event in this novel, it is also
evident within individual characters in that, like Kate, they vary their
own perspectives from moment to moment. Particularly evident is the
way in which they identify themselves to the reader or challenge their
own views of themselves at key moments.

The sense of becoming a new character becomes crucial to Kate
as she must rely on 'that unknown quantity: herself' to survive.[39] It
is a tragedy of the novel that such a convincingly resourceful character evades death so many times only to be killed at the end. Kate,
however, serves a greater fictional role than simply to demonstrate
survival strategies. Part of Cormier's teenage dialectic is that his novels
challenge the face of things in a world that otherwise accepts them as
truth. His characters, like Kate, are extended by extremity to comprehend truths that would otherwise seem beyond them. As Patricia
Campbell describes, Cormier's 'focus [is] not just on adolescent

concerns but also on the basic moral and spiritual issues of the larger human condition'.[40] Individual revelations of teenage crisis – often of private things that teenagers wish to keep hidden – strike wider messages about human experience.

Kate's beauty and popularity, for example, hide a secret that is not part of the identity she shows to the world: her weak bladder. She cannot control this in moments of crisis or excitement. Ironically it is the vulnerability of the 'weak bladder'[41] she tries to hide that presents her with a glimpse of hope in her attempt to get Miro to 'look upon her as a human being'.[42] Needing to remove her saturated panties, she seeks the semi-privacy of the back of the bus – the drugged children are all asleep – but, as she does so, catches Miro watching her undress. She recognises his attraction to her in this unguarded moment. This sudden glimpse of her nakedness excites and intrigues his sense of her vulnerable humanity.[43] Kate suddenly appears 'unprotected'.[44] She is not simply that 'American schoolgirl, one of those hollow, empty-faced girls without any purpose in life'[45] who can be labelled and discarded: her identity, in his eyes, has shifted.

Like the reference to Kate's impending period, which is made at a moment when Kate feels Miro's dangerous physical proximity confusing and disturbingly sexual, Cormier makes teenage sensitivity to personal embarrassment a revealing part of his narrative realism. At times he does so in a way that deliberately undercuts, it seems, the high-seriousness of the subject matter to add a more convincing sense of how a real teenager might react to such extremity rather than present a stereotypical characterisation. In this example, as Kate sits in the driving seat with Miro's gun 'pointing at her',[46] Miro is 'thrown slightly against her' by the lurching bus and she feels 'his body against her shoulder only for a moment' just as her migraine and a 'small pimple' appear to signal that her period might 'come ahead of time while she was here on the bus'.[47] Kate wants to cry like a 'little girl', faced as she is by this confusion of adult responsibility for the children with her own childlike vulnerability.[48] Cormier's teenagers are frank about their bodies – in their private narratives at least – and their physical embarrassment betrays a self-consciousness they wish to avoid. This sense of the body betraying one's identity is evident in this destabilisation that sexual tension brings into the already precarious Kate–Miro relationship. Miro sees bodies as potential 'traitors'.[49] His betrayal into sexual fascination and Kate's betrayal by her weak bladder or her untimely period are all part of the psychological and physical truthfulness in Cormier's teenage characterisation.

Emotional vulnerability becomes all the more redeeming in a story that becomes decided finally by technological negotiations and mechanical surveillance that enable the 'big lies' to predominate against the stories of simple human interaction. Humans, after all, including children, become anonymous and therefore expendable. As General Marchand states in his self-justifying narrative, remembering the moment he walked his son as an unwitting sacrificial pawn towards the terrorists on the bridge, 'Expediency is the rule'.[50] The 'big lies' are part of the mechanical dehumanisation expressed by Artkin's rationalising of terror and the General's 'defense of this nation'[51] that make Ben, Kate, and the children on the bus collateral damage rather than human individuals with identities worth protecting. Kate defends the need to protect the children's human individuality when she notices that the drugged sweets Artkin has given them make them a mass of drowsy bodies that have 'ceased to have identities'.[52] When the first child dies from an overdose her particular concern is that 'she realised she didn't even know his name'.[53] It is not just the violence but the denial of identity by the hijackers that Kate fears.

The terrorists, however, do not think their brutality is unjustified. The question of whether or not Miro is a 'monster' haunts the latter stages of the novel up to and after the moment when he kills Kate. Even as Artkin lowers the body of the first dead child down into the ravine, Miro asserts to Kate that '"We are not animals, after all"'.[54] As with Eric Poole in *Tenderness* who believes himself to be good and moral despite his crimes and who does, after all, risk his life to attempt to save Lori Cranston from drowning, Miro has a complex inner dialogue about his own humanity that keeps both reader and Kate guessing throughout the story. Moments before her death, Kate still struggles to separate the human from the inhuman in Miro when she realises 'how innocent he was in the most terrible sense of innocence: the innocence of a monster'.[55]

Loving the monster

The oxymoronic seems a suitable medium for Cormier's characterisation at this point. His novels recognise that identification with brutal acts does not automatically make his characters inhuman or villains. That would be too simple or stereotypical. Cormier asks us, as he stated in an interview, to 'remember even those who aren't good are human. The monsters around us have that spark of humanity that somehow exists even as they deny it'.[56] In Cormier's view, people remain humanly complex even when they support or commit

'inhuman' acts. It is this that makes them interesting and, to use
another oxymoron, fictionally real. Miro's empathy, therefore, is all the
more convincing because of the way Cormier shows it as a strength
that wrestles in Miro with the terrorist's inculcated sense of human
expediency. An example of such empathy is revealed in the moment
when Miro witnesses the captive and naked Ben writhing in agony
in the hijackers' van on the bridge. He sees, not the agent of war
and deception that Artkin suspects him to be, but a 'trembling, timid
teenager' whose voice 'emerge[s] small and thin and quavering, as if an
even smaller boy inside of him were speaking'.[57] The American 'other'
that Miro has opposed all his life is now not so different when seen
close up. This sudden recognition of kinship in the midst of extremity
is characteristic of Cormier's fiction. Miro's emotional instability at
points like this wins some trust and even hope for readers that he is
capable of change in time to prevent his planned execution of Kate.

Kate's death is the most disturbing horror in a novel where deaths
of children provide shock enough. The reader has shared in the development of her identity: her intimate thoughts, fears, and even her
flashes of hope and humour in the midst of extremity. The sudden
extinguishing of her life when she is on the verge of womanhood is
a destruction of an identity that is still in progress. In many respects
Kate is still a child and unformed. After the fatal bullet her final words
address her 'mommy and daddy'[58] and reinforce the impression that
for all her bravery and resourcefulness, it is a child Kate Forrester
who is murdered. In the moments before her death Kate's thoughts
are about her identity: the question of how she will be remembered.
After she is shot by Miro her syntax disintegrates with her breathing
even as she gasps for the chance to tell her story and be recognised as
the brave daughter who did the right thing.[59]

The tragic irony for Kate is that she persists in her belief that she can
unlock Miro's humanity with appeals to kinship. Her identification of
Artkin as Miro's father is a clever observation but also a fatal strategy
because it proves to be a truth Miro 'could not acknowledge'.[60] As
with Jerry Renault in *The Chocolate War*, whose isolated and heroic
stand for the right to say '"No"'[61] and to 'do your thing'[62] does not
prevent his persecution and destruction, so, too, do Kate's admirable
skills of communication and observation fail to save her. Her death
exhibits what Myers calls Cormier's 'stark and uncompromising challenges to conventional happy endings'[63] and what Campbell terms his
'dark awareness of evil as an implacable obstacle in human affairs'.[64]

Until the final pages of the novel Cormier allows us to believe that
Miro's gunshot as he and Kate huddle in a 'small nestlike enclosure'

in the woods, 'locked together, legs entwined ... and the gun still wedged between them',[65] may have been an accident. We expect a desperate Miro to regret her death and recant over her lifeless body but no such romance is admissible for Cormier. As Kate cradles the injured Miro who cries 'from the depths of his being' with 'a cry that went beyond sorrow and pain and anguish',[66] she enacts a moment of instinctive love and compassion for the gunman's human suffering in an attempt to give him an identity worth living for. It is painfully ironic, however, that her presentation to Miro of the dead Artkin as his long-lost father, an association she felt would achieve a positive and merciful response, should ensure her swift, ultimately Artkin-directed, execution by Miro in a moment of desperate grief. Such revelations, like the emotions they unleash, become dangerous in Cormier's unpredictable narratives.

Gregory Maguire notes that the 'children,' as he calls the teenage heroes of *After the First Death,* 'are not privy to the information adults have about the world, and they are forced to interact with powerful opponents and the weapons those opponents wield without being adequately prepared'.[67] There is some salvation, however, for Cormier's young adult protagonists in their willingness to explore bigger truths about existence beyond the immediate, often doomed, situations in which they find themselves. Maguire acknowledges that 'Cormier, always pulling the rug out from underneath us, sets up hope against hope'.[68] Against the starkness and brutal lucidity of exposure in Cormier's novels, hope lies ultimately in the teenage consciousness. It is this consciousness – so engaging and adaptable yet so fragilely 'unprotected' – that Cormier foregrounds in all its questioning vulnerability. Identity in his teenage protagonists becomes paradoxically unstable yet truthful as it is challenged and exposed relentlessly by extremity and crisis.

While Kate's death ends a lively consciousness full of hope and future, Miro's survival seems to be at the expense of his humanity, a humanity that Kate provoked but which Miro himself fears has caused him to 'reveal[ed] too much of himself'.[69] Kate's death shifts him from a teenager who, as Kate first observes on the bus, 'could be anything. From anywhere',[70] into a cold, isolated, and deadly killer. Murdering Kate, it seems, closes down any dialogue within Miro. He will become, like his dead mentor Artkin, 'emotionless, a machine capable of sudden startling deeds'.[71] He has stopped questioning his identity: it has become fixed.

Patricia Head argues that 'this questioning of identify is a common theme in Cormier's narrative. As the identities of the characters are foregrounded, so the reader is encouraged to rethink the possibility (or the impossibility) that any unitary or stable sense of self can exist'.[72] Ben speaks, it seems, for many of Cormier's protagonists when he has 'the feeling that someone had turned our world upside down, topsy-turvy, and the pieces had not yet settled into place'.[73] Cormier's teenage characters have unstable identities and this, perhaps, makes them effective voices for the postmodern world they encounter. They appeal to readers, as the feisty Lori Cranston does to Eric Poole in *Tenderness*, through their 'ability to constantly surprise ... keeping [us] on the edge, off balance'.[74] Identity and character in Cormier's fictional world emerge through the struggle for self-realisation that is central to teenage development and self-consciousness. Cormier's is a world in which the adolescent must struggle with extremity to negotiate 'so many disguises' and accommodate 'the stranger slowly taking shape' within.

Notes

1. Robert Cormier, *After the First Death* [1979] (London: Penguin, 2006): 107.
2. Ibid.: 78.
3. Ibid.: 28.
4. Ibid.: 77–8.
5. Ibid.: 21.
6. Mitzi Myers, '"No Safe Place to Run to": An Interview with Robert Cormier', in *The Lion and the Unicorn*, 2(3) (September 2000): 445–64, at 449.
7. Robert Cormier, quoted in Patty Campbell, *Robert Cormier: Daring to Disturb the Universe* (New York: Random House, 2006): 37.
8. Robert Cormier, *Heroes* (London: Penguin, 1998): 86.
9. *After the First Death*: 205.
10. Ibid.: 243.
11. Ibid.: 23.
12. Ibid.: 48.
13. Ibid.: 142.
14. Ibid.: 225.
15. Ibid.: 102.
16. Ibid.: 5.
17. Ibid.: 30.
18. Ibid.: 5.
19. Ibid.: 233.
20. Ibid.: 9.
21. Ibid.: 11.
22. Ibid.: 20.
23. Ibid.: 99.

24. Ibid.: 64.
25. Ibid.: 15.
26. Patricia Head, 'Robert Cormier and the Postmodernist Possibilities of Young Adult Fiction', *Children's Literature Association Quarterly*, 21(1) (Spring 1996): 28–33, at 28.
27. Robert Cormier, *Tenderness* (New York: Delacorte Press, 1997): 212.
28. Head: 28.
29. *After the First Death*: 96.
30. Caroline Hunt, 'Young Adult Literature Evades the Theorists', *Children's Literature Association Quarterly*, 21(1) (Spring 1996): 4–11, at 6.
31. Robert Cormier quoted in Myers: 453.
32. Ibid.: 459.
33. *Heroes*: 59.
34. Ibid.: 79.
35. Ibid.: 82.
36. Ibid.: 80.
37. Ibid.: 82.
38. Mike Cadden, 'The Irony of Narration in the Young Adult Novel', *Children's Literature Association Quarterly*, 25(3) (Fall 2000): 146–54, at 148.
39. *After the First Death*: 176.
40. Campbell: 6.
41. *After the First Death*: 77.
42. Ibid.: 142.
43. Ibid.: 123.
44. Ibid.: 125.
45. Ibid.: 175–6.
46. Ibid.: 39.
47. Ibid.: 37.
48. Ibid.: 38.
49. Ibid.: 32.
50. Ibid.: 228.
51. Ibid.: 104.
52. Ibid.: 116.
53. Ibid.: 50.
54. Ibid.: 92.
55. Ibid.: 256.
56. Myers: 455.
57. *After the First Death*: 237.
58. Ibid.: 260.
59. Ibid.
60. Ibid.: 258.
61. Robert Cormier, *The Chocolate War* [1974] (London: Penguin, 2001): 161.
62. Ibid.: 205.
63. Myers: 445.
64. Campbell: 2.

65. *After the First Death*: 253.
66. Ibid.: 258.
67. Gregory Maguire, 'Belling the Cat: Heroism and the Little Hero', *The Lion and the Unicorn*, 13(1) (June 1989): 102–19, at 107–8.
68. Maguire: 108.
69. *After the First Death*: 149.
70. Ibid.: 73.
71. Ibid.: 22.
72. Head: 29.
73. *After the First Death*: 107.
74. *Tenderness*: 194–5.

3

Fascinated by Evil: Robert Cormier as a Catholic Novelist

Pat Pinsent

It is easy for any reader with even a slight familiarity with Catholicism to recognise the part it plays in much of Robert Cormier's work. 'Frenchtown', a suburb of 'Monument', the location of most of his novels, is a thinly veiled version of French Hill in Leominster, Massachusetts, the area where Cormier lived throughout his life. The presence in the suburb of St Jude's church – 'big as a cathedral … remote and mysterious', as it is portrayed in *Darcy* (1991; published in the US as *Other Bells for Us to Ring* in 1990)[1] – is so central that it could almost be said to brood over life there. His characters habitually (rather than, in many cases, devotionally) go to Mass and confession, and many of them are described as lighting candles and saying prayers, which include such specifically Catholic practices as the rosary and novenas. Crucial roles are played by members of Catholic religious orders. At one level, this background can be seen as enriching the novels by providing the kind of detail that gives three-dimensionality to a work of fiction, an aspect which recalls, for instance, the importance of the town setting in George Eliot's *Middlemarch* (1871–2).[2]

What is more significant, however, is that this creation of a Catholic ethos leads to the characters' moral judgements being central to Cormier's novels and to reader's responses to the characters' actions.

This essay will explore how Cormier's own Catholic upbringing seems to have coloured much of his work. It is particularly apposite to highlight some of his affinities with Graham Greene, probably the most illustrious twentieth-century English Catholic novelist, since Cormier's novels, like those of his predecessor, seem to present the question of individual salvation and redemption as a central theme. As in Greene's work, some of the 'accidentals' of Catholicism loom large in Cormier's novels, intensifying the sense of the church as a powerful formative agent on his protagonists. In an interview shortly before he died in 2000, Cormier pays tribute to Greene, describing the earlier writer as his own 'great mentor'.[3] This interview reveals how impressed he was by Greene's use in his writing of a 'cinematic' technique, together with the way the characters sometimes strike 'bargains with God'.[4] Filmic qualities, such as a use of light and dark especially characteristic of cinema's black and white era, an enhanced focus on a specific facet of a character, and rapid switching of scenes, are to be found in both writers' fiction, and are consistently employed to enhance the sense of the 'drama of salvation' that their work conveys. The employment of what might be termed 'the language of Catholicism' lends both authors' writing a supernatural perspective, reflecting the way in which the laws and practices of religion were far more present to the average Catholic in the pre-Vatican II church[5] than is the case today. It seems appropriate, therefore, to adduce parallels between their writing where relevant, since Greene could be said to provide a precedent for Cormier's presentation of the metaphysical questions of good and evil that underlie the decisions taken by his characters.

A recent article in the Catholic weekly review *The Tablet* about Beryl Bainbridge claims that 'like other, Catholic novelists (or novelists who happen to be Catholics), she believed strongly in sin and evil – that evil is a force in the human psyche that is destructive and has to be combated'.[6] The same words could equally be applied to Cormier, who in an interview in 2000 answered the question, '"Who is your favorite character from all your books?"' with the words, '"They're all my children, but Archie Costello in *The Chocolate War* and its sequel continues to fascinate me"'.[7] Cormier himself attributes his fascination with evil to his Catholic upbringing: '"I was made aware of evil … and I'm aware of it now"'.[8] This recalls a similar preoccupation in Greene's novels, notably *Brighton Rock* (1938),[9] though this does not preclude in either writer's work the possibility of goodness as a supernatural value transcending more everyday qualities.

Robert Cormier first came to general notice with *The Chocolate War* (1974), in which several relatively malevolent characters and the pessimistic nature of the final scene caused some critics to feel that it was unsuitable for young readers. His later fiction, including the sequel to that book, did little to dispel the impression that Cormier was prepared to address aspects of human behaviour and society that previously had little place in literature for young readers. While some of his novels also include characters who sustain a high level of virtue, the atmosphere created is generally sombre. Neither the good nor the evil characters, however, are in any way stereotypical, and throughout the text, the internal workings of their minds are displayed as they tackle serious moral issues.

Although all Cormier's works for young people deal with issues that are relevant to his Catholicism, the main focus here will be on those books in which such questions are notably central. These include *The Chocolate War* and *Beyond the Chocolate War* (1985), which are set in a Catholic High, *After the First Death* (1979), *Fade* (1988), and *Darcy*, in which there is more explicit presentation of the Catholic background than in some of the rest of his fiction. Aspects of the semi-autobiographical free-verse text, *Frenchtown Summer* (1999) are also germane to the argument.

The accidentals of Catholicism in Cormier's novels

In her study of Cormier's earlier works, Patricia J. Campbell indicates how important Cormier's Catholic belief was to him, although he found himself more at ease with the church as reformed by the Second Vatican Council (1962–5) than with the way Catholicism was manifested in his youth.[10] An appropriate analogy for much of the Catholic detail in Cormier's novels can perhaps be derived from the 'Penny Catechism', familiar to all Catholic children of the period of the 1940s and early 1950s in which Cormier grew up. Its answer to the question, 'What is a sacrament?' is: 'A Sacrament is an outward sign of inward grace'.[11] In more formal theological language, based on medieval logic, this concept can be expressed by using the term 'accident', defined by the *Shorter OED* as 'An attribute that is not part of the essence',[12] or, as expanded in a traditional Catholic authority: 'The essence or substance is that which constitutes the thing, which makes it what it is, and it is distinct from accidents or qualities which may change while the thing itself remains'.[13] What is being suggested here is that the explicit Catholic impedimenta of these novels provide a way of making concrete the otherwise abstract dilemmas the characters face, as well as being a means of giving an in-depth dimension to their actions. The 'essence' of Cormier's Catholicism in the novels is revealed in their morality and character depiction, but the 'accident'[al] is the surface detail of the characters' adherence to the Catholic church.

This kind of incidental detail sometimes occurs when it might seem to be irrelevant to the main action. For instance, in *I am the Cheese* (1977), the narrator, known as Adam Farmer, comes to recollect that his alias has been given to him by the people protecting his father, who was a witness to various crimes. His father objects that 'Farmer' is a Protestant surname, less than appropriate for him as an Italian or for his Irish wife, who is 'a devout Catholic who never misses mass on Sundays or on holydays'.[14] Consequently the security services have to improvise, including in the family's camouflage documentation that 'proves' that they were converts to Catholicism. This apparently superfluous information not only displays the authorities' thoroughness in creating false identities and, by implication, the seriousness of the threat to the life of Adam's father, but also indicates how important to him is the fact that his Catholic identity has always been integral to him rather than something taken on in later life. The effect is to intensify the focus on identity as such, a theme integral to the novel. Similarly, the fact that the school in *The Chocolate War* and *Beyond the Chocolate War* is run by Religious Brothers could be seen as an important part of the creation of atmosphere in these two novels (as discussed in more detail in the next section), since it immediately implies that the evil therein encountered is particularly sinister because it transcends the merely everyday dimension.

An interesting instance of the way in which the drama is intensified by reference to the Catholic background occurs in *Frenchtown Summer*, where it is implied that during the World War I, the uncle, Jules, of the narrator, Eugene, has been spared being 'sent overseas/ to die in the trenches in France' because: 'He had been hurt/ when prayers brought/ three hundred pounds/ of combs and brushes/ down on him as he walked by'.[15] It appears that Jules's father, Eugene's grandfather, 'had spent hours/ in St Jude's church/ kneeling in prayer/ lighting candles,/ rising each morning/ for the five o'clock nuns' Mass,/ gulping Holy Communion/ like a starving man. /At the end of nine days,/ the length of a novena,/ the crates fell/ in an avalanche of boxes'.[16] His son seems ungrateful for the minor miracle of his deliverance from the trenches, and never subsequently seeks his father's blessing. The kind of 'bargain with God' which Cormier portrays in this instance recalls his admiration for a similar element in the novels of Graham Greene, and is used in an analogous manner. In Greene's *The Heart of the Matter* (1948) Henry Scobie prays for a dying child: '"Father look after her. Give her peace … Take away my peace forever, but give her peace"', and this marks the beginning of a situation that engenders Scobie's later tragedy.[17] In both instances there seems at least the possibility that God is a participant in the action, and answers prayer in a way that is unanticipated by the supplicants.

Evil and good in *The Chocolate War* and *Beyond the Chocolate War*

Many readers, accustomed to happy endings in novels for young people, have been frustrated by the inability of the protagonist of *The Chocolate War*, Jerry Renault, to triumph over Archie Costello and his evil organisation, The Vigils. In fact a sense of evil pervades much of the action of this novel, which depicts the consequences of Jerry's refusal to sell chocolates on behalf of Trinity Catholic high school – a situation analogous to that actually experienced by Cormier's own son (although as the author admits, "'nothing terrible happened to him'"[18]). The novel's portrayal of the failings of some members of the religious order that runs the school, in allowing a mafia-like group to terrorise the pupils, appears to be an indictment of corruption both in Catholic schools and, by extension, in some areas of American society.

In this book, as in the rest of Cormier's work, most of the many allusions to church attendance and the sacraments focus on the light which these practices, and the spirit in which they are undertaken, throw on the character concerned. Early in *The Chocolate War*, for instance, Obie is chided by Archie for using the name Jesus as a swearword. Obie responds by querying how Archie has the nerve to receive Holy Communion, to which Archie answers: "'When you march down to the rail, you're receiving The Body, man. Me, I'm just chewing a wafer they buy by the pound in Worcester.'" He goes on: "'And when you say 'Jesus' you're talking about your leader. But when I say 'Jesus', I'm talking about a guy who walked the earth for thirty-three years like any other guy but caught the imagination of some PR cats.'"[19]

This passage highlights the difference between the basically well-meaning Obie who, in spite of himself, has been fascinated by Archie and consequently caught up into the anti-social activities of The Vigils, and the unashamedly evil Archie who hypocritically cloaks his creatively cruel treatment of others by a practice of religion that presumably ingratiates him with the Brothers. On the one hand this use of religion recalls, for instance, how Pinkie Brown in Greene's *Brighton Rock*, has no scruples about capitalising on a shared Catholic background in order to attract into marriage Rose, otherwise a potentially hostile witness. On the other hand, Archie's insouciance about what other people hold to be sacred contrasts with the way in which much of the drama of Greene's *The Heart of the Matter* depends on the intensity of Scobie's belief in the church, to the extent that he is prepared to kill himself rather than continue to receive communion in a state of 'mortal sin'.

Later, in *Beyond the Chocolate War*, there is an instance of the response of an 'ordinary' Catholic to the behaviour of the two pre-eminently 'evil' characters, Archie and Brother Leon, the head-teacher: 'Brian Cochran was not a saint by any means, although he went to communion every Sunday, had served as an altar boy until his sixteenth birthday, knelt and said his prayers every night. He considered himself a good Catholic.'[20]

Brian is watching the guillotine created by Ray Bannister, a pupil who practises 'magic', and conjures up mental pictures of its blade killing each of them in turn: 'Shuddering a bit, he tried to escape the images – and wondered whether these were sins he would have to tell the priest the next time he went to confession'.[21] Here the allusions to the feelings of a boy who clearly believes in the power of the two sacraments mentioned – communion and confession – intensifies the contrast between him and either Archie, who unscrupulously makes use of the trappings of religion, or Leon, who, equally culpably, makes religious ideology a tool in his own control of the school.

The perversion of religion in which both Archie and Brother Leon indulge could legitimately be described as sacrilegious, for it is the turning of holy things to evil ends. For those familiar with certain very specific New Testament texts often used during the period of Cormier's education as 'proofs' of Christ's divinity, there are some very significant echoes that establish Archie as an Antichrist figure. Early in *The Chocolate War* Archie asks Obie, '"What the hell do they think I am?"',[22] words that parody Jesus' question to his apostles, '"Whom do you say that I am?"',[23] while Archie's arrogant claim of identity, '"I am Archie, I cannot lose"'[24] reminds the reader of how Jesus' statement, '"Before Abraham was made, I am"', led his hearers to take up stones to punish him for this 'blasphemy'.[25] Later, Obie's conviction that with Archie 'Nothing was impossible'[26] echoes Jesus' comment to his disciples, '"With God all things are possible"'.[27]

The evil in the two 'Chocolate War' books is not confined to Archie and Leon, or even to the other characters who prop up their regime, such as Obie and Emile Janza. Perry Nodelman argues that 'the propensity of boys in school to do cruel blackguard things is merely the potential in us all to do evil'.[28] He bases this conclusion on the way in which the reader is drawn in 'to expect and even hope that David Caroni will kill Leon and Obie murder Archie,' to the extent that 'we must consider the significance of our hope that they succeed in their vicious acts of revenge – the significance of what our own response to Leon's and Archie's evil has made us become'.[29]

In his fascination with evil and his generally pessimistic outlook on life, as implied by these novels, Cormier reflects something of the ethos of Catholicism during the first part of the twentieth century, also exhibited by such Catholic novelists as Greene and François Mauriac. This period was before the attempt to bring the church into the modern world, as essayed by the Second Vatican Council, which sought to remove the tendency, largely initiated by the sixteenth-century, counter-Reformation, Council of Trent, to demand that the 'faithful' concentrate predominately on obeying rules as the appropriate way of being religious. Nevertheless, Cormier's work also reveals the conviction that it is possible, within a Catholic framework, to aspire to a form of good behaviour that transcends the everyday norms of religious practice, in aspiring to a supernatural good. In *Beyond the Chocolate War*, he presents this through the experience of Jerry Renault when he visits Canada and sits in what Jerry terms 'The Talking Church'. Jerry first relaxes and even smiles as he listens to the 'whispering sounds' made by the wind as it passes through the church, and gradually he starts to pray. As he is more and more drawn to this church building, he associates the peace he experiences there with the contemplative life of monks.[30] Despite his difficulties when eventually he returns to Monument, he finds himself reverting to this spiritual experience and being strengthened by it. We are given a hint that his future may lie in the priesthood. Thinking at first of the peace he might find in a cloister away from the world, he goes on to consider a more active opposition to evil. He contemplates the possibility of a religious vocation as he remembers 'those exquisite moments of peace in Canada'.[31] Finally, having confronted Janza but not given in to the temptation to repel violence with violence, Jerry decides on his future: 'He knew somehow he would make his way back to Canada. And especially to the Talking Church. And beyond that to something else. Something he could not even consider now. But first he had to return to Trinity'.[32]

Before his return to Canada, Jerry will presumably try to oppose the evil in the school. Cormier, characteristically, does not give any indication as to how far he will succeed against Archie's heirs, Bunting and Janza. However, Jerry has already morally defeated Janza, while Bunting's limitations have been made apparent to the reader, so that perhaps there is a small element of hope that, at a deeper level, Jerry's experiences have been redemptive for him and will be so for the school.

Darcy: the power of the good

Some of Cormier's other writings also make evident how powerful the good, generally presented within an explicitly religious framework, can be. The eponymous narrator of *Darcy*, the daughter of occasionally practising Unitarian parents, is led towards the Catholic Church by her friendship with Kathleen Mary O'Hara, who in turn is the agent in introducing Darcy to Sister Angela. Darcy first sees the 'tiny nun ... on a marble bench under a trellised archway where pink roses bloomed ... As the nun turned, I saw her eyes. Clear blue eyes, as if she had only looked at beautiful things'.[33] Kathleen explains, '"Some people say she's a saint. People come to her from miles around for cures"'.[34] Darcy witnesses the nun praying and making the sign of the cross over a young child wearing callipers; much later in the novel she meets the child again, apparently healed and healthy. The child's mother reveals how the cure was a miracle, which took place a week after the nun had blessed her. The incident inspires Darcy to seek Sister Angela's help for her own father, who is missing overseas on active service (the novel is set during World War II). The nun settles Darcy's own concerns about religion:

'God comes first, you see,' she said. 'Not whether you are this or that, Protestant or Catholic, young or old. Loving God is the first thing ... You must love God because without him we are nothing ... God gave you life, gave your mother and father life. Gave them the love they have for each other, the love they have for you.'
She touched my bare arm, her fingers as light as flower petals on my skin.
'Dear, dear Darcy,' she said, 'don't frown, don't be worried, don't be unhappy. God is letting you discover him.'[35]

She goes on to suggest that it is unimportant whether the cure of the little girl was a miracle or not, as God's miracles are around us every day. She prays for Darcy's father and the girl feels that: 'We seemed joined together in a bond that would never break, as if we were united forever, caught in a sweet silence so profound and lovely that I heard no birds, no distant hum of traffic, no cries of children or barking dogs.[36]

Whether or not her father's deliverance is a miracle, shortly after this incident, Darcy and her mother learn that he is alive: he had been reported safe on the very day that Sister Angela had offered a prayer for him. Darcy does not see the nun again before her death, but a final miracle is suggested when the girl hears the bells of St Jude's church ringing, at a time when, as she later learns, they have not done so in the physical world.

Cormier's depiction of goodness, intensified by the images of the nun's 'clear blue eyes', the association with flowers, and the vision of peace that her prayer engenders, suggest that despite, or perhaps because of, his conviction about the evil in the world, he possesses a counter-vision of the power of good. The bells which Darcy hears – 'joyous tumbles of sound, so joyous that I raised my face to the night, saw stars dancing in the sky as if in cadence to the bells'[37] – seem to serve as a kind of divine authentication of the nun's goodness, resonating with that of God. Cormier's use of the miraculous, while possibly surprising in what remains in most respects a work of realist fiction, may well have been influenced by the way that one of his mentors, Greene, notoriously suggests divine intervention through the prayers of the repentant Sarah in *The End of the Affair* (1951).[38] The sceptical narrator, Maurice Bendrix (no more Catholic than is Darcy in Cormier's novel), reluctantly records what appears to be the miraculous fading of a disfiguring birthmark on the face of the private detective, Smythe, a situation which leads him towards anger against the God in whom up to this time he had disbelieved. It seems well within the bounds of possibility that familiarity with this incident, the acceptability of which divides critics, gave Cormier the confidence to include Sister Angela's putative miracles in *Darcy*.

While *Darcy* contains Cormier's most fully developed portrayal of goodness, another novel of the same period, *Fade*, which is discussed in more detail in the next section, includes elderly Sister Anunciata, who seems to exemplify the force of good; her voice and calm presence offer the opportunity for redemption to Ozzie Slater, the nephew of the protagonist, Paul Moreaux, who, like his uncle, is a 'fader'. She tells Ozzie that for him she feels "'Compassion, boy. And love. What Our Lord feels for us all'".[39] Unfortunately, Ozzie does not seem to be open to the good (any more than, for instance, Archie Costello is) and rejects her concern, and the timeless battle between good and evil is left unresolved at the end of the novel, as will be seen below.

The religious context of moral problems in *After the First Death* and *Fade*

Themes of evil, and to a lesser extent good, pervade other Cormier novels, and provide a framework against which the moral decisions of the characters have to be taken. *After the First Death* has less explicit reference to Catholicism than the books examined above, but at one telling point, the protagonist and co-narrator, Ben Marchand, craves sacramental absolution. As the son of the general who is in charge of operations, he judges himself to be culpable because he has, under torture, 'betrayed' the time at which the security forces plan to attack the terrorists who have hijacked a bus containing young children. Looking back, Ben muses:

> Is Christmas the time of year that Catholics must go to confession ... Maybe that's what I need. Not to be a Catholic, but to confess. Because after confession comes forgiveness ... And yet I realize that I don't have to confess. He already knows what I've done. On the bridge. But I still have to ask forgiveness. If I do, will he [his father] forgive me?[40]

This reference succeeds in putting a theological dimension on to the father/son situations that dominate the novel. We learn in due course that as well as the general, who has voluntarily exposed his own son, Ben, to danger, torture, and breakdown, the terrorist Artkin is not only the leader but also possibly the father of Miro Shantas who has been instrumental in the capture of the bus and whose life is as much in danger as Ben's. Cormier implicitly parallels the way that both these fathers, on opposing sides, have orchestrated the events and blithely put the lives of their sons into jeopardy, with the traditional Christian belief that Jesus, as Divine Son, has by his death implemented the Father's plan for the redemption of humanity: 'For God so loved the world, as to give his only begotten Son',[41] itself echoing the willingness of Abraham to sacrifice his son Isaac.

Cormier's remarkably prescient portrayal of terrorism in this novel implicitly poses the question as to which is the more evil, the action of the terrorists who have threatened a bus load of children, or that of the general. Through Ben's voice and that of an omniscient narrator, Cormier gradually discloses the fact that the general actually wanted Ben to give way under torture, so that he would reveal to the terrorists the time at which he believed the security forces would act; this was, however, an incorrect time deliberately 'planted' by his father in order to mislead them so that they would not be on their guard when the actual attack took place. The complex treatment of moral judgment and betrayal here is reminiscent of much of Greene's work, for instance his first novel, *The Man Within* (1929),[42] described in *The Cambridge Guide to Literature in English* as reflecting 'many of the themes of pursuit, guilt, treachery and failure which became the hallmark of his fiction'.[43]

One of Cormier's most powerful novels, *Fade*, the story of Paul Moreaux, who discovers he has inherited the ability to become invisible at will, poses a number of moral problems, all of which, like the ending of the book itself, are finally left unresolved. The use of this element of fantasy in a novel which, perhaps more than most of Cormier's work, continually highlights moral problems, could have the effect of making more general the ethical dilemmas that Paul faces.[44] From Paul's early agonising about the Confessional, via his role in the death of the Frenchtown villain Rudolphe Toubert, to the culmination of the novel with his killing of his nephew Ozzie who is using the 'gift' for evil purposes, a position of uncertainty is generated about the rightness or wrongness of Paul's moral choices. As in Cormier's other books, the shadow of St Jude's Church seems always to loom over the characters, in effect providing a concrete reminder of the supernatural dimension to the action. Much of the narrative is told in the first person by Paul, and although the first explicit treatment of the moral dimension of his deeds is concerned with the relatively trivial issue of his teenage sexual peccadilloes, the gravity of these is heightened by being seen in the context of religion. His 'crush' on his aunt Rosanna is verbalised in the poem he writes to her, comparing his feelings for her to 'a silent prayer at vespers',[45] though as he states, his love for her is 'hot with desire for her body. I wanted to caress her, to gorge myself on her'.[46] He judges that 'bringing church and prayer into the poem [was] a sacrilege'.[47] Sometime later, with his aunt's encouragement, he caresses her breast[48] with the result that the regular visit to the confessional, insisted on by the nuns who teach him, causes problems. He has always found confession an ordeal, because of the need to mention 'that sly act at night in bed when I summoned the visions that brought me both ecstasy and shame',[49] but now he fears he has committed 'a mortal sin … I had held a woman's breast in my hand'.[50] As a result of this fear, he skives off from confession, consequently creating an additional problem: if he does not receive communion at Sunday Mass, his mother will suspect him of missing confession. To avoid this, he goes to an earlier Mass than his parents, but this means 'More deception. More sins', and he says extra prayers to be on the safe side.[51] The strategy here is very reminiscent of how in Greene's The Heart of the Matter Scobie avoids going to the same Mass as his wife, Louise, so that she will not deduce from his failure to receive Holy Communion, that he has been refused absolution: in his confession of adultery Scobie was unable to give a promise that he would not continue to see his mistress, Helen.[52]

By the time that Paul is eventually ready to go to confession, the admission of his carnal contact with his aunt is less of a problem than are his feelings of guilt about the way he has increasingly been 'fading' and consequently seeing people behaving in ways they thought secret. That he manages, without too much soul-searching, to mention the sexual 'sin' that had previously caused him anguish, puts into perspective the seriousness of his anxiety about fading. He can find no other way to tell the priest about it than by referring to it as 'spying',[53] but the religious context is likely to generate the anticipation that his invisibility may provide an opportunity for sins much more heinous than either his youthful masturbatory fantasies or his touching of his aunt's breast.

Fading does in fact lead Paul to his responsibility for the death of Rudolphe Toubert; he deliberately invites the 'fade' in order to confront the man he sees as the cause of his father's injury in a strike at Toubert's works.[54] Though initially it is not Paul's fault that Toubert runs on to the knife in Paul's invisible hands, Paul continues to stab him, showing perhaps that in spite of himself, the 'Fade' has somehow turned his actions towards evil.[55]

Earlier than this, Paul's uncle Adelard, who also is a fader, had expressed his anxieties about this power falling into evil hands, and consequently suggested that it was Paul's vocation to look for the next 'fader' to ensure that no evil outcome should occur.[56] While Toubert's death in itself has revealed to Paul the dangers of the fade, it is not until he searches out his nephew Ozzie that we witness how powerful this 'gift' can be when used in the wrong way. Ozzie has already discovered his ability to become invisible and has used this in order to kill his step-father, an act which could perhaps be justified on grounds of protecting his mother. Unlike Paul, however, Ozzie is increasingly directed by a Voice which incites him to perform evil acts, notably that of killing kindly Sister Anunciata: '*You kill her in front of the nuns, in front of witnesses. Make yourself unseen and then hit her. Hard. And she'll fall down and die in her tracks and nobody will see it was you. They'll think it was a heart attack*'.[57] Finally, in a desperate, mutually invisible, confrontation, Paul succeeds in killing Ozzie despite the fact that he feels round his neck 'not the hands of a thirteen-year-old boy but the steel-like hands of a deadly enemy, ageless and mad, gaining strength from the madness'.[58] The impression conveyed here by Cormier, notably though the words 'enemy, ageless', is that this alien voice is that of diabolical possession, presumably the result of the fader being too ready to use the invisibility to evil ends. The concept of possession by the devil has always been more acceptable to Catholicism than to most mainstream Protestant denominations, and even in post-Vatican II enlightened days, the rite of exorcism is still occasionally practiced by those priests qualified through prayer and study. Numerous incidents in the gospels portray Jesus as casting out devils, which generally cry out in loud voices unlike those of the people whose bodies they are inhabiting.[59] However as Ozzie dies, there seems the possibility of redemption: 'knowing he had finally overcome the voice,' he hears instead his mother's voice.[60]

Before his own death at 42, Paul seems to have led a quietly solitary life, 'fading' away in the more usual sense of the word, occasionally attending Mass but not receiving communion.[61] The final section of this novel is narrated by Paul's great-niece, Susan, who has read his autobiographical narrative in the truth of which she has gradually come to believe. Newspaper reports lead her to the conviction that there is another 'fader' out there, committing arson and consequently being responsible for large-scale loss of life, yet her final statement 'God, I don't know what to do',[62] cannot be seen as totally negative even though it voices her feeling of powerlessness since it can also be seen as a prayer: if evil is so strong, then Christianity teaches that God is even stronger.

Conclusion

Throughout the Cormier novels which have been considered above, and indeed in others, which it has not been possible to examine here, such as *The Bumblebee Flies Anyway* (1983), *Tunes for Bears to Dance to* (1992), and *Heroes* (1998), there is a constant sense of both the power of evil and, by implication, the countering potential force of good. As in much of Graham Greene's work, God could be said always to be a character within the development of the plot. The moral problems that face Cormier's characters are nearly always located in a setting that is explicitly Catholic, with the presence of the actual church building being often mentioned. This setting is the thinly veiled disguise for the area in which Cormier himself lived his whole life, and some works, notably *Frenchtown Summer* and *Fade*, seem to have an implicitly autobiographical element. In the latter, there is a sense in which there is much in common between Paul Moreaux and Robert Cormier: both are novelists, and 'fading' seems to serve as a metaphor for the invisibility of the writer, who is conscious that he is making use of people he once knew, and feeling somewhat guilty about being an observer to their lives.

It is not necessary to see Graham Greene as a major influence on Cormier in order to accept that Cormier's debt to him includes the fact that the moral problems integral to the novels of both writers are given an added depth by being set within a framework of explicitly Catholic belief and practice. The encounter with values which, in his pre-Vatican II Catholic education, were presented to the young

Cormier as absolutes, together with the soul searching that was necessitated by preparation for the frequent visits to the confessional that were then the norm, encouraged in him a preoccupation with the kind of themes so important not only to Greene but also to other novelists who 'happened to be Catholics' such as François Mauriac, Muriel Spark, Alice Thomas Ellis, and Beryl Bainbridge. It could be conjectured that the very fact that some distinguished novelists had explicitly portrayed Catholicism in their novels could have been seen by him to create a precedent for the abundant Catholic references in his works. A question that suggests itself particularly to readers who have experienced both the pre-Vatican II church, often preoccupied with rules and regulations especially governing worthy reception of the sacraments, and the rather different Catholic perspective post-Vatican II, is whether readers who lack familiarity with either of these expressions of Church will have the same kind of engagement with the issues in his novels. What does appear clear is that the Catholic dimension adds a richness of texture to Cormier's work – and while there is no doubt that evil is strongly present, the possibility of redeeming grace is also there.

Notes

1. Robert Cormier, *Darcy* (London: Victor Gollancz, 1991): 63.
2. George Eliot, *Middlemarch* (London: William Blackwood and Sons, 1871–2).
3. 'Robert Cormier Meets Melvin Burgess: Part Two': www.achuka.co.uk/special/cormburg2.htm (accessed 7 May 2012).
4. Though the concept of striking a bargain with God would today probably seem as alien to most Catholics as to other Christians, it could be seen to be authenticated by scripture, as in Abraham's bargaining with God for the cities of the plain (*Genesis* 18, 23–32). All biblical quotations are taken from the Douay-Rheims translation, the one used in Catholic circles during Cormier's youth.
5. The Second Vatican Council (also known as Vatican II) addressed relations between the Roman Catholic Church and the modern world. It started under Pope John XXIII on 11 October 1962 and finished under Pope Paul VI on 8 December 1965.
6. Robin Baird-Smith, 'A not so quiet life', *The Tablet*, 10 July 2010: 15.
7. 'Author Profile: Robert Cormier', *Teenreads*: www.teenreads.com/authors/au-cormier-robert.asp (accessed 15 July 2010).
8. Robert Cormier quoted in Patricia J. Campbell, *Presenting Robert Cormier* (Boston: Twayne, 1985): 33.
9. Graham Greene, *Brighton Rock* (New York: Viking Press, 1938).
10. Campbell: 33.

11. *A Catechism of Christian Doctrine* (London: Catholic Truth Society, 1971): 42–3.
12. *Shorter Oxford English Dictionary*, (Oxford: Clarendon Press, 1978): 11.
13. *A Catholic Dictionary* (London:Virtue & Co., 1954): 313.
14. Robert Cormier, *I am the Cheese* [1977] (London: Collins, 1979): 120.
15. Robert Cormier, *Frenchtown Summer* [1999] (London: Puffin, 2000): 83–4.
16. Ibid.
17. Graham Greene, *The Heart of the Matter* (London: Heinemann, 1958): 127.
18. Quoted in Perry Nodelman, 'Robert Cormier's *The Chocolate War*: Paranoia and Paradox', in Dennis Butts (ed.) *Stories and Society: Children's Literature in its Social Context*, ed. by (Basingstoke: Macmillan, 1992): 22–36, at 23.
19. Robert Cormier, *The Chocolate War* [1974] (London: Collins, 1984): 11.
20. Robert Cormier, *Beyond the Chocolate War* [1985] (London: Collins, 1987): 247.
21. Ibid.: 14.
22. *The Chocolate War*: 14.
23. *Matthew* 16: 15.
24. *The Chocolate War*: 33.
25. *John* 8: 58.
26. *Beyond the Chocolate War*: 167.
27. *Matthew* 19: 26.
28. Nodelman: 34.
29. Ibid.: 34–5.
30. *Beyond the Chocolate War*: 108.
31. Ibid.: 160.
32. Ibid.: 225.
33. *Darcy*: 47–8.
34. Ibid.: 48.
35. Ibid.: 97.
36. Ibid.: 99.
37. Ibid.: 103.
38. Graham Greene, *The End of the Affair* (New York:Viking Press, 1951).
39. Robert Cormier, *Fade* (London:Victor Gollancz, 1988): 183.
40. Robert Cormier, *After the First Death* (London:Victor Gollancz, 1979): 91.
41. *John* 3: 16.
42. Graham Greene, *The Man Within* (New York:Viking Press, 1929).
43. Ian Ousby (ed.), *The Cambridge Guide to Literature in English* (Cambridge: University Press, 1988): 413.
44. Compare the use of fantasy to 'Help readers of all ages understand that people in all circumstances, times and places have to face vital moral issues', as discussed by Darja Mazi-Leskovar in 'Power and Ethics in Lois Lowry's *The Giver* and *Gathering Blue*', *Journal of Children's Literature Studies*, 2(3) (2005): 1–13, at 12.
45. *Fade*: 24.
46. Ibid.

47. Ibid.
48. Ibid.: 42.
49. Ibid.: 47.
50. Ibid.
51. Ibid.: 48.
52. Greene (1958): 238–9.
53. *Fade*: 102.
54. Ibid.: 117.
55. Ibid.: 171.
56. Ibid.: 86–7.
57. Ibid.: 217, italics in original.
58. Ibid.: 234.
59. Among the many Gospel references to Jesus casting out devils are *Mark* 3.11, 5.7, 9.17. Interestingly, Graham Greene uses the idea of an internal voice in *The Heart of the Matter* (218), but in a contrasted sense, to indicate Jesus pleading with Scobie not to kill himself. A situation closer to that in Cormier's novel is in C. S. Lewis's *Perelandra/Out of the Silent Planet* (London: Bodley Head, 1938) where the aptly named Ransom is confronted with Weston, the 'Un-Man' who seems to have sold his soul to the devil.
60. *Fade*: 236.
61. Ibid.: 244.
62. Ibid.: 246.

4

'Nobody out of context': Representations of Child Corruption in Robert Cormier's Crime Novels

Stefania Ciocia

Robert Cormier made his name as a groundbreaking writer of young adult fiction, particularly in view of his realistic, hardnosed, and unedulcorated portrayal of American society, where gratuitous violence lurks around corners, and evil is found in the most unsuspected of places. Given his thematic concerns with violence and evil, Cormier's writing frequently focuses on the investigation of delinquent behaviour, and therefore often revisits the conventions of crime fiction. In contemporary literature, one need not look at genre writing for candid portrayals of young people involved in brutal and unlawful activities. In fact, in recent years, there has been a noticeable increase in memorable, mainstream fictional representations of children, both as victims and as perpetrators of violent crimes, possibly inspired by the number of real incidents that have received media visibility. Prize-winning, bestselling novels such as Jonathan Trigell's *Boy A* (2004)[1] and Lionel Shriver's *We Need to Talk About Kevin* (2005)[2] – loosely inspired, respectively, by the 1993 murder of two-year-old Jamie Bulger by two ten-year-olds in Britain and by the phenomenon of high-school shootings in the United States – are clearly part of an ongoing, revisionist debate about the myth of childhood innocence.

In the face of the sensationalisation of stories of crime involving children as willing participants and schemers, rather than as helpless victims, sociologists are keen to highlight that events of a similar, tragic kind have been as frequent in the past as they are now; what has changed is our awareness of, and perhaps our voyeuristic curiosity for, such (real and fictional) narratives of tainted childhood.

For this reason, the representation of child corruption in Cormier's later crime novels – the main focus of the present analysis – will be prefaced by a brief outline of recent debates about young people's proclivity to immorality and delinquency. The essay will then explore the extent to which Cormier's *We All Fall Down* (1991), *Tenderness* (1997), and the posthumously published *The Rag and Bone Shop* (2001) participate in the debunking of the myth of childhood innocence. Since these novels can all be described as crime fiction, the following discussion will also offer observations on the presence of child characters in, and the appeal to child readers of, this very popular variety of genre fiction.

The received view of Cormier is that he 'den[ies] his readership a romantic view of society'[3] and that he is one of the few writers of young adult fiction who 'creates genuinely evil characters',[4] fully rounded, villainous figures who often make it to the end of the narrative triumphant and unpunished. It is indeed generally true that Cormier's protagonists 'are alone, physically and emotionally' and that 'their seemingly benign middle-class environments are in reality Orwellian landscapes where life is illogical, betrayal is commonplace and decent people, including children, are victims'.[5] Having said that, later texts such as *We All Fall Down*, *Tenderness*, and *The Rag and Bone Shop*, in which young characters are guilty of terrible crimes against equally young people, contextualise, or otherwise tone down, the apparent evil nature of their underage villains. Short of subscribing to the now wide-spread rhetoric of 'the criminalisation of youth', and contrary to Cormier's reputation as a relentless pessimist, these later texts in fact seem to perpetuate the traditional notion of childhood innocence, clearly suggesting that a child criminal is *made*, and not born.

The criminalisation of childhood

From circa 1960 we have been witnessing a revision and a fore-grounding of the debate about competing notions of what constitutes the realm of childhood, and this has had repercussions on our collective appreciation of experiences and phenomena pertaining to such realm. The 'seemingly unprecedented increase in child abuse in Western societies'[6] in the final four decades of the twentieth century is perhaps the most obvious by-product of the recent trend in Western culture towards the intensification of the scrutiny and surveillance of relationships between children and adults. This closer focus on child–adult interactions, now perceived as a collective social duty, itself relies on the (often unspoken) assumption that childhood is self-evidently in need of protection, vulnerable to adult malice, and obviously distinct from – and at risk of being tainted by – the world of grown-ups. According to Chris Jenks, the phenomenal, and relatively sudden, outbreak of the plague of child abuse has occurred 'not because of any significant alteration in the pattern of our behaviour towards children but because of changing patterns of personal, political and moral control in social life ... which have, in turn, affected our vision of childhood'.[7] Jenks's argument about the change in our general responsiveness to 'child corruption' is even more persuasive when we consider the remarkable amnesia that seized the public in the wake of the Jamie Bulger murder in Britain in 1993, and that underpinned a revival of neo-Puritan rhetoric about humankind's original sinfulness – the other side of the coin of the exceptionalism of childhood, positing the child's inherent sinfulness and its need for the civilising influence of society, as opposed to the Rousseauvian model of infant purity and childhood's innate moral instincts. This abduction, torture, and killing of a toddler by two ten-year-old boys triggered a debate of unprecedented scale about the nature of childhood, its predisposition to violence or 'evil', and the age of criminal responsibility. As Jenks points out, however, the common identification of the Bulger murder as a brutal awakening from the Rousseauvian ideal of innocence is predicated, in part, on the British public, and Western culture at large, forgetting 'the spectacular precedent provided by the double child-murder committed by the 12-year-old Mary Bell in the UK in 1968, ... and the largely unwritten history of child-by-child murders that undoubtedly preceded it'.[8]

In 1993 Britain reconsidered its conception of childhood as it had not been ready to do 25 years before, possibly because this time it was faced with the chilling incongruity between the CCTV footage of three children walking along, holding hands, in a shopping mall, and the terrible knowledge of where and how this activity, so seemingly above suspicion, would end. If the Bulger case provides a recent, significant watershed in late-twentieth-century conceptions of childhood,[9] the Columbine High School massacre in 1999 marks a similar epochal shift in the perception of adolescence, particularly, of course, in the United States. In this case too, the shootings were not the first of their kind, although previous school massacres had typically been committed by adult offenders. What distinguished Columbine, apart from the age of the shooters, the level of violence, the premeditation involved in the killings, and the high number of victims, was the suburban setting of the tragedy; for this reason, 'the Columbine incident completely shattered whatever faith Americans had in the idea that gunfire and death only plagued urban inner-city schools'.[10] Typically set in a small-town environment, Cormier's novels seem to have anticipated the disassociation, in our collective imagination, between violent, youthful crime and the metropolitan phenomenon of gang culture, which is now no longer commonly identified with the main, most visible locus of underage illegal activities.

Writing about childhood and crime

Cormier's novels have also reinvigorated the fertile crosspollination between young adult fiction – generally regarded as a post-World War II publishing phenomenon, much as adolescence itself is sometimes viewed as an invention of 1950s America – and the more time-honoured tradition of crime writing, whose most popular, codified formula – the clue-puzzle mystery, to be solved by a skilful detective – dates back at least to Poe's tales of ratiocination of the 1840s. In fact, Cormier's success as a storyteller has been associated with his ability to harness some of the conventions of crime writing in order to craft credible, uncompromising representations of the dark side of adolescent experience. Cormier's *noir* sensibility is evident in his adoption of the generic conventions of the thriller: a fast-paced narrative, spine-tingling atmospheres, the implicit promise of a surprising denouement, sharp psychological insights into characters' motives and into the implications of their actions (or, conversely, of their failure to act), and a relentless scrutiny of environmental influences and other external pressures on the individual. Cormier's chilling studies of the power struggles, easy temptations, and inevitable lapses facing his young protagonists work both as compelling page turners and as provocative invitations to readers to reflect on the least palatable aspects of contemporary culture. '[B]y placing his young heroes and heroines in … grim circumstances,' as Deanna Zitterkopf notes, 'Cormier not only creates powerful, suspense-filled narratives which unfold like detective novels – he also encourages his youthful readers to confront some of the major moral and ethical issues of our age'.[11] More specifically, the startling revelations in his plots and their mood of resigned acceptance of a widespread moral decadence in which his characters find themselves inextricably implicated is reminiscent of the sense of general corruption surrounding, and often compromising, the cynical private-eye of the American hard-boiled tradition of detective fiction. For the gritty realism of his stories, the emphasis on the fragility of his characters, the lack of flawless protagonists, and the general absence of clear-cut distinctions between good and evil, Cormier's narratives are definitely more akin to the hard-boiled formula of Dashiell Hammett and Raymond Chandler than to the more rarefied, genteel, and cerebral British tradition of the locked room mystery.

Crime fiction does not typically feature children among its main characters, and when it does, it tends to portray them as victims rather than perpetrators. Paradoxically, it is in young adult fiction, whose focus is often on power relations and conflicts, that we are more likely to find an unsentimental representation of young people as violent figures. Indeed, this is a theme of one of the pioneering examples of the genre, S. E. Hinton's *The Outsiders* (1967),[12] with its depiction of gang violence and juvenile criminal behaviour. The 'pack' mentality that fosters more or less extreme forms of bullying, psychological cruelty, and physical aggressiveness among youths – often the central theme in young adult novels, such as *The Chocolate War* (1974), Cormier's first and most famous foray into the genre – is not solely the fictional preserve of adolescents, as the descent into savagery of the prepubescent protagonists of William Golding's classic novel *Lord of the Flies* (1954) testifies.[13] Besides superficial thematic considerations, such as the unsurprising frequency of accounts of gang mentality, mob rule, and peer pressure involving young characters, it ought to be pointed out that the presence of a criminal plot or the need for clarity and/or justice in the face of devious behaviour is a popular feature in writing for a young readership for obvious narrative reasons. Cormier himself has openly acknowledged the genre's investment in providing its audience with a good plot, praising the ability of detective fiction to create and sustain the reader's interest: 'I love crime stories and mysteries because they always deliver – they give you a beginning, a middle, and a climax (which isn't always the case with mainstream novels praised by the critics as precious)'.[14]

The conventions of detective fiction have a further, undeniable appeal in the realm of children's literature, where '[p]erhaps even more than in its adult incarnation, the formal problem of "whodunit" ... allows the investigation of other kinds of mystery – mysteries that become apparent during childhood itself and concerning issues such as identity, economic power and social status'.[15] Enid Blyton's detective novels, for example, thematise the protagonists' marginal position within, and their challenge to, the world of adulthood and its phoney rules. The marginality of classic child–detectives recalls the eccentricity/foreignness/self-imposed seclusion from society and imperviousness to romantic and family relationships that remains one of the most resilient clichés about the figure of the investigator in popular fiction. As we will see, Cormier's crime novels also highlight the loneliness of their young protagonists – a stand-in for the fundamental alienation of the human condition which, together with the creation of a climate of general moral decay and a focus on the influence of a shady milieu on individual characters, is a concern that aligns Cormier with the hard-boiled tradition. In a further appropriation of a twist to the formula – the fact that the private eye sometimes turns out to have been used as a pawn in obscure machinations and conspiracies reaching out beyond the case that he or she has been called on to solve – Cormier's children typically feature as the passive objects, rather than the driving forces, of the investigation, and are therefore ultimately configured as victims of circumstances, rather than moral agents in full control of their options.

Cormier's fiction often focuses on aggressive forms of intimidation and peer pressure, but in his earlier narratives these conflicts usually climax in relatively minor incidents; the final fight in *The Chocolate War*, for example, gory as it is, ends with no fatalities. In more serious cases of physical and psychological violence – such as the murders and the psychological manipulation in *I Am the Cheese* (1977), or the hostage-taking and killings in *After the First Death* (1979) – the villains are invariably adults (or damaged, hence impressionable, young characters), and children only number among the victims. What distinguishes *We All Fall Down*, *Tenderness*, and *The Rag and Bone Shop* is that they all figure child or adolescent perpetrators of brutal crimes against their peers. Despite this, and despite Cormier's allegedly unsentimental view and treatment of young people, these texts also subtly perpetuate the notion of the Romantic child, whose innocence is corrupted by external forces. Like Miro Shantas in *After the First Death*, whose career as a hijacker is clearly the result of his having been 'adopted', as an orphan, into the ranks of a terrorist organisation, the young villains in Cormier's later crime novels have extenuating circumstances because of their upbringing and/or due to strong environmental pressures. Interestingly, when this line of reasoning does not fully hold, as in the case of the serial killers in *We All Fall Down* and *Tenderness*, or of the fratricide in *The Rag and Bone Shop*, Cormier makes narrative choices that reveal his investment in the fundamental decency of the child: he shows his villains to be aberrations, reduces them to two-dimensional characters, or sidelines them into functions of the plot.

We All Fall Down

We All Fall Down starts with an episode of vandalism spiralling out of control, when 14-year-old Karen Jerome walks into her home to find it being 'trashed' by a group of four teenagers. In an ensuing tussle, which threatens to escalate into a sexual assault, Karen slips down the basement stairs and falls into a coma. The novel then pursues two interrelated strands in the development of the events, focusing on how Jane – Karen's elder sister – and her family cope with the tragedy, as well as on the feelings of guilt of one of the culprits, Buddy Walker, and his fraught relationship with Harry Flowers, the group's ringleader and mastermind of the attack. Buddy's own predicament gets more complicated when, having taken to follow-ing Jane, with a mixture of curiosity and compassion for 'that poor poor girl',[16] he finally meets her and the two of them fall in love. This twist in the plot is an obvious source of dramatic irony since, as Buddy and the reader know, Jane is unaware of her boyfriend's involvement in the traumatic event that has turned her life upside down. The question of whether, and how, Buddy's secret will come to light is not the only source of suspense in the novel, which contains a much more disturbing mystery in the identity of the Avenger, an 11-year-old, self-appointed, murderous righter of wrongs who witnessed the trashing and is determined to find and punish its perpetrators – an act of retaliation partly motivated by this character's rather sinister obsession with Jane. The general bleakness of this scenario, and the flawed nature of its protagonists – even Jane has a secret of her own, for it is her loss of the house-keys that provides the trashers with an easy way into the Jeromes' residence – should not blind readers to the fact that the young characters' behaviour is all in some measure justifiable in view of their family circumstances.

Buddy is still reeling from the failure of his parents' marriage. His father, who has never been an exceptional role model – as Buddy gloomily muses, 'He always left a trail of disarray and debris behind him. Kept losing things. Didn't hang up his clothes. Ironic: in this house, the son was neater than the father'[17] – has recently left home for a younger woman, and his only regular contact with Buddy consists of a weekly $25 cheque sent through the post. Buddy's mother also seems to have abdicated her parental role, busy as she is trying to pull herself together. Interestingly, and in tune with current alertness to this phenomenon, Buddy's sensible younger sister, Abby, thinks of herself and her brother as victims of a subtle form of 'child abuse'.[18] The novel also makes an explicit link between Buddy's sense of abandonment and his vulnerability to the wild, charismatic Harry Flowers, whose offer of diversion in the guise of daring exploits, and drink-fuelled 'funtime' becomes virtually irresistible.[19] Buddy's quest for solace and oblivion in alcohol is presented as an understandable course of action, for it seems to run in the family, as it transpires when readers finally meet the absentee Mr Walker, whose new circumstances have clearly not yielded the happiness they had promised. During an overdue, awkward father-and-son encounter over lunch, Buddy suddenly realises his father's misery and his dependence on alcohol – both of which he understands only too well. Aware of these shared experiences, Buddy is left wondering whether he is doomed 'to grow up like his father, still drinking, his face filled with the tiny flowers',[20] while this description of the small veins on Mr Walker's nose and cheeks, the visible sign of his excessive alcohol consumption, subliminally aligns him with Harry Flowers, the other corrupting influence on Buddy.

Harry, for his part, is the product of a different, perhaps even more insidious, kind of parental neglect. He comes from a rich, permissive family, where, in return for compliance with the most superficial of filial duties, his 'big-name architect'[21] father is happy to demonstrate unconditional love by buying his son out of mischief. Mr Flowers' *laissez-faire* attitude to the education of his offspring, compounded by the ostensible passivity of his wife, paints a picture of extreme privilege, which in turn offers a convenient (if clichéd) explanation for Harry's rebellious behaviour.[22] A spoilt, bored, intelligent teenager, with the benefit of a good education and striking 'people skills', Harry immediately spots the potential for maximum damage with minimum risk, when he picks up the house-keys inadvertently dropped by Jane. Having instructed his fellow trashers not to break any windows, he proceeds to vandalise the Jeromes' family home, secure in the knowledge that he will not incur serious criminal charges, and that his actions will be tacitly condoned, as an out-of-control prank, by his father.

Even Jane's parents are not beyond reproach in the chain of events that lead up to the trashing, and this in spite of the characterisation of the Jeromes as an undoubtedly decent, even exemplary, family, whose textbook reaction to the vandalism would not be out of place as a counselling case-study. Artie, the youngest sibling, has nightmares, Mrs Jerome buys new furnishings to wipe out all traces of the attack, while Mr Jerome steps up to the traditional role of the level-headed patriarch, in charge of keeping the household together. As provider of comfort and safety, and custodian of the family unit, it falls to the father figure to rally the troops and give them a pep talk; thus, Mr Jerome invites his family not to let the incident intimidate them, but rather to talk and support one another, and to keep their faith in Karen's recovery.[23] This laudable illustration of model parental behaviour, however, is soon followed by a less commendable attitude

towards Jane's absent-mindedness. In complete contrast to its portrayal
of the Jeromes as tolerant, open, sympathetic parents, the novel also
intimates that they are somewhat to blame in the way they mishandle
their daughter's tendency to lose things; afraid of incurring parental
censure, Jane deliberately fails to mention that she is missing her
house-keys. This first breakdown in trust is later blown out of propor-
tion when Jane feels accused by her parents of having given her keys
to Harry, as he maintains during his interrogation.

Unsurprisingly, it is the Avenger, the only intentional killer in the
text – for Karen recovers, and her death would have been manslaugh-
ter anyway – who can claim the most deprived family circumstances,
while also providing a breathtaking conclusion to the novel. In a final
coup de théâtre, outraged by Jane's relationship with Buddy, he kidnaps
and threatens to kill her, but eventually turns the knife on himself,
having first opened her eyes to Buddy's responsibility in the trashing.
A pivotal character to the resolution of the plot, the Avenger turns out
not to be the geeky kid who had been set up as a red herring for this
role. In fact, he is not a child after all. Known as Mickey Looney, he is
the eccentric, local odd-job man, whose self-perception as an 11-year-
old dates back to the time when he committed two murders. Armed
with his grandfather's rifle, Mickey had killed a young bully, in a well-
meaning but tragically misguided attempt to mete out justice. Mickey
had subsequently felt compelled to dispatch his own grandfather,
who had begun to harbour dangerous suspicions about the identity
of the one person, beside himself, who had easy access to the murder
weapon. With the exception of the caring figure of this grandparent,
Mickey's family background is suitably squalid. His father has walked
out on his family 'without saying goodbye or leaving a note',[24] while
his mother has clung to the implausible hope 'that he'd somehow
lost his memory'[25] and that, presumably, he might be back one day.
Quite apart from his association with dire circumstances, which
provide an alibi of sorts for the Avenger's skewed sense of justice and
moral degradation, Mickey is also explicitly characterised as mentally
unstable, the local 'loon' whose facade of harmless eccentricity and
underdeveloped social skills hide much more serious disorders (such
as his continuing self-perception as an 11-year-old boy, or his obsessive interest in and morbid possessiveness towards Jane).

Tenderness

The language of pathology is also present in the characterisation of
the protagonists of *Tenderness*, which charts the dangerous liaison

between Lori Cranston, a 15-year-old runaway, and 18-year-old Eric
Poole, a convicted parricide recently released from a juvenile correc-
tional facility. As if Eric's back-story were not dark enough, readers
soon discover that he is correctly suspected of having killed two
teenage girls, and that, unbeknown to her, Lori might be able to link
him to the murder of a third. As it happens, years earlier she had met
him as he had been leaving the scene of this third crime. Given the
age of Eric's preferred victims, and his need to get rid of an inconve-
nient potential witness, readers have more than one reason to fear for
Lori's life when the two renew their acquaintance. Still, Eric's career as
a serial killer is not the initial focus of the novel, which opens instead
by detailing Lori's own strange compulsion: whenever she develops
a crush, she gets 'fixated' on the object of that crush, and will not be
cured of her obsession until she has tracked the man down and kissed
him.[26] Self-evidently much less threatening than Eric's compulsion
for asphyxiating first kittens, then young girls, Lori's 'fixation' reprises
some of its disturbing motifs, albeit in a lower key, as shown by her
own description of her attack on Throb, a popular singer and her
latest 'victim': 'I reach out and cup his face in my hands and plant
this monstrous kiss on his mouth, my lips devouring his mouth, my
tongue slipping between his lips …'.[27]

   Although 'technically' a virgin,[28] Lori is used to attracting a lot
of male attention, particularly from men much older than she is; her
'conquests' include her mother's previous boyfriend, Dexter, a violent
man who, as she recalls, 'got mean and nasty when he drank and hit my
mother once in a while'.[29] Lori's mother, a 36-year-old waitress, has
been in a string of (often abusive) relationships after the sudden death of
Lori's father, when her daughter was only two years old; since then, the
two female characters have often been on the move, '[a]lways looking
for a better job or following somebody … who makes promises that
are always broken'.[30] In spite of her censorious attitude to liars and
schemers, Lori herself is quite capable of exploiting to her advantage,
through carefully calculated advances, her irresistible 'sexy and innocent'
aura.[31] Nonetheless, she decides to leave home when Gary, her current
step-father (and one of the few kind men that her mother has ever
dated), starts showing her clumsy attentions. Even if she likes his 'tender'
touch,[32] Lori runs away, both for her mother's sake and because she
must pursue her new 'fixation' for the recently freed Eric Poole. Three
years before, aged only 15, Eric had carefully plotted the murder of his
own mother and step-father, having self-harmed in order to give the
impression of acting in self-defence, as the desperate victim of abuse.
The reality of Eric's family background is much less violent than he

would have people believe, but there is no doubt that he suffered from lack of affection and received clear hostility from his step-father.

Both Lori and Eric, then, come from broken families, and have suffered from neglect, and worse, because of this – hence their obsessive quest for tenderness, which the two epigraphs to *Tenderness* explicitly connect to pain and hurt: 'To know the pain of too much tenderness' reads a lyrical fragment by Kahlil Gibran, while the second, anonymous quotation recites, more prosaically, 'A part of the body that has been injured is often tender to the touch'. Besides sharing with Lori a sad personal history, Eric is characterised as incapable of feeling sympathy and as a master manipulator, highly skilled in turning on 'The Charm'.[33] What is more, his career as a serial killer is presented almost as a case of necrophilia, as the description of the aftermath to the murder of Laura Andersun, Eric's first teenage victim, intimates: 'As Eric lay beside the girl, ... he sighed with contentment. ... For some reason, he trailed his mouth along her flesh, so warm and moist against his lips. Bliss filled him. He had never known such tenderness before, his body trembling with it. He knew he must find it again'.[34] The detective who obsessively investigates the case (and uses unorthodox expedients in trying to frame Eric) does not hesitate to brand Eric a 'psychopath'[35] and a 'monster'.[36] This is how the boy comes to think of himself at the end of the narrative, when – in a dark, ironic twist, typical of Cormier – he ends up back in jail, accused of the one killing of which he is actually innocent. Lori's drowning, which Eric could not prevent, is the last, tragic piece of evidence of the girl's low self-esteem and self-destructive nature. Like the Avenger in *We All Fall Down*, the protagonists of *Tenderness* are the product of a lethal cocktail of psychological disturbances, familial neglect, and abuse.

The Rag and Bone Shop

The link between environmental influences and child corruption is even more evident in *The Rag and Bone Shop*, where it is undiluted by references to aberrations and pathologies, although Alicia Bartlett, the seven-year-old victim whose murder triggers the narrative, is described as having 'little-old-lady features' and manners,[37] unrepresentative of her age-group. Under pressure to bring the perpetrator of this shocking crime to justice, the local police require the assistance of Trent, an officer with an unbroken record of obtaining confessions from his suspects, and with a penchant for cultivating an extreme form of reserve, as his refusal to disclose even the most basic information about himself makes clear: 'No first-name greetings, no first name given. He wanted to operate alone, travel light'.[38] The only (tenuous) lead in this investigation is to Jason Dorrant, the 12-year-old boy who last saw Alicia alive. Trapped by his own formidable reputation, and lured by the prospect of career advancement, Trent does not balk at the idea of using his subtle psychological tricks in the interrogation of a child. Trent's careful control of his formal introduction to Jason is a good case in point, with the distancing strategy in withholding his own first name doubling up as a way to patronise and intimidate the child: 'You're Jason?' Omitting the family name, establishing a sense of familiarity but maintaining a degree of authority for himself, announcing only his family name. 'I'm Trent.'[39] Trent's ruthless exploitation of his command of the subtleties of language continues when he lulls Jason into a false sense of security through a calculated, avuncular readiness in explaining to him difficult concepts, such as the idea of somebody being suspiciously 'out of context'.[40] Only too eager to please, Jason will later repeat this very same expression, '[g]lad to be using one of Mr. Trent's phrases'[41] – a sign that he is being drawn into telling Trent exactly want he wants to hear.

In the face of Trent's manipulative abuse of power, Jason is utterly helpless; he inevitably gets crushed in this mechanism and confesses to a crime that he has not committed. By the end of his ordeal, when he is finally set free because the real culprit has been found, Jason is entertaining thoughts of killing a bully, having been virtually brainwashed into thinking himself capable of murderous actions. The instrument of such a chilling conclusion, Trent, is one of Cormier's most dislikeable creations. His mercenary manipulation of Jason is painfully transparent to the reader, and his cynical, self-loathing, corrupt personality contrasts starkly with the youthful integrity represented by the 'freshness and crispness'[42] of Sarah Downes, assistant to the district attorney. Sarah's unsullied honesty is replicated, even more poignantly, in the figure of Lottie, Trent's daughter and moral compass, even if in absentia. By the time the narrative begins, Lottie has been dead for 18 months, the victim of a car accident 'in which the air bag and seat belt conspired to cause her death – trapped by safety devices suddenly turned lethal'.[43] The manner of her tragic demise foreshadows the novel's ending, when another young character, Jason, gets destroyed by a malfunctioning cog in the machine – the corrupt investigator in the police force – designed to protect him.

The entire story is thus constructed around the dichotomy between the innocence of the young and the decay and evil embodied by the jaded, crooked cop, a conventional figure in crime narratives. This opposition is further exemplified, in slightly different terms, by the final exchange between Trent and his daughter, the day before her fatal car accident. In answer to Lottie's implicit accusation that she does not know him anymore, Trent replies with a disingenuous 'What you see is what you get'.[44] Trent's unconvincing appeal to the transparency of signs, to a non-existent coincidence between beings and appearances is met by the anti-essentialist, performative view of identity denoted in Lottie's sharp corrective, 'You are what you do'.[45] Significantly, this is the very principle that Trent implicitly subscribes to during his interrogation of Jason. After cornering the boy into admitting that he enjoys Stephen King, mysteries, and horror, he exploits this alleged 'disposition for violent movies and stories'[46] to make his case for the suspect's appetite for cruelty. Never one to shy away from a further turn of the screw, Cormier ends the novel with the revelation that Trent's corrupting influence has worked on Jason, who leaves the police station puzzled about his confession, and slowly drawn to the conclusion that 'if you said you did it, maybe you *could* do it'.[47] In this way, childhood innocence is shown to have crumbled in the face of the realisation that individual identity is not a matter of crystallised definitions, but something we renegotiate, through words and actions, every moment of our lives. Ironically, however, Cormier's staunch belief in moral responsibility and his endorsement of a performative notion of identity are underpinned, as we have seen, by a counterintuitive, insistent representation of children who are fundamentally corrupted by their environment – a view which presupposes as a starting point the common, essentialist view of childhood as an inherently innocent state.

Cormier's recuperation of innocence

Cormier does not usually indulge in the comforting narrative that it is always possible to rationalise the provenance of evil, and it is certainly true that he does not offer a 'picture of the world in which all will be well if everyone just tries a little harder'.[48] Still, possibly because of the particularly violent nature of the crimes depicted, and of the young age of their protagonists, the three narratives under analysis, most notably *The Rag and Bone Shop*, all give a plausible background to the various trajectories of degradation which they chart. Besides, the detrimental effect of corrupting influences and degrading environments is often compounded by the association of criminal behaviour with the sphere of pathology – as witnessed by the characters' abnormal fixations and self-delusions, for example – as if to reiterate the belief that a criminal child is a damaged child.

In the absence of these qualifications, as in the case of Brad Bartlett, Alicia's 13-year-old brother and the real murderer in *The Rag and Bone Shop*, Cormier makes sure that the narrative focus is firmly on other matters. That novel concentrates on Jason's tragic degeneration with very little space devoted either to what remains a sketchy (and fairly unsympathetic) characterisation of the victim, or to that of her murderer, who features as a mere function of the plot, and is conveniently introduced as a lover of 'practical jokes'.[49] This detail, added to the description of Alicia's body, laid down by her killer with apparent 'tenderness'[50] opens up the possibility that the girl's death might be legitimately construed as an accident – notwithstanding the ambivalence of the term 'tenderness' in Cormier's work.

Cormier is careful to allow comparatively limited access to the villains in the other two novels too: the focalisation in the third-person narrative in *We All Fall Down* is either through Jane or Buddy, and never through Harry Flowers, while *Tenderness* alternates Lori's first-person account, in the present tense, with a third-person focalisation, in the past tense, for the sections about Eric. While these three novels do not necessarily fully explain, let alone justify, the terrible crimes they are about, through his narrative choices Cormier makes sure to hold a firm grip on the reader's sympathy. Having thus ostracised and accounted for the more 'anomalous' child characters, the novels proceed to paint a picture where the young protagonists' behaviour, no matter how careless, destructive, or brutal, begins to make sense and is ameliorated by extenuating circumstances. This still makes for an uncomfortable view, but not quite for the unflinching representation of evil for which Cormier is known: as far as his child criminals are concerned, Cormier paints a picture where – in the words of officer Trent – 'nobody [is] out of context'.[51]

Notes

1. Jonathan Trigell, *Boy A* (London: Serpent's Tail, 2004).
2. Lionel Shriver, *We Need to Talk about Kevin* (New York: Counterpoint, 2003).
3. Patricia Head, 'Robert Cormier and the Postmodernist Possibilities of Young Adult Fiction', *Children's Literature Association Quarterly*, 21(1) (1996): 28–33, at 28.
4. Nancy Veglahn, 'The Bland Face of Evil in the Novels of Robert Cormier', *The Lion and the Unicorn*, 12(1) (1988): 12–18, at 12. In her article, published before the three novels discussed here, Veglahn also points out that the (adult) killers and kidnappers who are otherwise present in young adult mysteries tend to be 'flat characters, never

developed enough to take on real stature, always defeated in the end'
(12). The present essay shows that the same can be argued of Cormier's
child villains – like the murderer in *The Rag and Bone Shop*, for example –
in those cases when the narrative does not provide clear extenuating
circumstances.

5. Deanna Zitterkopf, 'Robert Cormier', *Children's Literature Association Quarterly*, 11(1) (1986): 42–3, at 42.
6. Chris Jenks, *Childhood* (London and New York: Routledge, 1996): 85.
7. Ibid.: 86.
8. Ibid.: 119.
9. Here childhood is meant in the narrowest sense of the term, referring to prepubescent individuals. The 1989 UNO 'Convention on the Rights of the Child' gives a broader definition of the category, classifying as children all people under the age of 18.
10. Katie Marsico, *The Columbine High School Massacre: Murder in the Classroom* (Terrytown, NY: Marshall Cavendish Corporation, 2011): 13.
11. Zitterkopf: 42.
12. S. E. Hinton, *The Outsiders* (New York: Viking Press, 1967).
13. Golding's most famous novel, *Lord of the Flies* (London: Faber and Faber, 1954), has been reclaimed by some critics as part of the young adult fiction canon; on the matter see, for example, Jonathan Stephens, 'Young Adult: A Book by Any Other Name... : Defining the Genre', *The ALAN Review*, 35(1) (2007): 34–42. Of course, teenage gang culture is at the heart of other classics of twentieth-century literature, such as Anthony Burgess's *A Clockwork Orange* (London: Heinemann, 1962).
14. Robert Cormier, 'A Character by Any Other Name', *English Journal*, 90(3) (2001), 31–2, at 32).
15. Christopher Routledge, 'Children's Detective Fiction and the "Perfect Crime" of Adulthood', in Adrienne E. Gavin and Christopher Routledge (eds), *Mystery in Children's Literature: From the Rational to the Supernatural* (Basingstoke: Palgrave, 2001): 64–81, at 64.
16. Robert Cormier, *We All Fall Down* [1991] (Oxford: Heinemann, 1994): 101.
17. Ibid.: 23.
18. Ibid.: 70.
19. Ibid.: 42–3.
20. Ibid.: 136.
21. Ibid.: 76.
22. Early on in the narrative, Buddy thinks to himself that Harry, who has taken to calling his cronies 'bloods', is 'probably the whitest kid [he] knew' (12). This is further evidence of Harry's cultivated, superficial disavowal of his privileged background.
23. *We all Fall Down*: 34.
24. Ibid.: 59.
25. Ibid.
26. Robert Cormier, *Tenderness* [1997] (New York: Delacorte Press, 2004): 1.

27. Ibid.: 24–5.
28. Ibid.: 9, 194.
29. Ibid.: 4.
30. Ibid.: 7.
31. Ibid.: 167.
32. Ibid.: 5.
33. Ibid.: 42.
34. Ibid.: 45.
35. Ibid.: 37, 41.
36. Ibid.: 37.
37. Robert Cormier, *The Rag and Bone Shop* [2001] (London: Puffin, 2002): 22.
38. Ibid.: 70.
39. Ibid.: 79.
40. Ibid.: 89.
41. Ibid.: 113.
42. Ibid.: 64.
43. Ibid.: 68.
44. Ibid.: 67.
45. Ibid.: 68.
46. Ibid.: 85.
47. Ibid.: 152.
48. Veglahn: 12.
49. *The Rag and Bone Shop*: 15.
50. Ibid.: 17.
51. Ibid.: 113.

5

'You have to outlast them': Bullying in *The Chocolate War* and *Beyond the Chocolate War*

Amy Cummins

In Robert Cormier's *The Chocolate War* (1974) and *Beyond the Chocolate War* (1985), Trinity high school suffers from a bullying climate. The behaviour of Brother Leon, as a teacher and assistant headmaster who later becomes the headmaster, exemplifies workplace bullying, while peer harassment pollutes the student environment. This sequence of two novels describes one full school year and forms a narrative that reveals how Trinity school perpetuates a bully culture. Protagonist Jerry Renault embodies the victim role. Vigils members John Carter, Emile Janza, and Bunting bully peers, while Obie both harasses and gets victimised. Roland Goubert and fellow Trinity students become both onlookers and victims. Archie Costello and Brother Leon enact the worst bullying practices, and intimidation by The Vigils and the headmaster will persist without systemic changes and the removal of Leon as administrator at Trinity.

Education research about bullying provides a scholarly lens through which to analyse the peer and administrator intimidation that cause the bleak tone of Cormier's texts. The patterns of bullying in *The Chocolate War* and *Beyond the Chocolate War* correlate with observed reality in schools, revealing ways in which bullying gets perpetuated and factors that can either interrupt or perpetuate unhealthy experiences for students and teachers.

Jerry and the Chocolate War at Trinity school

Bullying, another term for 'peer victimisation' or 'peer harassment,' is a social experience in which there is a power differential and 'intent to cause physical or psychological harm'.[1] A bullying triad includes the victim, the perpetrator(s), and bystanders, and in bullying verbal, physical, and/or psychological harassment occur. Teasing remains 'the most commonly observed and experienced form' of school bullying,[2] and bullying is more common than many school personnel realise. Typical attributes of victims of bullying include 'submissive personality', 'low self-esteem', and 'being a member of the "out-group" as opposed to the powerful "in-group"'.[3] Students may not report being victimised due to fear of retaliation from the bully and doubt 'that reporting incidents will lead to effective resolutions'.[4] Such a sense of hopelessness is palpable at Trinity.

When Jerry Renault, aged 14, challenges the code of mandatory chocolate selling, he briefly becomes a rebel hero. But The Vigils and Leon stigmatise him when he continues refusing to sell beyond the ten days assigned by The Vigils. His hard-fought decision to 'disturb the universe' almost costs Jerry his life.[5] Quoted on Jerry's poster, T. S. Eliot's poem 'The Love Song of J. Alfred Prufrock' (1915) asks: 'Do I dare / Disturb the universe?';[6] the allusion amplifies Jerry's efforts at defining himself without conforming. The indecisive speaker of the poem, composed by Eliot 'in his early twenties', is middle-aged but can be interpreted as an adolescent.[7] For a teen, the awkwardness of human interactions may be so severe as to be akin to challenging the universe. Cormier's novel and Eliot's poem mean different things to readers as they age, evoking the frustration of trying to define one's own roles in an automated world of rules and codes.

C. Anita Tarr argues that in Jerry, 'Cormier presents only the *illusion* of decision making and the *illusion* of a rebel hero',[8] but in truth, as Anne Lundin suggests, Jerry does take a stand in 'defiance of the institutional and peer pressure' to do as directed by The Vigils and school administration.[9] As Zibby Oneal observes, Jerry's act of 'refusal truly does seem a way to disturb the universe'.[10] Anti-bullying advocate C. J. Bott explains that many adolescents will 'trade away' everything they are and believe in order to 'fit in'.[11] Jerry resists the pressure to conform while his Trinity classmates take the path of least resistance and comply with The Vigils' demands.

Jerry becomes a victim of 'social exclusion'.[12] During and after the ten days he fulfils The Vigils' assignment not to sell the chocolates, Jerry is ostracised. He feels invisible and 'isolated' by having this secret task.[13] He is publicly humiliated and harassed by his classmates and by Leon. Jerry endures telephone calls to his home, vandalism of his locker, defacement of his poster, and theft of the painting assignment he has submitted to a teacher's desk. Teachers not only fail to intervene in this isolation but also start ignoring Jerry when he becomes a pariah to peers, which makes him feel that they, too, are involved in the conspiracy.[14]

Teachers possess influence to prevent or minimise bullying, but teachers may also inadvertently 'foster bullying by failing to promote respectful interactions among students, modeling disrespectful behaviors, declining to intervene in bullying episodes or intervening ineffectively'.[15] Pretending the situation is not happening only enables it, for teachers' 'lack of response' to bullying gets interpreted 'as permission'.[16] Because teachers may lack legal protection in case of injury sustained while stopping student fights, schools need to develop policies that enable teachers to enforce the 'zero tolerance policy' recommended by many specialists.[17] A school fails the victims, bullies, and witnesses if there is no 'schoolwide anti-bullying program'.[18] Exercises with victims, bullies, and bystanders can be used in schools 'to assist students in identifying their role in bully prevention'.[19] Students can be empowered by discussing young adult literature such as *The Chocolate War* and using 'process drama' strategies for enacting ways to 'stop bullying and violence'.[20] Teaching 'adaptive coping strategies' to victims can help them in social situations both in and out of school.[21]

None of these productive approaches happens at Trinity. The instructors neglect to take any action to stop bullying, and students who have been assigned dangerous tasks by The Vigils feel that they have no choice but to complete them. Jerry's responses are typical of a victim who has no faith in the system. When he is beaten up, he wants to hide, internalising the hatred from his peers and authorities, and not reporting the crime. He realises the irony of this, thinking, 'Funny, someone does violence to you but you're the one who has to hide, as if you're the criminal',[22] yet still he does not report it.

Jerry's interactions with Emile Janza support the strategy of responding to a bully by refusing to fight back and 'avoid[ing] giving the bully an emotional payoff'.[23] Nonresponsiveness is the strategy Jerry adopts late in *Beyond the Chocolate War* when Janza continues antagonising Jerry, beating him up again, and vowing to do so whenever he sees him. Jerry's refusal to fight back, a strategy of 'passive resistance',[24] removes some of Janza's pleasure. Janza feels 'something missing' physically and emotionally because he does not get the same satisfaction from beating up Jerry.[25] The implication is that Janza will not continue to beat up Jerry, and Jerry tells Goober, '"You can really lose only if you fight them. ... You have to outlast them"'.[26] The word *them* connotes the bullies like Archie Costello, Emile Janza, and Leon.

After a period away in Canada, Jerry's resolve to return to Trinity strengthens. He has been changed by his experiences with the Talking Church in Quebec, and he contemplates becoming 'a good and kind brother like Brother Eugene',[27] dedicated to service and a simple life that honours God. But Brother Eugene is an ambiguous role model, and Cormier never reveals whether Jerry's strategy to 'outlast' the bullies will work in the long run.

The Vigils: peer harassment at Trinity

Cormier shows that Trinity high school perpetuates peer harassment by allowing the existence of The Vigils. The secret society serves a useful function to the school authorities by regulating student actions, for 'Trinity brothers wanted peace at any price'.[28] This noninterference by teachers allows the bullying to continue, creating an unhealthy school climate for the sake of maintaining order: 'The brothers knew the organization existed but preferred to ignore it, allowing it to function because it served a purpose: kept peace at Trinity'.[29] Archie expects credit and praise from Leon because Trinity does not have the external problems nearby Monument High School faces with 'student misbehavior, bomb scares, vandalism'.[30] The student body shows more deference to the secret society than to school authority. As Jen Menzel observes, *The Chocolate War* has the 'most overt depiction' of peer intimidation in any novel by Cormier.[31] The Vigils run the school yet seem led by rituals such as the marbles, by very few appointed positions, and by an indefinite membership.

Archie Costello, a senior, directs the peer intimidation campaign at Trinity. As assigner for The Vigils, Archie bullies his classmates by dreaming up the tasks and victims for assignments. From behind the scenes, Archie takes advantage of other people and creates chaos at school. His influence is such that he is, as Rickey Cotten states, 'the ruthless antagonist of both novels'.[32] Archie revels in directing The Vigils' power. Archie's style is to 'let the victim be his own torturer' by finding a task that matches the victim ironically, such as forcing an overweight student to gain more weight.[33] Archie targets Jerry, not despite knowing, but because he knows, that Jerry is deeply mourning the recent death of his mother.

It does not excuse Archie to suggest that he is a bully who strikes back against exploitation by Leon. Archie has little choice but to accept when Leon requests Vigils influence for the chocolate sale. When Archie watches all of the furniture in Brother Eugene's homeroom fall apart and relishes 'a sweet moment of triumph', Leon sneaks up to castigate Archie while gripping Archie's shoulder so hard that he 'wince[s] with pain'.[34] Archie, embarrassed at being 'humiliated by this sniveling bastard of a teacher', consoles himself by 'drinking in the beautiful debris of Room Nineteen – his masterpiece' and watching Brother Eugene weep.[35] Leon threatens to expose Archie and eradicate his Vigils if the sale fails, but Leon's intimidation does not pardon Archie from practicing the same techniques on others.

Archie negatively directs fellow students who likewise bully – John Carter, Emile Janza, and Bunting – as well as Obie, who becomes both victim and persecutor. Carter, a varsity football player, boxer, and appointed president of The Vigils, bangs the gavel but has no control over the organisation; his feeble remonstrations are overcome by Archie. Carter hates Archie for making everyone feel 'dirty, contaminated, polluted,' but he goes along with him.[36] His world changes at the start of *Beyond the Chocolate War* when Leon disbands the boxing team, costing Carter his athletic identity. He anonymously reports to Leon Archie's plan to ruin the Bishop's visit, and he helps Obie in his plan for revenge against Archie. Archie considers Carter a traitor and removes the sports trophies temporarily to remind Carter of his power. Yet Carter or any other Vigils member could have halted the violence at any time. The Vigils' perpetuation of bullying reveals a human tendency to allow violence to continue rather than intervening, an inclination for self-concern that requires deliberate correction.

Although the word rarely appears, each instance of the word 'bully' across the two novels refers to Emile Janza. Janza is the thuggish 'voice of all the bullies' who want to provoke Jerry into starting a fight because, as Jerry thinks, 'That's the way bullies worked so they could be held blameless after the slaughter'.[37] Janza's private beating of Jerry is a precursor to the public fight in the boxing match. Patricia Campbell interprets Janza as a 'villain' on par with Archie and Leon, all three of whom 'are completely devoid of any sense of guilt'.[38] Janza is not yet equivalent to Archie and Leon, but by the end of the second novel, he is implicitly on track for the subsequent school year to become a tormentor at their level.

Bunting, the sophomore Archie grooms to replace Obie as Vigils secretary, appears only in the sequel but is a violent, destructive force. Bunting organises the surprise attack on Obie and his girlfriend Laurie Gundarson at Purgatory Chasm. The assault traumatises Laurie through physical violation and the threat of rape. Bunting derives pleasure from this cruelty under cover of darkness. Because Bunting is physically violent and imagines creative ideas of how to inflict suffering, Archie knows Bunting will wreak havoc when given free rein after Archie's graduation. Archie's awarding leadership of The Vigils to Bunting and insisting on Janza as his assistant will escalate the bodily traumas caused by The Vigils.

Obie is both bully and victim. He does not resign from or expose The Vigils, even after losing his enthusiasm for his role as The Vigils secretary, keeper of the information notebook, and finder of victims for assignments. The attack at the chasm devastates him, but Obie accepts Cornacchio's falsehood that the attack on Laurie was a Vigils' assignment. When he learns Bunting is to blame, Obie still considers Archie ultimately at fault. He further blames The Vigils for the fact that he earns an indifferent high school grade record of 'a dull B average' and gets fired from his after-school job.[39] Obie rebels secretly against Archie, using Ray Bannister, the new student who becomes bully bait, to plot violent retribution.

The four sections of *Beyond the Chocolate War* are structured to emphasise Obie's struggle with Archie. The attack at the chasm ends part one, and at the end of part two, Obie realises he has 'lost Laurie Gundarson forever'.[40] Part three ends with Archie's acting sympathetically about Obie's loss while also saying '"Welcome back"' as if assuming Obie will do more with The Vigils now that his former girlfriend has rejected him.[41] At the end of part four, Obie strikes back at Archie, and only Ray's preparation as a magician saves Archie from death by the guillotine. Obie knows that Archie's power has twisted him into becoming an attempted murderer; he is no better than his nemesis.[42] Archie himself insists on their similarity, telling Obie: '"I'm all the things you hide inside you"'.[43] The cruelty he has regularly witnessed makes Obie violent. Readers sympathise with Laurie and Obie as victims, but Obie, as a Vigils officer, remains an active participant in the system that causes his own misery.

Unlike the remorseless bullies in The Vigils, victim and bystander Roland Goubert, known as Goober, feels complicity in Brother Eugene's death and in Jerry's beatings. Goober endures guilt and shame for unscrewing the desks as ordered by The Vigils and later dwells on the news of Brother Eugene's death, a loss attributable in part to the bullying climate. After The Vigils' Room Nineteen prank in which Eugene's homeroom falls apart, he disappears from school. Eugene has 'a nervous breakdown,' never recovers, and dies in the Manchester infirmary during spring semester.[44] The famous opening line 'They murdered him' applies even more literally to Eugene than to Jerry.[45] Goober also feels that he has been a 'traitor' to Jerry.[46] In a common manifestation for a victim within the bullying triad, Goober

becomes physically ill. While Janza beats up Jerry, Goober is forced
to be first a bystander then a physical victim. Although Jerry tries 'to
convince Goober that he was not to blame,' Goober decides to transfer to Monument High School for the next year.[47]

For only the price of a raffle ticket, Jerry's classmates direct his fight
with Emile Janza and become accountable for the brutalisation he
endures: 'Everybody who bought a ticket – and who could refuse? –
had a chance to be involved in the fight ... with no danger of getting
hurt'.[48] As Oneal suggests, readers too, are participants in the book's
events, literally 'there, yelling in the stands', having 'become the mob,
participants in the very evil we profess to despise'.[49] No one speaks
out when Janza enacts prohibited blows to the groin and head or
when he beats Jerry unconscious after Jerry has fallen to the ground.
In this way bystanders become active contributors to, even exacerba-
tors of, the bullying. Education researchers Dawn Newman, Arthur
Horne, and Christi Bartolomucci explain that peers often 'positively
reinforce' bullying behaviours by showing 'interest and admiration
for the manipulations of the bully'.[50] The students who gather in the
bleachers on the athletic grounds know exactly what they are there
to see.

Adrienne Nishina emphasises the multiplicity of possibilities for
the third position in the bullying triad. In addition to the bully and
the victim are people in various other roles such as 'reinforcer, assistant, defendant, bystander'.[51] Alternatively, Allison Baer and Jacqueline
Glasgow see the 'bystander' as a term encompassing the roles of
'assistants, reinforcers, outsiders, or defenders'.[52] Bystanders have
varying degrees of involvement and culpability, and working with the
witnesses of bullying 'is essential to reducing the occurrence of bullying in an organization'.[53] Punishing the bully 'does not address the
roles that other students may have played' and thus does not stop the
problem.[54] When one aggressor gets removed, someone else typically
takes his or her place. This reality bodes poorly for Trinity because
only Archie leaves at the end of the school year, with Bunting and
Janza set to take his place at the head of The Vigils. With the school
climate unchanged and Leon still in charge, Trinity high school is
likely to get worse, not better.

Brother Leon: the administrator as bully

Brother Leon is an adult who has power over, and responsibility for,
the care of his charges. Leon's violations betray his educational and
religious commitments to lead the school. Cormier's texts do not

support Martha Westwater's assertion that Archie is 'the real evil influence' and 'the more vile and violent' of the two 'arch villains' of both books.[55] Nancy Veglahn observes that in multiple novels, Cormier features 'moral monsters' who 'use the authority and power they have to destroy the young',[56] and Leon exemplifies this trope. When Leon claims, "'I love this school,'" Archie thinks, 'Like a criminal loves his crime',[57] equating Leon's school with desecration. In both chocolate war novels, Leon is the *ur*-bully, the unethical criminal who makes the student body and his fellow teachers into victims.

Granted, school administrators in young adult novels serve as convenient antagonists who tend to be ridiculed or opposed by students and teachers reacting against authority figures. Administrators are rarely portrayed like the dedicated leader in Graham Gardner's *Inventing Elliot* (2003), in which the principal genuinely wants to stop the 'organized intimidation' of students by a secret society.[58] Educational administration professor Patricia Brieschke asserts that novels featuring principals constitute 'an interpretive data source' worthy of study by future principals, and she assigns such fiction in education courses.[59] Jacqueline Bach and Jennifer Jolly note that school administrators on film tend to be cast either as 'bumbling fools' distant from the classroom or as heroic leaders who help the school triumph over adversity.[60] Although Trinity School's Brother Leon, the prototype of the bad school administrator, is a fictional creation and not a living person, his characterisation falls into the pattern of the bullying principal.

The 'teacher stress literature' in educational research addresses the ways in which some principals mistreat teachers and students.[61] Principal bullying is a form of workplace incivility, and workplace bullies tend to outrank their targets[62]. A bully leader has major impact, because when 'incivility becomes the behavioral norm,' a "'spiral of silence" can then occur at the organizational level as it d[oes] with the observers to [a] bullying act'.[63] Principal bullying is defined as the 'persistent abuse of power that may impact negatively on the victims'.[64] Interviews of teachers who have experienced bullying reveal 'verbal abuse and public ridicule', 'unwarranted written reprimands', and 'reassignment or threatening victims with dismissal'.[65] Principals may deliberately create a 'state of fear' due to job stress or jealousy.[66] An 'authoritarian-abusive approach to school leadership' can result in the 'mistreatment of students' as well as teachers.[67]

Leon's classroom abuse of Gregory Bailey fits the pattern of the bully as 'an evildoer who often acts anti-normatively and without remorse'.[68] Leon falsely accuses Gregory of cheating, calls him to the front of the room, and strikes him in the face with a pointer, raising a welt 'like an evil stain', yet Leon contrives to blame the class for letting this happen.[69] The teachers rarely interact with Leon, who remains a shadowy figure; they are alienated from leadership, rendering Trinity a fiefdom for Leon. Schools should involve teachers in decision-making processes so teachers can 'see themselves as part of the picture in all aspects of school functioning' and make preventing violence such as bullying an in-role duty.[70] Furthermore, the 'social stratification' among adult employees at a school worsens bullying for students and staff.[71] Leon solicits no one's permission or approval before purchasing double the usual amount of fundraising chocolates; the brothers might have advised him that Trinity's educational mission does not include making every student responsible for selling 50 boxes of fancy chocolates.

Due to Leon's autocratic leadership, Trinity has 'a dysfunctional organizational culture' that is fundamentally unsound.[72] Far from sharing power, Leon disregards his colleagues and eliminates Brother Jacques by transferring him away. The act is retaliation because Jacques knows Leon abused his power of attorney by making unapproved purchases and overspending the school's budget during the headmaster's absence.[73]

The unnamed headmaster, hospitalised for an unstated illness, is never seen, and Leon effectively runs the school from the outset. There is an implication that the ambitious Leon has caused the illness of the headmaster. Leon is likely to be promoted to headmaster if the chocolate sale succeeds, but he will lose rank if his financial choices result in failure. Contributing to the inscrutability of Leon is the fact noted by Campbell that readers never hear his 'interior monologue', so Leon seems like 'pure unexplained evil'.[74] The novels also remain silent about the home lives of and family influences on Archie and Leon. Readers do not know if they continue a cycle of abuse they personally experienced while growing up, as bullies often do, nor would such information exonerate Leon, whose intimidation techniques have a ripple effect on everyone at Trinity.

Leon's leadership poisons school-day rituals. He makes roll call a source of stigma to Jerry. He turns assembly and the mass for Brother Eugene into sacrilege. He allows The Vigils to perpetrate assignments. During the boxing match between Janza and Jerry, Leon, who has been tipped off by Archie, watches and does not intervene. Readers do not know how much Leon sees – presumably everything. Yet Leon excuses and approves of Archie.

Leon revels in power over the students. In class he holds their attention 'like a cobra' and watches them 'like a hawk, suspicious,'

probing for 'weaknesses' which he then exploits.[75] His methods
centre on the teacher as authority and resemble the transmission
theory of learning, in which classroom practice 'revolves primarily
around the teacher as the center of instruction',[76] though no teacher-
educators would claim Leon as a model. His aggressive teaching style
is characterised by 'quick and sudden classroom movements in which
a student was usually the loser, struck with a teacher's pointer or a
piece of chalk'.[77] The incident with Gregory Bailey is not isolated.
As Westwater encapsulates, 'In his exercise of power Leon belittles
others – especially students'.[78] Leon has 'a cold intelligence in which
there [i]sn't an ounce of pity or mercy'.[79] In an earlier school year,
Leon makes Henry Boudreau fail out of school as retribution for 'a
devastating burlesque' of Leon on a Skit Night, complete with Henry's
onstage 'mincing' and wielding a baseball bat like Leon's pointer.[80]

Unjust grading and coercion characterise Leon's algebra teaching. Brian Cochran only accepts the duty of being treasurer for the
chocolate sale because he is in Leon's algebra class and cannot risk
'sudden unexplained Fs on exams'.[81] Due to designing test questions
which have 'ambiguous answers', Leon completely controls results:
'Could pass or fail students at will'.[82] Leon brings certain students
in for conferences in which he probes for information about other
students, 'dangling a possible F in front of them'.[83] Some readers
interpret Leon's threats as sexual predation. Tarr perceives Leon's
characterisation as 'a stereotype of the male homosexual' and argues
that 'Cormier indoctrinates readers with hatred against Leon because
Leon is homosexual',[84] but Leon's sexual orientation seems irrelevant
to his bullying.

Leon drives David Caroni into a downward spiral, and destroys the
boy's world by giving him an unmerited F even though David leaks
information about Jerry to Leon during the chocolate war. While
David originally is 'a certainty for valedictorian' with plans to become
a teacher, his grades plummet until he feels hopeless.[85] David realises
'how terrible a teacher could be, how rotten the world really was, a
world in which even teachers were corrupt'.[86] David accosts Leon in
his study during Fair Day but does not injure him, instead turning his
anger against himself and committing suicide 'to end this agony'.[87]
The tomato Henry Malloran throws at Leon's face during assembly
suggests student disdain for Leon's pretences.

Through the Trinity School Fund, the institution itself is implicated in the violence and unhealthy climate at the school. Like the
chocolate sale, the Fair Day at the end of the sequel raises money by
selling food and games to the public: 'All profits for the Trinity School

Fund'.[88] In addition to tolerating peer harassment, the institution itself requires students to raise money beyond tuition and fees – funds not for donating to charity or supporting a student activity but for the general operations of the school and the church that runs it.

Moreover, the Bishop's failure to observe Trinity School lets Leon get away with corrupt administration. Leon only stays accountable to higher authorities when he expects that he will be observed; freed from oversight, he rampages. *The Chocolate War* contains no references to the Bishop or any governing board for the school, and in the sequel, the Bishop cancels his scheduled visit due to a conflict and does not reschedule.[89] The Bishop's noninvolvement requires criticism; he does not effectively oversee the school although it is a Catholic institution requiring guidance. Certainly, the decision to promote Leon to headmaster reveals a lack of awareness by authorities about what is taking place.

After the ending: can the bullying be stopped?

The ending of *Beyond the Chocolate War* does not reassure readers because the bullying situation and the climate at Trinity have not improved. Only replacing Leon, stopping The Vigils, and instituting a programme against bullying might solve the problems. Both books emanate bleakness. Campbell asserts that 'there is hope for next year', asking, 'Doesn't Brother Leon know very well how to squelch the kind of disturbance Bunting and Janza have in mind?'[90] Such optimism, however, overlooks the fact that Leon is a worse problem than The Vigils' officers. Near the end of the sequel, Goober, mourning the environment at Trinity School, says to Jerry: '"It's the school itself. Brother Leon, who lets The Vigils and guys like Archie get away with murder'.[91] Goober recognises that the headmaster and the institution are at fault in allowing the bullying culture that wrecks the learning environment.

There is no indication that the teaching practices or school climate will change for the better after Archie's departure. The leadership he establishes to succeed him in The Vigils will make student life worse. Life at Trinity is unlikely to improve because the 'peer ecology' still has a stratified 'status hierarchy' rather than the egalitarian one associated with 'positive youth outcomes'.[92] Vigils' tyranny overpowers any representative student leadership, and conditions remain conducive to bullying. A more positive environment would be created by 'teachers who actively address aggression and bullying'.[93] Perpetuation of The Vigils and Leon counters any chance of life improving at Trinity.

For bullies continue to bully after they leave school. In the boxing ring, when Jerry is told of the twisted rules for the raffle, he thinks ruefully of the larger significance, mourning what people like Archie and Janza 'did to Goober, to Brother Eugene ... to the school. What they would do to the world when they left Trinity'.[94] Jerry sees that the bullies will impact in the same way upon the wider world because schooling has not disciplined injustice. Readers of Cormier's *Chocolate War* novels likewise wonder about the future actions of Vigils' alumni such as Archie, Carter, Bunting, and Janza, who learned bullying techniques in school and will inflict more pain on people around them in the future unless there is intervention.

Reading young adult literature about bullying provides an opportunity for classroom or school programmes to counteract bullying. The study of a classic text like *The Chocolate War* can be combined effectively with student choice of a newer book. In James Howe's *The Misfits* (2001) and Doug Wilhelm's *The Revealers* (2003), middle school victims take productive action to stop bullying by exposing the harassment and seeking to understand the bullies.[95] Graham Gardner's *Inventing Elliot* (2003) and Alex Flinn's *Breaking Point* (2003) chronicle high school victims who become bullies in reaction to their sufferings but realise their mistake.[96] Paul Volponi's *Crossing Lines* (2011) and James Preller's *Bystander* (2009) give the perspective of classmates who witness bullying and struggle to do the right thing to stop it.[97] Meriting teen readership, new young adult titles examining the impact of bullying frequently appear.[98] Teachers and librarians can consult C. J. Bott's *The Bully in the Book and in the Classroom* (2004) or *More Bullies in More Books* (2009) for annotated entries and discussion questions about fiction on bullying.[99] Searches of the online Children's Literature Comprehensive Database (CLCD) yield professional reviews of young adult fiction on bullying and other subjects important to contemporary students.

Education research underscores the importance of teacher intervention in bullying, the value of school-wide awareness for all students, and the need for leadership that creates a healthy climate for learning and teaching. Pretending the bullying situations do not happen only enables them to worsen, as teacher nonresponsiveness becomes permission. To focus on the bullying in Cormier's *The Chocolate War* and *Beyond the Chocolate War* builds understanding of how peer harassment by The Vigils and Leon's intimidation of teachers and students – through his manipulation of power as a teacher and administrator – cause unhappy experiences at Trinity high school. Viewing both novels as a whole reveals the consequences of individual actions. Victims like Jerry Renault can overcome the experiences of their freshman year. Bystanders may become victims or bullies – or both – while bullies who go uncorrected during their school years are likely to continue the pattern as adults. In this chocolate war, there are no winners, only survivors.

Notes

1. Adrienne Nishina, 'A Theoretical View of Bullying: Can It Be Eliminated?' in Cheryl E. Sanders and Gary D. Phye (eds), *Bullying: Implications for the Classroom* (San Diego, CA: Elsevier Press, 2004): 35–62, at 36.
2. Melissa Holt, Melissa Keyes and Brian Koenig, 'Teachers' Attitudes Toward Bullying', in Dorothy L. Espelage and Susan M. Swearer (eds), *Bullying in North American Schools*, 2nd edn (New York and London: Routledge, 2011): 119–31, at 126.
3. Michael G. Harvey, M. Ronald Buckley, Joyce T. Heames, Robert Zinko, Robyn L. Brouer and Gerald R. Ferris, 'A Bully as an Archetypal Destructive Leader', *Journal of Leadership and Organizational Studies*, 14(2) (November 2007): 117–29, at 123.
4. Holt, Keyes and Koenig: 120.
5. Robert Cormier, *The Chocolate War*, 1974 (New York: Dell Laurel Leaf, 2000): 129.
6. T. S. Eliot 'The Love Song of J. Alfred Prufrock' [1915], *Prufrock and Other Observations* (London: The Egoist Ltd, 1917).
7. Roberta Seelinger Trites, *Disturbing the Universe: Power and Repression in Adolescent Literature* (Iowa City: University of Iowa Press, 2001): 1.
8. C. Anita Tarr, 'The Absence of Moral Agency in Robert Cormier's *The Chocolate War*', *Children's Literature*, 30 (2002): 96–124, at 96 (emphasis in original).
9. Anne Lundin, 'A Stranger in a World Unmade: Landscape in Robert Cormier's Chocolate War Novels', in Alethea Helbig and Agnes Perkins (eds), *The Phoenix Award of the Children's Literature Association, 1995–1999* (Lanham, MD: Scarecrow Press, 2001): 127–32, at 129.
10. Zibby Oneal, '"They tell you to do your own thing, but they don't mean it": Censorship and *The Chocolate War*', in Nicholas Karolides, Lee Burress and John Kean (eds), *Censored Books: Critical Viewpoints* (Lanham, MD: Scarecrow, 2001): 179–84, at 181.
11. C. J. Bott, *More Bullies in More Books* (Lanham, MD: Scarecrow Press, 2009): 79.
12. Melissa Holt, Melissa Keyes and Brian Koenig: 121.
13. *The Chocolate War*: 132.
14. Ibid.: 224.
15. Holt, Keyes and Koenig: 129.
16. Dawn A. Newman, Arthur M. Horne and Christi L. Bartolomucci, *Bully Busters: A Teacher's Manual for Helping Bullies, Victims, and Bystanders* (Champaign, IL: Research Press, 2000): 103.

17. Ibid.: 157.
18. William Broz, 'Professional Resource Connection: The Bully in the Book and in the Classroom', *The ALAN Review*, 34(2) (Winter 2007): 34–8, at 36.
19. Newman, Horne and Bartolomucci: 40.
20. Allison L. Baer and Jacqueline N. Glasgow, 'Take the Bullies to Task: Using Process Drama to Make a Stand', *English Journal*, 97(6) (July 2008): 79–86, at 80.
21. Nishina: 54.
22. *The Chocolate War*: 215
23. Dawn A. Newman, Arthur M. Horne and Christi L. Bartolomucci: 134.
24. Patricia Campbell, *Robert Cormier: Daring to Disturb the Universe* (New York: Delacorte, 2006): 88.
25. Robert Cormier, *Beyond the Chocolate War* (New York: Dell Laurel Leaf, 1985): 222.
26. *Beyond the Chocolate War*: 224.
27. Ibid.: 160.
28. *The Chocolate War*: 12.
29. *Beyond the Chocolate War*: 33.
30. Ibid.: 80
31. Jen Menzel, 'Intimidation in Cormier's *Tunes for Bears to Dance to*, *We All Fall Down*, and *The Chocolate War*', *The ALAN Review*, 31(1) (Fall 2003): 21–3, at 20.
32. Rickey Cotten, 'Engaging the Religious Dimension in Significant Adolescent Literature', *Literature and Belief*, 30 (2) (2010): 81–93, at 86
33. *Beyond the Chocolate War*: 174.
34. *The Chocolate War*: 71, 73.
35. Ibid.: 73, 74.
36. Ibid.: 241.
37. Ibid.: 208, 211.
38. Campbell: 61.
39. *Beyond the Chocolate War*: 181.
40. Ibid.: 170.
41. Ibid.: 184.
42. Ibid.: 261.
43. Ibid.: 264.
44. *The Chocolate War*: 80; *Beyond the Chocolate War*: 43.
45. *The Chocolate War*: 1.
46. Ibid.: 207.
47. *Beyond the Chocolate War*: 158.
48. *The Chocolate War*: 240.
49. Oneal: 183.
50. Newman, Horne and Bartolomucci: 54.
51. Nishina: 53.
52. Baer and Glasgow: 80.

53. Harvey et al.: 123.
54. Nishina: 53.
55. Martha Westwater, *Giant Despair Meets Hopeful: Kristevan Readings in Adolescent Fiction* (Edmonton, Alberta: University of Alberta Press, 2000): 122, 121.
56. Nancy Veglahn, 'The Bland Face of Evil in the Novels of Robert Cormier', *The Lion and the Unicorn*, 12(1) (June 1988): 12–18, at 13.
57. *Beyond the Chocolate War*. 45.
58. Graham Gardner, *Inventing Elliot* (London: Orion, 2003; repr. New York: Dial, 2004): 109.
59. Patricia Brieschke, 'The Administrator in Fiction: Using the Novel to Teach Educational Administration', *Educational Administration Quarterly*, 26(4) (November 1990): 376–93, 378.
60. Jacqueline Bach and Jennifer Jolly, 'Chalking the Profession: Unintended Lessons about Teaching', *Journal of Curriculum Theorizing*, 27(1) (April 2011): 87–98, at 94.
61. Joseph Blase and Jo Blase, 'The Dark Side of Leadership: Teacher Perspectives of Principal Mistreatment', *Educational Administration Quarterly*, 38(5) (December 2002): 671–727, at 718.
62. Ibid.: 678.
63. Harvey et al.: 125.
64. Corene De Wet, 'The Reasons for and the Impact of Principal-on-Teacher Bullying on the Victims' Private and Personal lives', *Teaching and Teacher Education*, 26(7) (October 2010): 1450–9, 1451.
65. Ibid.: 1453.
66. Blase and Blase: 696.
67. Ibid.: 697.
68. Ibid.: 1455.
69. *The Chocolate War*. 42.
70. Anit Somech and Izhar Oplatka, 'Coping with School Violence through the Lens of Teachers' Role Breadth: The Impact of Participative Management and Job Autonomy', *Educational Administration Quarterly*, 45(3) (August 2009), 424–49, at 443.
71. Nishina: 52.
72. Harvey et al.: 126.
73. *The Chocolate War*. 162.
74. Campbell: 87.
75. *The Chocolate War*. 24–5.
76. Richard Beach, Deborah Appleman, Susan Hynds, and Jeffrey Wilhelm, *Teaching Literature to Adolescents*, 2nd edn (New York and London: Routledge, 2011): 7.
77. *Beyond the Chocolate War*. 37.
78. Westwater: 121.
79. *Beyond the Chocolate War*. 37.
80. Ibid.: 246.
81. *The Chocolate War*. 99.

82. *Beyond the Chocolate War*: 235.
83. Ibid.
84. Tarr: 109.
85. *Beyond the Chocolate War*: 236.
86. Ibid.: 235.
87. Ibid.: 239.
88. Ibid.: 228.
89. Ibid.: 81.
90. Campbell: 95.
91. *Beyond the Chocolate War*: 223.
92. Philip C. Rodkin and Scott D. Gest, 'Teaching Practices, Classroom Peer Ecologies, and Bullying Behaviors Among Schoolchildren', in Dorothy L. Espelage and Susan M. Swearer (eds), *Bullying in North American Schools*, 2nd edn (New York and London: Routledge, 2011): 75–90, at 77.
93. Ibid. 77.
94. *The Chocolate War*: 236.
95. James Howe, *The Misfits* (New York: Atheneum, 2001); Doug Wilhelm, *The Revealers* (New York: Farrar, Straus, and Giroux, 2003).
96. Gardner; Alex Flinn, *Breaking Point* (New York: HarperTeen, 2003).
97. Paul Volponi, *Crossing Lines* (New York: Viking, 2011); James Preller, *Bystander* (New York: Feiwel and Friends, 2009).
98. Broz: 37.
99. C. J. Bott, *The Bully in the Book and in the Classroom* (Lanham, MD: Scarecrow Press, 2004); Bott (2009).

6

Männerbund and Hitler-Jugend: Queer Perceptions of Nazis In and Beyond Robert Cormier's The Chocolate War

Holly Blackford

> By the late 1950s and early 1960s ... new interpretations of Nazism took hold. ... [I]t was stressed that the Nazi movement was strongly motivated by homosexual impulses (even as the Nazi persecution and murder of homosexuals were completely suppressed). Young people born during or shortly after the war ... were offered only the most selective (not to say distorted) stories about sexuality under Nazism. ... [A] man who grew up in the 1950s Rhineland noted that 'all I ever heard about was the queer Nazi'.[1]

In *The Chocolate War* (1974), Robert Cormier encourages readers to view the events at Trinity high school as analogous to Nazi Germany. He embeds references to the hydrogen bomb,[2] concentration camp dogs,[3] prisoners[4] 'resigned to execution',[5] survivors,[6] and World War II movies.[7] The reference to movies calls attention to the highly mediated relationship between the 1960s and the Holocaust, a relationship pressed in this essay to specify why *The Chocolate War* foregrounds male characters who take pleasure in brutalising others. In a particularly disturbing classroom scene, the acting head teacher Brother Leon humiliates student Gregory Bailey, after which he encourages the class to view its participation in the student's humiliation as simulating Nazi Germany.[8] Hardly a benign lesson, Brother Leon's perverse classroom 'game' inspires the students' 'horrible fascination'.[9] When Leon's pointer strikes Bailey, the resulting mark becomes an 'evil stain', making Bailey appear as if he 'had committed an error ... and caused his own misfortune'.[10] The novel draws many similarities between Trinity and the German *Männerbund*, which, as

Dagmar Herzog analyses, scapegoated European Jewry for all sorts of sexual and moral transgressions.

Like Bailey, protagonist Jerry Renault comes to feel shamed and polluted[11] by persecutions against him for not selling chocolates and thus failing to conform to the 'school spirit' of 'true sons of Trinity', Leon's words for the healthy *Volk* committed to the nation-state of Trinity's *Männerbund*. Masculinity played an important role in 'the military nationalism which rose up in opposition to the democratic system of the Weimar Republic':

> During the Nazi era several books were published in which the trenches of the First World War were glorified. ... The *Männerbund*, the community of men united in emotional attachment ... was the model for the National Socialist ideal of manliness, of male solidarity and superiority over foreigners. ... [As] one Nazi functionary for education expressed, .. 'The *Männerbund* of the army and of the SA, the SS, and the Labor Service are all prolongations of the HJ [*Hitler-Jugend*, the Nazi youth movement] into the years of manhood'.[12]

The Nazi elevation of male warrior society (*Männerbund*), committed to nation above all else, created the conditions under which those perceived as threats to the state were vilified, tortured, and eradicated.

The Chocolate War generally advances a situation approximating *Hitler-Jugend*. Its young men must prove school spirit in a *Männerbund* setting that discharges female presences from the picture, rendering them to a lower order and therefore irrelevant to the true mission of school excellence. Jerry, for example, is initially interested in girls but by the time his friend Goober pleads with him to sell chocolates and capitulate to the state that Goober knows is 'evil',[13] the girl is no longer at the bus stop, where they are talking.[14] During the scene she *disappears*, just as Archie finds no time for girls given Vigils' pressures, as if heterosexuality and *Männerbund* principles cannot cohabitate. Indeed female presence is systemically expunged from the boxes of chocolates when mothers' day ribbons are removed and the boxes recast as male capital. The youths who are ritualistically polled for chocolate sales each morning parallel a new military order – Leon gives Archie the *order*[15] to support his chocolate sale – and in the end the students become a blood-thirsty mob witnessing, in what Leon defends as a display of 'high spirits',[16] the spectacle of Jerry's beating. Any crimes or corruptions performed for the benefit of the school are acceptable to the *Führer* Leon. Language of impending doom permeates the novel, Jerry feels 'murdered' and obliterated when his locker is invaded and then traces of invasion erased, and even 'the final humiliation'[17] of Archie's probation from The Vigils echoes the Nazi phrase 'the final solution'. Cormier's very title, of course, foregrounds *war*.

Cormier's novel not only simulates *Männerbund* ideology, but it also conveys the specific thesis that 1960s Americans and West Germans argued about Nazis. Some liberals and leftists maintained that the Holocaust was the result of sexual repression, a misremembering reconstructed by Herzog in *Sex After Fascism: Memory and Morality in Twentieth-Century Germany* (2005). The New Left – called the 1968ers – of West Germany persisted with this line of reasoning because the post-fascist generation (the parents of the 1968ers) had reacted to war with a newly rigid sexual conservatism, rewriting the memory of fascism. In *The Chocolate War*, Jerry's victimisation is accompanied by a shift in The Vigils, which moves from a student organisation annoying the teachers to one promoting the school and keeping in check the advancement of 1960s liberals and hippies. Viewed as antithetical to a sexually liberated world, the students of Trinity play out 1960s fantasies that Nazi Germany had been marked by sexual repressions, which found expression in torture, violence, and murder.

The idea that Nazi excesses had been the result of repressed homosexuality originated among leftist German exiles after the 1934 murder of openly gay stormtrooper SA leader Ernst Röhm,[18] but the idea also achieved popular legitimacy in mid-century American magazines and films. In *Monsters in the Closet* (1997), Harry Benshoff explains that Hollywood films of the World War II era, seeking to promote patriotic masculinity, demonised effeminacy and 'homosexual connotation crept into the movies of the war years ... to further delineate Nazi villains as evil'.[19] Popular magazines created a dichotomy between sexually normal Americans and the unmentionable sexual deviances of the Nazis'.[20] An article by George W. Herald, 'Sex is a Nazi Weapon', published in *The American Mercury* (June 1942), claimed that '"the whole Nazi movement arose in large measure out of the sexual frustrations of some groups in the German population. Certainly, distorted personalities have been prominent among the leaders. ... A telltale hatred for the morality of the Western Christian world runs through the writings of Nazi leaders"'.[21] Not only did many post-war and 1960s magazine articles remind readers that most Nazis were homosexuals, as if this were common knowledge, but even post-Stonewall articles sometimes voiced this theory.[22] The association of repressed homosexuality and

Nazis continued even in 1990s American political rhetoric.[23] For example, in 1996 Pat Buchanan reiterated the theory that people involved with Hitler were both homosexual and Satanic. Likewise, Tim Pursell observes, 'Controversial work continues to theorise that the Nazi leadership was populated with closeted or repressed homosexuals, including even Hitler, according to a recent psychobiography'.[24]

Cormier's most pronounced villains in *The Chocolate War*, Brother Leon, Archie Costello, and Emile Janza, are gay-coded to various degrees, associating Nazi sadism and repressed homosexuality. The novel's suggestion of closeted 'perversions' fits squarely with Cold-War American ideology, which perceived 'perverts' as a threat to the state yet veiled the dangerous congruence between persecutions of gay people and Nazism. For example, when the Hoey Committee, charged in 1950 with investigating homosexuals in government, reflected on the presumed reason for discharge – homosexuals' vulnerability to blackmail – 'the committee was caught in a conundrum – blackmail served as both a cause and effect of government antigay policies'.[25] Similarly, Janza and Archie shame Jerry by calling him '"a fairy. A queer. Living in the closet, hiding away"',[26] but the accusers understand this as scapegoating: '"Of course [he's] not. That's why he blew up"', Archie tells Janza.[27] Further, both Archie and Janza can be read as closeted characters with queer characteristics. Arranging his closeted meetings in the sweaty 'polluted atmosphere of the gymnasium',[28] Archie is represented as the tortured artist whose unappreciated genius and Vigils pressures accord with dominant stereotypes of repressed homosexuals as both geniuses[29] and tortured, predatory souls.[30] As the only character to continually crave and devour chocolate, Archie embodies the decadent degenerate whose desires for chocolate echo, for example, the sexual-sadistic characters of the torturers in Marquis de Sade's *120 Days of Sodom* (written in 1785)[31] or Dorian Gray in Oscar Wilde's *The Picture of Dorian Gray* (1891),[32] who awakes the day after murdering Basil Hallward to enjoy a steaming cup of hot chocolate.

More overtly, Janza gets 'horny' from physical contact with male youths, particularly Jerry; he also masturbates in the bathroom, and the connection between masturbation and homosexuality as perversions (one leading to the other) are as old as Havelock Ellis's *Sexual Inversion* (1896).[33] Archie blackmails Janza by pretending to have a photograph of him masturbating, but the two characters are connected more than separated on the moral binary. Janza believes Archie would understand the sexual arousal that stems from physical violence, and even Archie sees the similarity of their characters as fellow torturers,[34] as if Janza is an aspect of Archie that Archie would prefer not to acknowledge.

Queerness is embedded in the *Männerbund* environment, however, and therefore hardly limited to particular characters. At Trinity, which taps into the tradition of queerness in male school stories,[35] students ask other students about masturbation,[36] bathroom doors lack locks, lockers are regularly violated, and faculty encourage games and sports with intense physical contact. For example, Jerry's pride in carrying out his coach's 'assignment' to 'get Carter' during football[37] echoes his appropriation of 'the assignment' not to sell chocolates. Jerry's internalisation of 'the assignment' can be situated in American 1960s scholarship on the Holocaust, which, in an effort to understand victimisation and challenge Cold War politics, circulated the theory that the concentration camp engendered a particular type of personality.

In a well-known 1960 book on prisoner mentality, *The Informed Heart*, Bruno Bettelheim argued that concentration camp inmates were 'so infantilized and emasculated by Nazi brutality that they came to admire their captors and enforce SS rules themselves'.[38] A former inmate of Dachau and Buchenwald, Bettelheim advanced a thesis similar to that argued by Raul Hilberg in *The Destruction of the European Jews* (1961) and Hannah Arendt in *Eichmann in Jerusalem* (1963).[39] Arendt used Adolf Eichmann's defence that he was 'following orders' to suggest problems with the dehumanising structure of bureaucracy. Similarly, Jewish scholar Stanley Elkins, whose work was commended in the early 1960s, connected the concentration camp inmate to the 'Black Sambo' personality that he believed typified American slaves.[40] Elkins relied on evidence such as that of Elie Cohen, a physician who had survived Auschwitz, who said that long-time prisoners adapted SS uniforms as their own, took pride in standing to attention during roll call, enforced SS rules even more than SS guards themselves, adopted Nazi values, and used violence against other prisoners.[41] Cohen's observation that prisoners enforced camp rules long after SS guards had abandoned them is echoed in Jerry's decision to keep refusing to sell chocolates even after his 'assignment' has expired.[42] Jerry asks himself *why* he will not sell, and in his inner dialogue he becomes *both* 'tough cop and hounded prisoner',[43] in line with 1960s scholarship.

Cormier depicts a culture that at once scapegoats gay people and embraces an inherent queerness in the *Männerbund*, where being 'patted' 'on the ass' is 'an old Trinity mark of distinction',[44] a queer refrain[45] indicating the ambivalence of male–male camaraderie that similarly marked the German context, as discussed below. By featuring a broadly queer environment that expresses pleasure through torture,

Cormier's novel debunks as much as supports the refusal of liberals to see Nazism and sexual pleasure as compatible. A queer reading unlocks the perilous similarity between Cold-War closeting and Nazi Germany. Preoccupied with bodies that collide and glean violent masculinity in gymnastics, boxing, and football, Trinity's *Männerbund* points to conflicts in American masculinity as it was constructed against the queer and the Nazi, oppositions that had collapsed.

The assignment

The Chocolate War stands in a long line of Nazi simulations and concentration camp analogies, which were applied liberally in the US in the 1960s. Brother Leon's sadistic classroom experiment brings to mind Stanley Milgram's famous obedience experiments, which encouraged Americans throughout the 1960s and early 1970s to consider how seemingly normal citizens could harm others because they are ordered to do so. Milgram's experiments received much press in the years preceding 1974, when his book *The Perils of Obedience* was published.[46] Milgram wished to understand how horrific orders could have been carried out on a mass scale. Feeling it only an 'accident of geography' that he was not a concentration camp inmate – when many of his relatives were – he designed obedience experiments at Yale University. Pretending to be studying learning, Milgram found that 65 percent of the recruited subjects would, under orders, administer increasingly high shocks to the 'learner', despite hearing screams of distress. Initially published in 1963, Milgram's research became famous during the next 15 years, featuring in all kinds of media from magazines to talk shows to classrooms, where a prepared film, *Obedience*, was used. The Stanford prison experiment and 'the Third Wave', simulating Hitler Youth in a Californian high school, followed suit, showing broad interest in how 'murderous bureaucracy'[47] in the US and Nazi Germany might share an uncomfortable kinship.

In *The Chocolate War*, Leon's accusations that the *observers* of Bailey's shaming spectacle are equally at fault echo Milgram's own unpublished notes: 'I feel, … that the reactions of observers – those who sit by "enjoying the show" are profoundly relevant to an understanding of the actions of the subject'.[48] The novel ties this observer effect to nuclear anxiety; the hydrogen bomb, which 'makes no noise', characterises the watchful silence 'that blaze[s] in the classroom'.[49] In the post-war boom, following a war in which many people's sexuality 'came out under fire',[50] the prototype of 'the organisation man' emerged, and Cormier, like other critics, found this prototype dangerous. The 'organisation man' was a nonaggressive, domesticated type who navigated corporate hierarchies by depending 'less on personal ambition and individual initiative than on respect for authority, loyalty to one's superiors, and an ability to get along with others'.[51] *The Chocolate War* features this type in the Treasurer of the chocolate sale, Brian Cochran, who exemplifies what Arendt called 'the banality of evil'[52] when he sells tickets for the boxing match that serves Jerry on a silver platter to the perverse Janza. Nancy Veglahn bases her essay title 'The Bland Face of Evil in the Novels of Robert Cormier' on Cormier's own words, showing a conscious echo of Arendt's description of Eichmann.[53]

Simulating Milgram's experiment, *The Chocolate War* fleshes out how economic machinery and obedience assignments collaborate for social and sexual repression. Leon is so obsessed with money and career-building that he facilitates atrocity. Archie sees through Leon's façade and believes him to be vulnerable and scared, like most adults .[54] In contrast, Archie's uncertainty about backing the chocolate sale testifies to his own paradoxical presence in the 'war'. Archie objects to his treatment as a 'machine. … What did they know about the agonies of it all? The nights he tossed and turned?'[55] Archie believes himself 'artistic', his personalised assignments his 'art'[56] and – for Jerry – 'Therapy', a 'terrible word' denoting the postwar approach to policing character.[57] However, just as Leon repels Archie, Archie repels Vigils members, and in turn Janza repels Archie, showing a broad circulation of what Eve Sedgwick analyses as the 'epistemology of the closet'.[58]

Archie has a dual role as the enforcer of bureaucracy and the queer outsider, unsure about his part in promoting either school or Vigils machinery, in front of which he must maintain a veneer of calm detachment, *passing* by selecting white marbles from the black box. When he is put on probation by Carter, the normative jock-type who says Jerry is making 'patsies' of The Vigils, he keeps a 'smile on his face until he fe[els] his cheeks would crack'.[59] Archie believes that the secret society The Vigils are allowed to exist because they keep more radical 1960s forces at bay. Paradoxically, then, Archie, in great personal anguish and ironically embracing and abhorring his alienation, embodies the force of sexual repression. This is pursued further in *Beyond the Chocolate War* (1985), when Obie's relationship with a girl threatens Archie and when it becomes clear that Obie *is* his surrogate girlfriend. Archie distils Cormier's study of the type of anguish caused by the 'murderous bureaucracy' and the closet it built inside a 'polluted' gymnasium.

Nazi queerness and male relations

German *Männerbund* culture emerged from a distinctly homoerotic subculture that placed high value on male-male relationships, bodies, and noble 'Greek' bonds. Harry Oosterhuis traces homosexual emancipation in Germany before 1933 in his collection of selected articles from Adolf Brand's German journal *Der Eigene* ('the unique one'), which after 1898 evolved into a literary and artistic homosexual journal for readers who, 'as Brand declared, would be men who "thirst for a revival of Greek times and Hellenic standards of beauty after centuries of Christian barbarism"'.[60] Brand's 'celebration of virile masculinity' opposed the 'third sex' theory of Magnus Hirschfeld and his followers, which emphasised effeminacy, androgynous appearances, and cross-dressing as homosexual norms. To Brand, '[i]t was hyper-masculinity, not effeminacy, that accounted for a man's attraction to other men'.[61] The emphasis on Greek aestheticism (some preferred Nordic) and male devotion to state, 'manifest in ancient sculpture, in which the male body was the main object',[62] echoes the associations between Hellenism and homosexuality operative in England[63] and articulated by Oscar Wilde in his 1895 trial, when he identified love of boys as noble Greek love. However, while the political leanings of British and American embrace of 'Greek love' tended toward democracy and/or socialism, the German claiming of this classical culture leant itself toward nationalism through the German youth movement (the *Wandervogel*).[64] *Der Eigene* promoted love among men and youths (*Münner-und Jünglingsliebe*), and viewed it as more noble than reproductive and domestic relations with women. In *The Chocolate War*, the brief depiction of a woman with small children – to whom a student attempts to sell chocolate – signifies disgust.[65]

Anita Tarr discusses Trinity misogyny, ranging from 'rape by eyeball' to the treatment of Jerry's late mother,[66] but the novel focuses on how male devotion to state affects relationships between men. In a telling moment in *Beyond the Chocolate War*, Goober feels the need to express regret to Jerry, but the intimacy of Jerry's response cannot be expressed.[67] Jerry can only 'almost say' to Goober, '"You held me in your arms when I was all broken inside and out"'.[68] Similarly, male–male friendship had been viewed with passion in the German Romantic period, idealism in the Weimer Republic and ambivalence in the early Nazi regime, when 'national regeneration' was linked to manliness and camaraderie,[69] but changes in Nazi policy censored the emotions that men could express to one another. Although Nazi prosecutions of homosexuals were not as systematic or consistent as

prosecutions of Jewry, and although some homosexuals and homosexual artists were not prosecuted or were thought curable,[70] after the
murder of Röhm Hitler took a hard line against homosexuality by
becoming virtually obsessed with its danger in all-male organisations,
about which he had been warned by Heinrich Himmler. Himmler
thought organisations like the SS and Hitler Youth could inspire
homosexuality partly because of lack of exposure to women and
partly because of the 'too powerful masculinization and militariza-
tion' of the movement.[71] After Himmler helped tighten regulations
in 1935, men could be prosecuted for any physical contact or even
expressions of feelings.

The story of the *Männerbund* as both inciting desire and policing
repression underwent dramatic transformation in the 1960s. In 1962,
writers such as Theodor Adorno, Fritz Bauer, and Hans Joachim
Schoeps began to draw a parallel between Nazi persecutions and the
continuing homophobia articulated in Paragraph 175, which crimi-
nalised homosexual acts:

> [A] different version of the Third Reich [came] into public discussion …
> when *Der Spiegel* approvingly cited a comment made by one of the pros-
> ecutors in the Frankfurt trial of Auschwitz perpetrators, to the effect that
> Auschwitz had been built by *Spiesser* – the term typically used by liberals
> and leftists to describe not only generally banal and conventional but also
> sexually uptight conservatives.[72]

In the context of sexual liberation, writers began to understand
fascism as suppressed sexual drives expressed through cruelty. Christian
conservatives were compared with Nazis, the role of the Church in
Nazi Germany was investigated, and the radicals known as the 1968ers
continually advanced the unstoppable thesis that – as Arno Plack put
it in *Die Gesellschaft und das Böse* (*Society and Evil*, 1967) – unexpressed
sexual impulses lead to murder and aggression.[73]

Plack argued that seemingly normal citizens 'celebrated true orgies
of sadism' in the camps; Freudian theorists like Erich Fromm argued
that fascists had an overabundance of pregenital and anal impulses,
evident both in their concerns with orderliness and with split sexual
orientation.[74] Journals such as *Das Argument* deployed Freudian
approaches to National Socialism and to Hitler. Associating fascism
with the bourgeois family, such positions attributed intensified anal-
and phallic-sadistic tendencies and masochistic or sadomasochistic
personalities to the sexually repressed era. A 1965 article claimed that
'"the latent homosexual component among the Nazis" expressed
itself in "the fanatic persecution of manifest homosexuality"',[75] and

writers like Dieter Duhm, in his 1972 *Angst im Kapitalismus* (*Fear in Capitalism*), advanced the repressive thesis even further.[76] Critics such as Klaus Theweleit in *Männerphantasien* (*Male Fantasies*) (1977)[77] and Andrew Hewitt in *Political Inversions* (1996)[78] continue this line of thought.[79] In *Nationalism and Sexuality* (1985), George Mosse observed that Himmler tried to keep within the bounds of respectability what '[f]ascism thus threatened to bring to the surface' – homoeroticism, most evident in France, where many homosexuals became Nazi collaborators.[80] American films that gay-code Nazis may seem an odd permutation of popular culture, but this gay-coding embodies both West German influence and American perceptions of homosexuality as a spreading threat especially for youth, a panic put in place after the 1948 Kinsey report demonstrated that homosexuality was much more prominent than presumed.

Male–male relationships in *The Chocolate War* become an arte-fact of closeting, 'anal-sadistic' tendencies, and gymnastic violence at once idealised and queered. The most obvious example, Janza, derives pleasure exclusively from violence since he cannot express pleasure in other ways. He feels horny 'when he roughhoused a kid or tackled a guy viciously in football and gave him an extra jab when he had him on the ground. How could you tell anybody about that? And yet he felt that Archie would understand. Birds of a feather, that was it'.[81] Cormier is careful to express Janza's perversion as only the enhanced consequence of pleasure that many characters – even Jerry – feel from physical contact sports, since pain earns coach approval. Janza's intu-ition that Archie would understand demonstrates the repressive thesis characterising popular interpretations of SS guards. Archie himself is disgusted by Janza, yet he admires Janza siphoning gas and exploiting a freshman for cigarettes. Just as Archie is fascinated and repelled by watching athletes, he is 'fascinated by Janza, crude and gross as he was', Janza's giggle 'chill[ing]' him, even though Archie himself is someone 'considered capable of hurting little old ladies and tripping cripples'.[82] Archie's self-recognition suggests that Janza is Archie in monstrous form, a connection solidified by their co-manipulation of Jerry in calling him a queer, which Jerry feels the 'worst thing in the world'.[83]

The scene in which Janza calls Jerry a 'fairy' emphasises Janza's *own* imagination of Trinity through a gay lens. Janza expresses 'mock, exag-gerated admiration' that Jerry has passed Trinity's 'ways of weeding out homos'. Janza taunts, '"You must be creaming all over – wow, four hundred ripe young bodies to rub against…"', then he pleads for a kiss, 'puckering his lips grotesquely'.[84] The accusation actually communicates Janza's own fantasies, resonating with earlier scenes.

Beyond the Chocolate War similarly characterises Janza as a repressed homosexual:

> Other things made him horny as well. ... He noticed it first in football during plays in which he tackled his opponents bruisingly and without mercy. A distinct wave of sexual pleasure swept him on these occasions. Sometimes when he engaged in a scuffle in the parking lot – Trinity was a very physical place – he would be instantly aroused. He had felt that kind of swift pleasure last fall when he had faced the Renault kid. ... The beauty [of that feeling] had returned the other day when he spotted Renault in the park. ... He wanted to keep Renault for himself. ... Janza picked up the telephone book. Looked up the *R*'s. Felt nice and sexy.[85]

Janza is disarmed only when Jerry refuses to fight back, for his sexual arousal depends on aggression. While Yoshida Junko views Leon and Archie as the normative males against whom Jerry rebels,[86] Tarr views Jerry as the normative male,[87] a reading that accentuates the queerness of the victimisers. Whereas Jerry feels 'queer' is shameful, Janza (later speaking to Archie) is merely curious about Jerry's orientation, and Archie merely shrugs and notes that if Jerry were in fact queer, the name-calling would not matter. The repressed and artistic Archie provides a more complex example of how a troubled, alienated youth might turn his talents to torture because the environment does not facilitate the career of the non-jock.

Archie's status as an artist and 'different' outsider offers a more comprehensive study of the repressive thesis. Cormier dwells on Archie's curious distaste for male bodies, for example. Archie is repulsed by 'secretions of the human body. ... He couldn't stand the sight of greasy, oozing athletes drenched in their own body fluids. ... Take a guy like Carter, bulging with muscles, every pore oozing sweat'.[88] The proliferation of impossible prohibitions (like avoiding the gym and athletes) and disgust exemplifies the sort of sexually repressive thesis articulated by Erich Fromm. Distinctly reminiscent of Archie's disgust at Janza, this disgust overcompensates for attraction. Archie does not in fact avoid athletes; he is watching football with Obie the first time the reader meets him, he meets The Vigils in a closeted section of the gym, and he arranges the boxing match to create a pleasurable arena – a fight in slow motion, such that every contact can be savoured. Even in the initial scene in the football bleachers, Archie is craving chocolate – implicitly conveying both insatiable lust and the observer posture – and Obie is struggling to satisfy him. Cormier also dwells on Archie's athletic body. He moves 'languidly, the walk of an athlete although he hated all sports and had nothing but contempt for athletes. Particularly football players and boxers'.[89] For someone repulsed by male bodies, shapes, and fluids, he certainly engineers queer sites of exploitation.

Beyond the Chocolate War continues this portrayal of Archie as a closeted character, enjoying 'the surge of satisfaction' gleaned from secret assignments and the knowledge that 'he was apart from other people. It was a dark and beautiful secret he shared with no one'.[90] Whereas Archie imagines he likes girls, when he is actually with one, he is 'missing Obie, missing the way he could bounce ideas off Obie, gauging his future actions by Obie's reactions. ... Meanwhile, he had Morton. She gave him what Obie could never give him and he responded now to her touch'.[91] When Archie describes Carter to Jill Morton, she replies that his description makes Carter seem the perfect guy. Archie replies that everyone has a secret – that no one is perfect – which is a philosophy he espouses throughout the sequel. Archie's continual voicing of his dark views makes readers ask why a youth might be so disturbed. His artist persona in the first novel, along with his longing for male camaraderie in the second, suggests he embodies the monstrous Cold-War closet.

Beyond the Chocolate War culminates by offering Archie as a generalised repression – whether of artistic tendencies, queerness, sensitivity, or femininity – by giving him a long speech in which he claims he is 'inside' everyone:

> You blame me for everything, right, Obie? ... But it's not me ... It's you, Obie. ... [H]ow you loved it all, didn't you, Obie? ... Oh, I'm an easy scapegoat, Obie. For you and everybody else at Trinity. Always have been. ... You'll always have me wherever you go and whatever you do. ... Because I'm you. I'm all the things you hide inside you'.[92]

This final speech draws out the lesson of both novels – that Archie embodies the unhealthy repressions implicit in *Männerbund* culture. *Beyond the Chocolate War* shows that heterosexuality (Obie's love for a girl) threatens the *Männerbund* and must be squashed. Echoing Eichmann's defence and reflecting the problem of 'the organisation man', as well as the fragility of heterosexual masculinity, Cornacchio feels no personal responsibility in attacking Obie and his girlfriend because 'Bunting said later that it was all Archie Costello's idea, an unofficial assignment. This knowledge had greatly relieved Cornacchio. The involvement of Archie and the Vigils made it seem less serious, not such a rotten thing, more like a kind of stunt'.[93] The novels, to the end of Trinity graduation, link 'murderous bureaucracy' to shaming apparatus. Yet paradoxically, Cormier offers Archie as a distinctly artistic outsider to Leon's games, increasingly alienated from The Vigils because of his uniqueness.

Although the seemingly imminent murder of Jerry preoccupies the first novel, the potential murder of Archie preoccupies the second, drawing a parallel victim status between them.[94] On the school's carnival day, Archie calmly volunteers for the guillotine demonstration by Obie, who really wants Archie dead, and Ray Bannister, a magician in training. The guillotine is a symbol of how a revolution in the name of liberty turned into a murderous engine against civil liberty. Likewise, it symbolises the separation between Archie and Obie, who have moved from partners in crime to Obie's interest in girls and distaste for a 'wifely' role serving Archie. Just as Cormier takes pains to show that intimate sentiments between Goober and Jerry remain unsaid, he foregrounds Archie's double life when he must walk into the guillotine to stay true to his public, projected face. In a culture of 'the epistemology of the closet', what male youths really mean to one another can only surface in grotesque carnival mockeries or violent moments of contact, as glimpsed in Janza's taunting of Jerry and in the skits of a student who impersonates Leon in 'a prissy voice'[95] but then flunks out of school by Leon's hand. This skit not only interprets Leon as queer, but it also reveals that Bakhtinian carnival days can draw out hidden queerness, but only temporarily.

In *The Chocolate War*, Archie's role-playing of a World War II movie scene, as he makes Goober say 'yes, sir',[96] disgusts him and shows that he has been split into an acting and spectating self. Continually role-playing and revolted by the overwhelming environment of a simulated – even clichéd – Nazi Germany, Archie is almost too aware of being the stereotypical 'Nazi queer' that writers of the 1960s made popular. Ultimately, the story of shaming 'the resister' into selling chocolates is both a study of concentration camp personality (Jerry) and the torturous games played by people aroused by *Männerbund* culture and repressed by its homophobic policy. The final glimpse of Leon's face, watching Jerry's beating in *The Chocolate War*, disgusts Archie, for Archie stands against the pretence of male success. While *The Chocolate War* utilises 1960s scholarship on the Holocaust, its stance on repressed homosexuality is paradoxical. On the one hand, it offers the lesson that forced closeting is precariously Nazi-like; on the other hand, its thinly veiled gay-coded Nazi perpetrators reinforce stereotypes. However, Archie's own sense of his part in a clichéd movie is almost camp. While his sinister queerness might be campy, the damaged male intimacies recurrent across many relationships, even between Jerry and his father, suggests a wider-reaching critique of gymnastic *Männerbund*.

Notes

1. Dagmar Herzog, *Sex After Fascism: Memory and Morality in Twentieth-Century Germany* (Princeton: Princeton University Press, 2005): 63.
2. Robert Cormier, *The Chocolate War* (New York: Dell Laurel-Leaf, 1974): 42, 146.
3. Ibid.: 137.
4. Ibid.: 119.
5. Ibid.: 126.
6. Ibid.: 131.
7. Ibid.: 30, 137.
8. Ibid.: 46.
9. Ibid.: 40.
10. Ibid.: 42.
11. Ibid.: 122.
12. Harry Oosterhuis, 'Homosexual Emancipation in Germany Before 1933: Two Traditions', in Harry Oosterhuis (ed.), *Homosexuality and Male Bonding in Pre-Nazi Germany: The Youth Movement, the Gay Movement, and Male Bonding before Hitler's Rise, Original Transcripts from* Der Eigene, *the First Gay Journal in the World*, trans. (of transcripts) Hubert Kennedy (New York: Haworth Press, 1991): 1–28, at 252–3.
13. *The Chocolate War*: 159.
14. Ibid.: 160.
15. Ibid.: 165.
16. Ibid.: 248.
17. Ibid.: 187.
18. Tim Pursell, 'Queer Eyes and Wagnerian Guys: Homoeroticism in the Art of the Third Reich', *Journal of the History of Sexuality*, 17(1) (January 2008), 1–17, at 2.
19. Harry Benshoff, *Monsters in the Closet: Homosexuality and the Horror Film* (New York: Manchester University Press, 1997): 86.
20. Ibid.
21. Quoted in Benshoff: 86.
22. Benshoff: 180.
23. Ibid.: 241.
24. Pursell: 2.
25. David K. Johnson, *The Lavender Scare: The Cold War Persecution of Gays and Lesbians in the Federal Government* (Chicago: University of Chicago Press, 2004): 111.
26. *The Chocolate War*: 211.
27. Ibid.: 221.
28. Ibid.: 149.
29. Gavin Butt, *Between You and Me: Queer Disclosures in the New York Art World, 1948–1963* (Durham, NC: Duke University Press, 2005): 56–7.
30. Anita Tarr agrees with Roberta Seelinger Trites that the reader is supposed to view Leon and Archie as so corrupt that they have reached

the pinnacle of debauchery in homosexuality, but the present essay suggests that the 1960s saw homosexuality as the cause rather than consequence of corruption. See Anita Tarr, 'The Absence of Moral Agency in Robert Cormier's *The Chocolate War*', *Children's Literature*, 30 (2002), 96–124, at 109); Roberta Seelinger Trites, *Disturbing the Universe: Power and Repression in Adolescent Literature* (Iowa City: University of Iowa Press, 2000): 37–8.

31. Marquis de Sade, *The 120 Days of Sodom* [1785] (London: Arrow Books, 1989).
32. Oscar Wilde, *The Picture of Dorian Gray*, [1890] (London: Ward Lock, 1891).
33. For a discussion of masturbation and homosexuality as boys' school vices, see Diane Mason, *The Secret Vice: Masturbation in Victorian Fiction and Medical Culture* (Manchester: Manchester University Press, 2008); Havelock Ellis, *Sexual Inversion* [1896] (Philadelphia: F. A. Davis Company, 1928).
34. *The Chocolate War*: 106.
35. See Tison Pugh and David Wallace, 'Heteronormative Heroism and Queering the School Story in J. K. Rowling's Harry Potter Series', *Children's Literature Association Quarterly*, 31(3) (2006): 260–81.
36. *The Chocolate War*: 170.
37. Ibid.: 189.
38. Cited in Kristen Fermaglich, *American Dreams and Nazi Nightmares: Early Holocaust Consciousness and Liberal America, 1857–1965* (Waltham, MA: Brandeis, University Press, 2006): 22.
39. Raul Hilberg, *The Destruction of the European Jews* (New York: Quadrangle Books, 1961); Hannah Arendt, *Eichmann in Jerusalem: A Report on the Banality of Evil* (New York: Viking Press, 1963).
40. Fermaglich: 24.
41. Ibid: 27.
42. Anita Tarr agrees with Perry Nodelman that Jerry does not know whom he is fighting or why, which contradicts scholars and teachers who view Jerry as a heroic resister: 96–7. See Nodelman, 'Robert Cormier's *The Chocolate* War: Paranoia and Paradox', in Dennis Butts (ed.), *Stories and Society: Children's Literature in Social Context*, (London: Macmillan, 1992): 22–36, at 30.
43. *The Chocolate War*: 119.
44. Ibid.: 80.
45. Ibid.: 78, 127.
46. Stanley Milgram, 'The Perils of Obedience', *Harpers Magazine* (1974).
47. Fermaglich: 22.
48. Quoted in Fermaglich: 104.
49. *The Chocolate War*: 42.
50. See Allan Bérubé, *Coming Out Under Fire: The History of Gay Men and Women in World War Two* (New York: Macmillan, 1990).
51. Robert Corber, *Homosexuality in Cold War America: Resistance and the Crisis of Masculinity* (Durham: Duke University Press, 1997): 5–6.

52. Hannah Arendt, *Eichmann in Jerusalem: A Report on the Banality of Evil* (New York: Viking Press, 1963).

53. Nancy Veglahn, 'The Bland Face of Evil in the Novels of Robert Cormier', *The Lion and the Unicorn*, 12(1) (June 1988): 1–5.

54. *The Chocolate War:* 22.

55. Ibid.: 33.

56. Ibid.: 15.

57. Ibid.: 142.

58. Eve Sedgwick, *Epistemology of the Closet* (Berkeley: University of California Press, 2008).

59. *The Chocolate War:* 187.

60. Harry Oosterhuis, 'Homosexual Emancipation in Germany Before 1933: Two Traditions', in Harry Oosterhuis (ed.), (1991): 3.

61. Pursell: 2.

62. Harry Oosterhuis, 'Eros and Male Bonding in Society: Introduction', in Harry Oosterhuis (ed.), (1991): 119–25, at 120.

63. See Linda Dowling, *Hellenism and Homosexuality in Victorian Oxford* (Ithaca, NY: Cornell University Press, 1996), and Louis Crompton, *Byron and Greek Love: Homophobia in Nineteenth-Century England* (Trowbridge, UK: Gay Men's Press, 1998).

64. Oosterhuis, 'Male Bonding and Homosexuality in German Nationalism', in Harry Oosterhuis (ed.), (1991): 241–64, at 242.

65. See Karen Coats, 'Abjection and Adolescent Fiction', *JPCS: Journal for the Psychoanalysis of Culture & Society* 5(2) (Fall 2000): 290–300, at 295.

66. Tarr: 104–9.

67. Robert Cormier, *Beyond the Chocolate War* (New York: Dell Laurel-Leaf, 1985).

68. Ibid.: 150.

69. Oosterhuis, 'Male Bonding and Homosexuality', in Harry Oosterhuis (ed.), (1991): 243.

70. Ibid.: 248–50.

71. Quoted in Oosterhuis, 'Male Bonding and Homosexuality', in Harry Oosterhuis (ed.), (1991): 255.

72. Herzog: 135.

73. Ibid.: 156.

74. Ibid.: 156.

75. Herzog: 157.

76. Ibid.: 157.

77. An edition is: Klaus Theweleit, *Male Fantasies* (Cambridge: Polity Press, vol. 1., 1987, vol. 2 1989).

78. An edition is: Andrew Hewitt, *Political Inversions* (Stanford, CA. Stanford University Press, 1996).

79. 'At the fantasmatic foundation of he-men's masculinity and projected symbolic virility is a lie; the so-called "tough guys" within a totalitarian regime, according to Adorno, are really effeminate and need those who are weak or disempowered as their victims so as to prove that

they are not similar to them. As agents of repression, as sadists, however, tough guys repress their own homosexuality, performing repressed homosexuality as the only approved form of heterosexuality.' (William Spurlin, *Lost Intimacies: Rethinking Homosexuality under National Socialism* (New York: Peter Lang, 2009): 69).

80. George L. Mosse, *Nationalism and Sexuality: Respectability and Abnormal Sexuality in Modern Europe* (New York: Howard Fertig, 1985): 176.
81. *The Chocolate War.* 51.
82. Ibid.: 106.
83. Ibid.: 212.
84. Ibid.
85. *Beyond the Chocolate War.* 176.
86. Yoshida Junko, 'The Quest for Masculinity in *The Chocolate War.* Changing Conceptions of Masculinity in the 1970s', *Children's Literature,* 26 (1998), 105–22, at 109–12).
87. Tarr: 100–1.
88. *The Chocolate War.* 143.
89. Ibid.: 11.
90. *Beyond the Chocolate War.* 46.
91. Ibid.: 144.
92. Ibid.: 263–4.
93. Ibid.: 167.
94. Junko: 118.
95. *Beyond the Chocolate War.* 256.
96. *The Chocolate War.* 30.

7

Inducing Despair?: A Study of Robert Cormier's Young Adult Fiction

Clare Walsh

Since Robert Cormier's unconventional approach to narrative closure has perhaps attracted more negative criticism than any other aspect of his work, this essay will begin in a somewhat unorthodox fashion with reference to the endings of his three best known young adult novels: *The Chocolate War* (1974), *I Am the Cheese* (1977) and *After the First Death* (1979). The endings of these novels are not just bleak, but respectively involve their young protagonists in utter abjection and self-betrayal (Jerry Renault); either regression to childhood dependency or authorised State termination (Adam Farmer/Paul Delmonte); suicide (Ben Marchand), a violent death at the hands of a terrorist (Kate Forrester), and emotional death (Miro Shantas). All three novels are, in their different ways, anti-*Bildungsromans*, thwarting their young protagonists' transition to adulthood. The key questions this essay will investigate are what subject positions these novels offer young adult readers, and how they contain the potential to make them compliant or interrogative readers.

Critical discourse analysis

Norman Fairclough's approach to critical discourse analysis (hereafter CDA) seeks to identify the covert *traces* text producers leave of their own ideological stance, as well as *cues* that invite readers to adopt preferred subject positions, while suppressing others.[1] In relation to the discourse of narrative fiction, this leads primarily to a focus on strategies by which a point of view is established. Cormier's use of a shifting narrative perspective in his fiction would seem to make him a subversive writer located at the radically transgressive end of John Stephens's continuum of interrogative texts, that is texts which call into question the assumptions embedded in the intertexts to which they refer.[2] This technique ostensibly cedes power to readers, permitting them to make up their own minds about characters and events. However, one of the insights of CDA is that power which is backgrounded can be more difficult to contest precisely because it is covertly embedded. For instance, the narrator can align himself or herself with a particular character's point of view through instances of Free Indirect Discourse (FID) in which the words and/or thoughts of the character and the words and/or thoughts of the narrator are blended, but with no reporting clause. Likewise, how different characters' points of view are ordered in respect of one another can be significant. Moreover, it will be suggested that shifts in narrative point of view in Cormier's fiction are not necessarily dialogic in a Bakhtinian sense, and can also be temporally and spatially disorientating for readers.

The Chocolate War

Critical discourse analysis stresses the importance of locating texts within the context of their production and reception. *The Chocolate War*'s acquired status as a classic work of young adult fiction has obscured its origins as a novel aimed at an implied *adult* readership. It was Cormier's publisher who recognised its potential appeal to adolescent readers and who advised publishing it under a young adult imprint, perhaps because the novel is focalised exclusively through the consciousness of its adolescent protagonists. Mike Cadden points out that this makes it double-voiced discourse: 'Novels constructed by adults to simulate an adolescent's voice are inherently ironic because the so-called adolescent voice is never – and can never be – truly authentic'.[3] Indeed, there is a temptation for an adult writer addressing an implied adult readership to ironise the perspective of some or all of his young protagonists due to the relative immaturity of their worldview. Such irony can operate at the expense of both the protagonists and, by implication, actual adolescent readers. *The Chocolate War*, in fact, veers uncertainly, and potentially uncomfortably for young readers, between parodying the conventions of the traditional school story, including the heroic credentials of its schoolboy protagonist, and investing its characters and themes with allegorical significance.

Ironising the point of view of the schoolboy 'hero'

The novel's title, with its incongruous collocation of 'war' and 'chocolate', hints at Cormier's ironic treatment of the power struggle at the heart of the story. In the traditional boys' school story team sports are invariably seen as 'character building'. By contrast, the football trials depicted in the opening chapter of *The Chocolate War* reduce the 14-year-old schoolboy protagonist, Jerry Renault, to a state of complete physical abjection. From the outset, the transitivity patterns in the text make clear that, far from being a natural hero, Jerry is a character who is acted upon by others. The hyperbolic opening sentence, 'They murdered him',[4] is followed by a series of tropes in which his body parts – head, stomach, mouth – are all subjected to violent assaults by his fellow football players, culminating in his objectification as 'a toy boat caught in a whirlpool'.[5] The latter metaphor, in fact, prefigures Jerry's condition throughout the novel.

While the reader is invited to admire Jerry's dogged physical determination at this stage, this is offset by his own admission that he is a moral coward: 'thinking one thing and saying another, planning one thing and doing another'.[6] This comment foreshadows his ultimate act of self-betrayal when he agrees to take part in the spectacle of a boxing match with the 'animal' Emile Janza. While the revelation that Jerry had recently lost his mother[7] invites reader sympathy, Cormier cannot resist a rather tasteless joke at his young hero's expense, albeit one uttered unwittingly by the Coach: '"You'd make a better end. Maybe"'.[8] These covert cataphoric allusions to Jerry's ultimate defeat call into question Millicent Lenz's view of Cormier as a romantic novelist whose fictions grow organically out of his characters' perspectives.[9] As Frank Myszor has shown convincingly in relation to *After the First Death*, his novels are, in fact, highly structured.[10] In *The Chocolate War* it would seem then that Jerry is set up to fail. This contrasts with C. Anita Tarr's view that the opening chapter creates the narrative expectation that Jerry will win out in the end.[11]

One of the consequences of backgrounding the heterodiegetic narrator's presence in the text is that readers often have to rely on the clues offered by characters participating in the novel's text world. For instance, when the focalisation switches to Obie in Chapter 2, he notes that the goal post shadows on the field look like 'grotesque crosses',[12] thereby cueing the reader to view Jerry as a Christ-like martyr-in-the-making. Yet it is clear that such clues cannot always be trusted, since the characters have their own agendas. For instance, Obie's figurative reading of the goal posts could, perhaps more plausibly, be viewed as a projection of his own guilt about his complicity in the assignment set for Jerry by The Vigils (unlike Archie Costello, Obie is a believer). Indeed, in a characteristic instance of self-irony Obie cautions himself, and by implication the reader, against reading too much into such things: 'That's enough symbolism for one day'.[13] Thus Cormier encourages an allegorical reading of Jerry's role one moment, only to call this into question the next.

In any case, as the events of the novel unfold, it is difficult to sustain a view of Jerry as a Christ-like hero. For instance, when he eventually says 'no' to the chocolate sale, to Brother Leon, and to The Vigils, the rhetoric employed by the narrator seems overly inflated: 'Cities fell. Earth opened. Planets tilted. Stars plummeted. And the awful silence'.[14] The reader is invited to wonder whether the refusal of a freshman to sell some chocolates can really be of such world-stopping significance. Much has been made of Jerry's subsequent epiphany triggered by the words from T. S. Eliot's poem 'The Love Song of J. Alfred Prufrock' (1915) on the poster in his locker: '*Do I dare disturb the Universe?*' (italics Cormier's) [15] Yet, this question appears on a mass produced poster and it is clear that Jerry had not previously understood its import. He had, like many teenagers before and since, been drawn to the vaguely profound meaning of the poster's caption and so its appropriation by him is likely to strike the reader as a rather grand *post hoc* justification for his instinctive refusal to sell the chocolates, rather than its cause. Indeed, Cormier suggests that, like many adolescents, Jerry finds it difficult to articulate just why he has taken the stance he has. All he can offer by way of explanation to his fellow students is the platitude: '"It's a free country"'.[16] This is one of the few occasions when the reader is invited to endorse Brother Leon's view that Jerry needed to do better than this. As Tarr points out, the perception of Jerry as a rebel hero is more of a reflection of how readers would like him to be, rather than a view warranted by textual evidence.[17]

Mythologising the point of view of the school bully

If Jerry's role as a schoolboy hero is ironised, Archie's nihilistic view that '"life is shit"'[18] seems to be positively endorsed in the text. The reader's first impressions of Archie are mediated through Obie's eyes and initially Obie seems determined to cut him down to size as simply 'a senior in a lousy little high school like Trinity'.[19] However, this is quickly forgotten as he is reminded of the 'uncanny'[20] power with which Archie appears to read his mind, and his ability to 'dazzle … with his brilliance'.[21] Obie is fascinated by the way in which Archie's voice can express soft concern[22] one moment, and then be 'cold as polar regions' the next.[23] His dangerous unpredictability contrasts with Jerry's predictable stubbornness. The reader is invited to share Obie's awe and this is all the more persuasive because it is grudgingly acknowledged both by him and the other members of The Vigils. At the same time, Cormier toys with readers by providing several false cues that create the expectation that Archie as arch-bully will, in accordance with the conventions of the school story genre, get his well-deserved comeuppance. Obie provides the first of these cues when he predicts to himself that one day Archie would take things 'too far and trip himself up',[24] but subsequent events in the novel reveal that Archie is far too sure-footed to do any such thing.

It would seem, then, that Cormier is of Archie's party whether he intends to be or not. For instance, Archie, more than any of the other characters, employs Cormier's favourite epithet 'beautiful', often with irony. Likewise, the narrator betrays an affinity with Archie's point of view in several instances of free indirect thought (FIT), in which the thoughts of the character and those of the narrator are blended, again without a reporting clause, as on the following occasion when he takes part in the theatrical Vigils' ritual involving the black box:

> Reaching inside, he grabbed a marble, concealed it in the palm of his hand. He withdrew his hand, held the arm straight out, calmly now, without shiver or tremor. He opened his hand. The marble was white. The corner of Archie's mouth twitched as the tension of his body relaxed. *He had beaten them again. He had won again.* I am Archie. I cannot lose.[25]

The narrator seems to share Archie's triumphalism here and appears to be seduced by him almost as readily as the members of The Vigils. This is not surprising since Archie is a kind of author surrogate. He is the arch plotter whose endlessly inventive assignments for The Vigils have made him a legend at Trinity. His master plan, of course, is the one by which he tricks Jerry – who is no match for 'his quick mind, his swift intelligence, his fertile imagination'[26] – into self-betrayal and abject defeat in front of the entire school. The danger is that readers are invited to admire Archie's cleverness, rather than to condemn the chilling lack of compassion he shows for Jerry.

Promoting moral ambiguity?

Even more reprehensible is the way in which Brother Leon, the corrupt acting headmaster of Trinity, is accorded a degree of moral authority in the novel. This follows a prolonged scene of psychological torture in which, in front of the whole class, he falsely accuses one of the boys, Gregory Bailey of cheating. When an anonymous student finally protests, Leon dismisses this as '"too little, too late"', and accuses the class of complicity, telling them that they had made their classroom: '"into

Nazi Germany'".[27] Several critics have accepted this sermonising at face value and have noted that Leon thus points to one of the central lessons of the novel: that sins of omission can be worse than those of commission (see, for instance, Nodelman).[28] However, this lets Leon off the hook, allowing the bully to deflect responsibility for his actions on to others. As elsewhere in the novel, this episode sows the seeds of moral confusion in the minds of readers, rather than of moral complexity.

A polyphony of voices?

In Chapters 14 and 21 the focalisation shifts between a number of minor characters in a technique reminiscent of cross-cutting in film. This has the potential to diffuse the prevailing claustrophobic atmosphere, since we are given a rare insight into the boys' lives beyond the confines of the school. Instead, as Perry Nodelman points out, the atmosphere of paranoia is heightened further by the fact that these characters, John Sulkey, Tubs Casper, Paul Consalvo, Kevin Chartier, Howie Anderson, and Richie Rondell, are all fixated on the chocolates.[29] They also share a remarkably similar attitude of distain for their parents' lives. In a comment calculated to amuse Cormier's implied adult readers, Consalvo reflects: 'what did they have to live for? They were too old for sex'.[30] Cormier has no qualms about exploring the budding sexuality of his adolescent protagonists, but he reveals them as all sharing a voyeuristic attitude towards girls, with Howie Anderson's comment about 'rape by eyeball'[31] being only the most extreme instance of this. This jaundiced and homogenising view of his young protagonists' attitude towards the opposite sex is likely to prove discomfiting for many of the novel's young adult readers. Thus as Robyn McCallum makes clear, the novel is multivoiced but not dialogic: 'there is on the one hand a sameness in the world views that these characters represent and on the other hand an inability on the part of characters to engage and enter into dialogue with each other'.[32] *The Chocolate War* is, then, a monologic text masquerading as a polyphonic one.

Reader positioning

Throughout *The Chocolate War* Cormier seems intent upon parodying the moral certainties of the traditional boys' school story, so it comes as no surprise when he deliberately subverts the ending in which the school boy hero wins out against the bullies. Critics have thus had to read *against* the text to interpret the novel's ending as anything other than unremittingly bleak. Rather than creating interrogative readers, the novel has the potential to induce paranoia, to promote morally confusing messages, and ultimately to offer compliant subject positions to its readers. Jerry becomes an eloquent apologist for conformity, although the irony is that he has been so badly beaten by Janza in the rigged boxing match that he cannot actually speak. His friend Roland Goubert (nicknamed The Goober) is the ostensible narratee at this point, although the actual addressee is, of course, the extratextual reader: "'They tell you to do your thing but they don't mean it. They don't want you to do your thing, not unless it happens to be their thing too ... Don't disturb the universe, Goober, no matter what the posters say'".[33] Readers are thus invited to accept Cormier's overarching cynical view of the futility of individuals taking a stand against corrupt institutions like Trinity.

In terms of reader reception, the puzzle remains as to why such a melodramatic and ultimately conservative work of fiction should have proved so popular with young adult readers. Nodelman comes closest to explaining this with his exploration of the pleasures of paranoia,[34] but it could be argued that such pleasures do not take young adult readers further than they already are. Although not originally intended for a young adult readership, the novel's popularity with this age group led young adult fiction into a cul-de-sac in which unhappy endings became the norm, not least in Cormier's own fiction. Fred Inglis perceptively points out that such allegedly 'realist' fictions promote the 'sentimentalities of disenchantment' by replacing the myth that the good guys always win out in the end with the equally homogenising myth that the bad guys always do.[35]

I Am the Cheese

Unlike *The Chocolate War*, *I Am the Cheese* was written with a young adult readership in mind and is a self-conscious attempt to push back the boundaries of fiction for this age group in terms of both subject matter and style. As an experiment in style, the novel is a *tour de force*. As a novel for young adults exploring the individual's relationship to the State, it is more problematic. In order to discuss the novel, it is necessary to *begin* with the ending, since this forces readers to revisit and revise their impressions of much of what has gone before. Strictly speaking, the novel's cyclical narrative structure means that the ending is identical to the opening. Yet, the one crucial difference is that the reader is now aware of the fact that Adam's bicycle ride is not going anywhere. As in *The Chocolate War*, shifting focalisation can ultimately be disempowering for readers, in this case with the parallel narrative strands leading them to draw erroneous inferences about the relationship of these strands to one another.

The bicycle ride sequences

On first encountering the novel, most readers are likely to take Adam's first-person account of his bicycle ride from Monument to Rutterburg at face value. Indeed, the deictic shift readers make into the text world of the bicycle sequence, their empathy with the sense that Adam *is* going somewhere, is what makes the alternating claustrophobic therapy sequences with Brint bearable. This is underlined by the obvious relish with which Adam describes the freedom the bicycle affords him: 'I swoop around the curve and sail steadily onward'.[36] The use of the instantaneous present tense, 'I am riding the bicycle … I'm pedaling furiously',[37] gives a sense of immediacy, but also timelessness to his journey, and it is this temporal ambivalence that Cormier exploits to fool the reader into thinking that the bicycle ride is real and that it either pre- or post-dates the therapy sessions. As Nodelman points out, there are hints that Adam may not be an entirely reliable narrator,[38] such as his reference to being on medication[39] and the gaps in his account of his hasty departure from home, but we are inclined to overlook these. The irony is that Adam *is* an unreliable narrator, but an unwitting one, since his journey and the people he encounters along the way are real to him. The cruel joke is played on the reader not by Adam, but by Cormier, and the effect is at best an uncomfortable one.

This, according to Nodelman, is the whole point, to make readers feel duped, just as Adam has been duped by Brint: 'By tricking readers into believing lies and then revealing the truth they hide, Cormier makes *us* undergo the same experience Adam does'.[40] Yet, this glosses over the terrible implications of this discovery for our understanding of Adam's fate. Viewed in retrospect, the bicycle ride becomes a travesty of the conceptual metaphor LIFE IS A JOURNEY. For Adam, 17 years old by the end of the novel, life proves to be a dead-end. Far from moving forward into adulthood, the signs are that he has regressed to childhood dependency, clinging to the stuffed toy, Pokey the Pig, and singing the nursery rhyme 'The Farmer in the Dell'.[41] Although some critics have tried to view his determination to keep pedalling as evidence of his indefatigable spirit (see, for instance, Tarr[42]), it is in fact utterly futile. The best that has been offered is a reading beyond the hopelessness of the text: 'we should be grateful for the distance between the lurid melodrama we love to imagine and the usually unexciting world we actually live in'.[43]

It is, however, possible to read the sections narrated by Adam more positively as his alternative route to the truth, constructed out of half-memories recalled on his bicycle ride around the grounds of the sanatorium, together with those he is able to piece together from his drug-induced dreams/nightmares. In this reading, he is courageously undertaking a *psychological* journey with the aim of facing up to his own fears on his own terms without prompting or probing from Brint. In this context, the obstacles he encounters along the way, such as the taunting and harassment he experiences at the hands of Whipper and his gang, and the subsequent theft of his bicycle, can be interpreted as devices for deferring the terrible truth about his mother's death, as well as for storing up courage to face it. Unlike in the coercive sessions with Brint, Adam is in control of this narrative, giving him some ownership over his own story. In fact, although he claims to be a coward, he casts himself as stubbornly immoveable in his confrontation with Whipper, in words that recall Jerry's final stand against Janza in *The Chocolate War*: 'I stand there like a tree. I will not bend'.[44] Likewise, he successfully wrestles with the menacing Junior Varney to regain possession of his bicycle.[45] Readers are invited to infer that Adam arrives independently at the traumatic truth about his past *before* he reveals this in detail to Brint in the final therapy sequence. The only doubt that remains in his mind is about whether his father is also dead, and he eventually faces up to this too without Brint's 'help'.[46]

Yet Cormier also uses the sections narrated by Adam to build up an image of a hostile world full of mutual suspicion and mistrust. The old man at the petrol pump seems to articulate the author's own conspiratorial view of the world in the wake of the Watergate scandal: '"It's a terrible world out there. Murders and assassinations. Nobody's safe on the streets. And you don't even know who to trust anymore. Do you know who the bad guys are? ... Of course you don't. Because you can't tell the good guys from the bad guys anymore. Nobody knows these days. Nobody."'[47] This paranoid vision is fully endorsed by events recounted in both of the novel's narrative strands.

The taped sequences

From the outset of the taped sequences there are clues that encourage the reader to mistrust Brint, notably the discrepancy between his name and his designation as 'T' in the transcript,[48] although Cormier teases the reader with the possibility that this could refer to his role as a therapist. Another sinister detail is the fact that the dates of the interviews have been deleted. A young adult reader in particular is likely to baulk at Brint's presumption in claiming to know what is best for Adam: 'The sooner we begin, the better it will be for you'.[49]

This sense of unease is reinforced by Adam's own uncertainty about Brint: 'although he seemed sympathetic and friendly, he wasn't entirely comfortable with him'.[50] Brint's construction of himself as a disinterested guide is undermined by his use of reformulation to put an innocent gloss on Adam's disturbing childhood memories,[51] and by the evasive answers he gives to Adam's questions about whether he is a doctor and what kind of institution they are in.[52] As the interviews progress, his questions become more and more coercive, leaving the reader in little doubt that he is an interrogator, not a therapist.

The long pauses between turns suggest that Adam is a less than cooperative interlocutor. He finds himself in an impossible double bind in that he relies on Brint to help him recover his memory and self-identity, and yet he becomes increasingly aware that Brint has an agenda which is at odds with Adam's own best interests. He has no choice but to collude in Brint's construction of him as an object of concern. The chilling significance of the novel's title comes into play here. Not only does it anticipate Adam's ultimate isolation, but it also cues readers to recognise that Adam is the bait by which Brint hopes to trap him. The interview process is, as McCallum notes, therefore 'metonymic of Adam's disempowered subject position'.[53] Despite this, Adam earns the reader's admiration for the strategies he employs to resist Brint's power over him. For instance, he appropriates Brint's prerogative to ask questions, placing him on the defensive on a number of occasions. He also shrewdly withholds information for his own protection: 'He could parcel out information as if he were dealing cards, a little at a time. But he would have to be clever, cunning'.[54] One of the most depressing aspects of the taped sequences is that all of Adam's strategies of resistance to Brint's questions fail to save him. The message to young readers seems to be the disempowering one that there is no point in trying to defy the agents of the State, since 'they' will get you in the end.

The retrospective third-person narrative strand provides a portrait of a loving family life, with no equivalent in The Chocolate War. However, these passages also chart an earlier identity crisis for Adam, based on a source of insecurity for many young people: the fear that their parents might not be their parents. His anxieties about this force Adam to become a reluctant spy within his own home. The subsequent discovery that his family is, in fact, part of a government re-identification programme initially serves to heighten, rather than dispel, this identity crisis: 'a small part of him was isolated and alone, a part that was not Adam Farmer any longer but Paul Delmonte'.[55]

It is rare in Cormier's novels for his young protagonists to achieve the first stirrings of reciprocal heterosexual desire, as happens in Adam's relationship with Amy Hertz. Yet, he plants a doubt in the reader's mind as to whether Amy is part of the plot to unmask Adam's family. The serendipitous nature of their meeting and her persistent probing about his past led numerous readers to question her innocence in letters to the author, although Patricia Campbell notes that Cormier denied that Amy was implicated.[56] In any case, Adam's need to protect his family's secret means that he has to sacrifice his relationship with Amy, thus thwarting yet another of his rites of passage to adulthood.

The increasingly close relationship that develops between Adam and his father and mother make it all the more poignant when both are killed, apparently with the collusion of the shadowy government agent, Mr Grey. There are hints that his mother's minor acts of rebellion against Grey's control over their lives may have sealed their fate. In an excruciatingly painful scene, Adam is forced to undergo the trauma of witnessing his mother's death, while retaining the false hope that his father may have survived, one of the last illusions he has to abandon.

This is a thwarted rites of passage narrative of an even bleaker kind than Jerry's in *The Chocolate War*. The impact of Adam/Paul's story may exacerbate young adult readers' anxieties about self-identity, as well as inducing in them what the novel suggests is well-founded paranoia about the State and its collusion with organised crime. The danger is that this bleak message is likely to disenfranchise young readers before they are even old enough to vote.

After the First Death

Whereas *The Chocolate War* depicts the power of Trinity's official and unofficial leaders as unassailable, and *I Am the Cheese* suggests that the fears of conspiracy theorists are well-founded, *After the First Death* shows the State as vulnerable to attack and its agents as susceptible to self-doubt. The novel is prescient in its exploration of what motivates terrorists and even more so in its radical troubling of the boundary between terrorism and patriotism. Although ultimately bleak, it is a genuinely polyphonic novel, establishing dialogues of difference between its characters, thus offering potentially interrogative subject positions to its young adult readers.

The framing narrative

A number of critics have pointed to the parallels the novel sets up between General Marchand and the terrorist leader Artkin. The

General acknowledges their kinship: 'We knew each other across the chasm; we had recognized each other across the ravine, although we had never met'.[57] Both share an unquestioning patriotism which in the General's case means never contemplating the possibility that his side could ever be 'the bad guys'.[58] Anne Scott MacLeod argues that: 'The coldness with which Artkin murders a child or tortures a boy is neither more nor less monstrous than Marchand's choice of Ben for the mission on the bridge, or his calculated anticipation and use of Ben's break under torture'.[59] The difference between them, however, is that Artkin never experiences any doubts, whereas the General evinces both regret and remorse, albeit retrospectively, for treating his son as a pawn in the deadly game with Artkin.

Cormier's achievement is to portray the General *not* as a monster, but as someone who deludes himself into believing that he is acting in the best interests of both his country and his son. Young adult readers may be appalled by the panoptic surveillance to which he has subjected every aspect of Ben's life, yet the General constructs this in his own mind as benignly paternalistic: 'I thought all this would make me a better father, provide me with a better understanding of you, making it easier for me to put myself in your place'.[60] Even more transparent than this self-justifying rhetoric is the General's use of euphemism when persuading Ben to act as a go-between in the negotiations with the terrorists. He warns him that they will 'question you intensively', on the grounds that the word 'torture [is] an old-fashioned archaic word'.[61] Likewise, he employs chillingly bureaucratic language to explain that the possibility that Artkin would actually kill Ben was 'computerized as a minimum risk'.[62] The reader is invited to recognise that this is at odds with his earlier claim to know 'exactly what [Artkin] was and to what lengths he would go'.[63] The implication is not that the General is an unfeeling hypocrite, but that he has 'surrender[ed] his moral will to the abstract concept of patriotism'.[64] These sections of the novel thus encourage young readers to be critical of the way in which officially sanctioned language can be used to gloss over unpalatable truths.

The bus and the bridge sequences

The choice of Kate, an all-American schoolgirl, as a foil for the young terrorist Miro in the bus and bridge sequences in the novel establishes a fascinating dialogue across cultural and ideological difference, as well as one charged with sexual tension. The subsequent exchanges between them provide the reader with a surprisingly sympathetic insight into the making of a young terrorist, not least because Kate's continuing survival depends on gaining Miro's trust and getting him to open up about his past. Likewise, he has been instructed by Artkin to 'win her confidence'.[65] While focalisation shifts back and forth between them, it becomes clear to the reader that theirs is by no means a dialogue of equals. Although Miro may have the gun, it is Kate who is the dominant interlocutor, initiating questions and self-consciously performing the role of sympathetic listener in thrall to his stories: 'She had to make it hard for him to kill her'.[66] Despite her powerlessness as a hostage, she thus manages to accrue interactional power. She is also a resistant, rather than co-operative, listener, quietly contesting in her own mind several of the claims Miro makes for and about himself and the other terrorists, such as when he insists that they are '"not animals after all"' and she thinks 'Yes, you are'.[67]

Again, Cormier's achievement is to portray Miro as more than an 'animal'. Despite having been indoctrinated in a terrorist training camp and thus speaking in slogans for much of the time, he does show some human emotion, not least when he recalls his grief when his brother Aniel was killed,[68] and when he reflects on the futility of the death of the first child on the bus: 'this child seemed so defenseless, and his death was without purpose'.[69] However, it is in his relationship with Kate that Miro reveals himself as most vulnerable. Cormier radically reverses the transitivity patterns in conventional romance fiction in which the heroine is acted upon: '[Miro's] skin was hot and flushed';[70] 'he was betrayed by his voice, which was suddenly too high and too false';[71] 'Her fingers on his arm startled him'.[72]

Whereas Kate experiences only pity for Miro, 'This strange, pathetic boy',[73] he veers from feelings of heterosexual desire for her,[74] through intense hatred,[75] to admiration for the initiative she shows in trying to get away: 'He was still astonished that the girl had tried to drive the bus from the bridge. Who would have thought that she could be so daring, so brave?'[76] Although, perhaps inevitably, Miro kills Kate in the end, this is not before she has proven herself to be a proactive heroine who has challenged almost every negative cultural stereotype associated with the figure of the blonde cheerleader.

Conclusion

The Chocolate War has been praised as a novel that introduced a radical new realism into young adult fiction, perhaps because it was originally intended for an adult readership. It undoubtedly calls into question the moral certainties of the traditional boys' school story, but a CDA approach reveals that it replaces these with morally confusing messages delivered via a pseudo-dialogic address. Under the guise of 'telling it like it is', Cormier indulges his readers' paranoid vision of how power operates in schools like Trinity, and endorses the conservative view that resistance to such power is futile. In *I Am the Cheese*, Cormier credits young readers with the ability to cope with a complex narrative structure, but the effect is ultimately a disempowering one. There is some space for resistant reading, as figured in the text by Adam's own courageous stance *vis-à-vis* Brint's sinister style of interrogation, but the novel's closure affirms Cormier's own conspiratorial post-Watergate view of the State as antithetical to the interests of the individual. By contrast, *After the First Death* offers its young readers more liberating subject positions by inviting them to question their own assumptions about the limits of patriotism, about terrorists as alien others, and, above all, about heroism being an exclusively male preserve. These are all highly pertinent lessons for our own times and ones capable of inducing hope for a less xenophobic and patriarchal society.

Notes

1. Norman Fairclough, *Language and Power*, 2nd edn (Harlow: Pearson Education, 2001).
2. John Stephens, *Language and Ideology in Children's Fiction* (Harlow: Longman, 1992): 126.
3. Mike Cadden, 'The Irony of Narration in the Young Adult Novel', *Children's Literature Association Quarterly*, 25(3) (2000): 146–54, at 146.
4. Robert Cormier, *The Chocolate War* [1974] (London: Puffin, 2001): 1.
5. Ibid.: 1.
6. Ibid.: 3.
7. Ibid.: 4.
8. Ibid.: 3.
9. Millicent Lenz, 'A Romantic Ironist's Vision of Evil: Robert Cormier's *After the First Death*' in Priscilla A. Ord (ed.), *Proceedings of the Eighth Annual Conference of the Children's Literature Association, University of Minnesota, March, 1981* (Boston: Children's Literature Assoc, 1982): 50–6.
10. Frank Myszor, 'The See-Saw and the Bridge in Robert Cormier's *After the First Death*', *Children's Literature* 16 (1988): 77–90.
11. C. Anita Tarr, 'The Absence of Moral Agency in Robert Cormier's *The Chocolate War*', *Children's Literature* 30 (2002), 96–124, at 99.
12. *The Chocolate War*: 12.
13. Ibid.
14. Ibid.: 93.
15. Ibid.: 155.

16. Ibid.: 162.
17. Tarr: 96.
18. *The Chocolate War*: 11.
19. Ibid.: 6.
20. Ibid.: 6.
21. Ibid.: 7.
22. Ibid.: 7.
23. Ibid.:11.
24. Ibid.: 9.
25. Ibid.: 38, emphasis added.
26. Ibid.: 24.
27. Ibid.: 36.
28. Perry Nodelman, 'Robert Cormier's *The Chocolate War*: Paranoia and Paradox', in Dennis Butts (ed.), *Stories and Society: Children's Literature in its Social Context* (Basingstoke: Macmillan, 1992): 22–36, at 31.
29. Ibid.: 24.
30. *The Chocolate War*: 75–6.
31. Ibid.: 111.
32. Robyn McCallum, *Ideologies of Identity in Adolescent Fiction: The Dialogic Construction of Subjectivity* (New York: Garland, 1999): 42.
33. *The Chocolate War*: 205.
34. Nodelman (1992): 28–9.
35. Fred Inglis, *The Promise of Happiness: Value and Meaning in Children's Fiction* (Cambridge: Cambridge University Press, 1981): 274.
36. Robert Cormier, *I Am the Cheese*, (New York: Dell Publishing Co, 1977): 37.
37. Ibid.: 11.
38. Perry Nodelman, 'Robert Cormier Does a Number', *Children's Literature in Education*, 14 (1983), 94–103, at 97.
39. *I Am the Cheese*: 14.
40. Nodelman (1983): 100.
41. *I Am the Cheese*: 216.
42. Tarr: 122–43.
43. Nodelman (1983): 103.
44. *I Am the Cheese*: 90.
45. Ibid.: 175.
46. Ibid.: 215.
47. Ibid.: 24.
48. Ibid.: 16.
49. Ibid.
50. Ibid.: 20.
51. Ibid.
52. Ibid.: 39.
53. McCallum: 206.
54. *I Am the Cheese*: 40.
55. Ibid.: 132.

56. Patricia J. Campbell, *Presenting Robert Cormier* (New York: Twayne Publishers, 1985): 89.
57. Robert Cormier, *After the First Death* [1979] (London: Puffin Modern Classics, 2006): 168.
58. Ibid.: 160.
59. Anne Scott MacLeod, 'Robert Cormier and the Adolescent Novel', *Children's Literature in Education*, 12 (1981): 74–81, at 79.
60. *After the First Death*: 222.
61. Ibid.: 226.
62. Ibid.
63. Ibid.: 227.
64. MacLeod: 78.
65. *After the First Death*: 49.
66. Ibid.: 142.
67. Ibid.: 92.
68. Ibid.: 31.
69. Ibid.: 43.
70. Ibid.: 125.
71. Ibid.: 126–7.
72. Ibid.: 203.
73. Ibid.: 144.
74. Ibid.: 174.
75. Ibid.: 199.
76. Ibid.: 240.

8

Framing the Truth: Robert Cormier, His Readers and 'Reality'

Susan Clancy

Robert Cormier's writing has been variously described in ways that reflect extreme contradictions and beliefs about the suitability of his writing for young people. His young adult fiction has been profusely praised by reviewers and won numerous awards. At the same time, it has been criticised and often banned for his inclusion of adolescent issues of apparently gratuitous and senseless vandalism and underage drinking, explicit physical and sexual violence, strong, uncompromising language, and dysfunctional families.

This essay considers such issues through the ways in which Cormier situates the concept of truth. First, given the diverse nature of responses to Cormier's work, it addresses a theoretical basis for the wide range of reader responses. Second, it identifies a range of Cormier's own views about truth and the place he believes it holds in his writing and society. Third, it provides a detailed analysis of three of his novels: *Tunes for Bears to Dance to* (1992), *We All Fall Down* (1991), and *Tenderness* (1997), as a means of exploring his framing of truth within these texts.

These novels not only demonstrate how Cormier integrates story, language, and culture in complex and challenging ways to explore truth as he sees it in contemporary society, but also, in a developmental sense, his use of protagonists to provide a continuum from early to later adolescence, showcasing his ability to write for a broad audience. The essay concludes with a consideration of some specific responses to Cormier's work and of the ways in which these link back to his framing of truth.

To explore the representation of truth in Cormier's work this discussion uses a body of ideas taken from literary theories embedded within the area of reader-oriented theories, including the works of Umberto Eco (2002),[1] Wolfgang Iser (1980)[2] and Louise Rosenblatt (1978).[3] Although such theories lack a predominant philosophical starting point, their shared focus on the concepts of readers, reading processes, and responses provides distinct areas for investigation.[4] They highlight the proposition that we cannot discuss the meanings of Cormier's literature without considering the reader's contribution to it.[5] These approaches provide a sound critical framework for exploring the polyphonic nature of the meanings embedded within and initiated through a text, from the writer's creation of the text to readers' interpretations of it. This requires acknowledgement that responses evolve from differing perspectives, while also recognising that they are bound by the hermeneutic truths within the text. As a consequence of this, it can be argued that no part of a text can be understood until the whole text can be understood and vice-versa. While Eco, Iser, and Rosenblatt all recognise the importance of the reader's role in understanding texts, they also believe that the reader is, to a degree, bound by the text. Eco suggests that 'the world of literature inspires the certainty that there are some unquestionable assumptions, and that literature therefore offers us a model, however fictitious of truth', but it also 'enables a universe in which it is possible to establish whether a reader had a sense of reality or is the victim of his own hallucinations'.[6] 7). Similarly, Iser suggests that 'By reading …. we uncover the unformulated part of a literary work and … what we uncover "represents its [the text's] intention". The text's intentions maybe manifold, they may even be infinite, but they are always present embryonically in the work itself, implied by it, circumscribed by it and finally traceable to it.'[7]

Iser highlights this by recognising the dialectical qualities of reading with his terms 'implied readers' and 'actual readers', relating to the artistic (the author's text) and aesthetic (the realisations of the text by the reader) nature of texts. Rosenblatt explores these ideas further by arguing that while a text offers both openness and constraint, it also has a complex role in its transaction with the reader. It is the sense, she conveys, of the complexity of the transaction between the reader, the text, and hence the author, that can lead to a more detailed analysis of the process of reader response to text.[8]

The process of identifying readers and their responses through different descriptors is highly problematic, as such descriptors and responses are intrinsically framed by different ideologies and theories. For example, in relation to literature for young people, John Rowe Townsend identifies critical readers (adult readers of young people's and children's books) as 'book people' and 'child people',[9] where the reading of the texts is approached with different intent, either to respond to it as a piece of literature or to make a judgement about its suitability for an assumed audience. While this sort of positioning in relation to a text may work for some critical responses, it is a narrow delineation of readers and leaves little space for the input of the writer, through his or her creation of the text, or for the diversity of responses elicited from many readers who choose, or are required, to read for many different purposes.

It can be argued that to enable a stronger analysis of Cormier's framing of truth, it is more appropriate to search for understanding somewhere within the intersection of the text, the writer, and a wide cohort of readers including Rowe Townsend's 'book people' and 'child people' and Iser's 'implied readers' and 'actual readers'. To this end, this essay will draw mainly on Rosenblatt's work, which centres around the transactional nature of reader response theory, taking into account both the reader's interpretation of the text, and a consideration of how the text (the writer's creation) produces or initiates responses in the reader. Rosenblatt argues that 'There is no such thing as a generic reader or a generic literary work ... [the] reading of any work of literature is, of necessity an individual and unique occurrence involving the mind and the emotions of a particular reader'.[10] Rosenblatt's work provides a scaffold for the relationship between the author and his or her work as an integral aspect of the reader's exploration and understanding of the text. This leaves room for an analysis of the author's thematic presence and the role of culture in the creation of a text.

The intent of Cormier's 'truth'

Many of Cormier's beliefs, understandings, and intentions about his writing are known due to his speeches and contributions to interviews and workshops. Cormier believes that in his writing he owes his readers an honest story that is neither exploitative nor sensational'.[11] Such thinking also relates directly to his statement that 'political correctness is one of the worst things to happen to literature. It's killing language and thought. It's evading real life. It's substituting euphemisms for truth'.[12] His concern is to write 'realistically and truthfully to affect the reader'.[13] These comments immediately alert readers to the issue of truth, and its importance to Cormier in his writing. In light of this, it is interesting to note further comments he has made which set up tensions between how he perceives truth as he writes it and truth within broader society. One of the most telling of these is the comment he makes to Herbert N. Foerstel that, 'Lying is part of our daily life. If we told the truth, people would stop talking to each other. We lie to them to protect them'.[14] However, he also thinks that for young adult novels to be realistic they should reflect themes evident in contemporary society in the hope they will 'make children wiser in the ways of the world without making them cynical'.[15]

Although these statements seem to reflect ambivalent views about truth, they also suggest that within his writing Cormier is seeking literary truth, truth that while not literal, resonates with his perception of truth in the broader cultural sense, and provides a basis for realist young adult texts. His predominant tools for producing literary truth are: the use of irony to establish the reality of his truth by expressing it in seemingly contradictory forms; an often cinematic narrative style, which develops 'in terms of scenes' and lets 'character growth come out of action rather than description';[16] and an almost forensic use of language.

In choosing to use irony, Cormier immediately demonstrates 'an implicit compliment to the intelligence of readers, who are invited to associate themselves with the author and the knowing minority who are not taken in by the ostensible meaning'.[17] When considering structures that Cormier uses in his writing, Sylvia Patterson Iskander particularly highlights his use of situational irony and the demands this makes on his readers to 'respond to ironies and qualifications'.[18] She argues that this enables readers 'to perceive the different levels of meaning or "reality"' in his texts.[19] This process challenges the reader to work through the representations of the socially given world, and the cultural level of reality to find a generic level of truth.[20]

His cinematic style is evident in the quick changes of focus, and time shifts, and contribute to the often old movie style black (his use of bleakness) and white (his use of innocence) approach to his narrative, as in *Tenderness*, or the depiction of the trashing in *We All Fall Down*, where the reader is fully aware of Cormier's real views about his protagonists. He is also very clear on his language selection: 'I watch whether I am indulging myself. I'm very aware of choosing certain words... [in *Tenderness*] I didn't even use the word "breast", I talked about her top, and that was a very careful selection, it wasn't being casual'.[21] While such language choices could be seen as euphemistic or acceding to political correctness, it can also be argued that they really highlight Cormier's intent on framing truth through his literary techniques. In understating the obvious truth of Lori's physical endowments, and using the first person narrative to show her own youthful insecurity and inability to use the anatomical term for her body parts, when she says 'I am sometimes embarrassed by how big I am on top',[22] he is in fact using the euphemism as irony: the ironic nature of this comment being directly paralleled with her seeming insecurity, and yet, also aligned with the blatant use of her sexual attributes to get what she wants.

This same ironic intent is evident in the titles of the texts this essay discusses. *Tunes for Bears to Dance to* is taken from a quotation about language by Gustave Flaubert, immediately alerting the reader to the duplicitous ways in which language can be used, and suggesting that readers, as well as characters, can be manipulated through the author's choice of language. *We All Fall Down* uses a simple line from a traditional nursery rhyme – one whose connotations time has changed, from its relationship to the Plague, to its current use as a harmless children's playground rhyme – to suggest that falling down in a metaphorical sense is integral to being a player in the contemporary world. The third title, *Tenderness*, is used as an ironic euphemism for gratuitous sex and murder.

While these texts are certainly different they also share some key ideas. All deal with aspects of guilt, deception, and powerlessness. Most of the young protagonists have recently moved from another place and are finding their new social spaces challenging and very different from their previous experiences. The relationships explored are all built around the naïve assumptions protagonists make when they are not prepared to face the truth of what is happening to them, and their initial failure to recognise their own powerlessness as, in a range of contexts, they are manipulated by other characters. In addition, addressing adolescent experiences across an age range from 11 to 18 years old provides evidence of Cormier's ability to construct texts that resonate with the truth of life for a broad range of young people, and his refusal to compromise his hard messages for particular ages. Cormier uses the 'interplay between individuals and their contexts'[23] to focus on the choices his protagonists must make. This process demonstrates his deep understanding of the adolescent psyche and his recognition that the truth of their existence is that each life is different, each life has its difficulties, each life has its challenges, but their choices must be made within contexts that resonate with the truth of any adolescent reader's existence.

The realisation of Cormier's 'truth'

While these three texts clearly have certain points of intersections, they are also quite different in their structure, content, and constructions of literary truth. *Tunes for Bears to Dance to* provides strong insight into the notion of truth in the world of 11-year-old Henry Cassavant. Cormier uses a range of moral dilemmas to develop consistent tensions between the truth of what Henry believes is a right action and his need to justify why he cannot always follow that path. Ironically, Cormier does this by deftly fashioning within Henry a constant burden of guilt, one which is initially unfounded, but which nevertheless emerges as a reality.

The reader knows that within his family, 'Henry felt guilty because he could go, oh, three or four hours without thinking about Eddie'[24] – his brother who was killed in a car accident – compared with his parents who 'seemed to be thinking of him every minute of the day'.[25] Although he does well at school, Henry does not have his brother's sporting ability, so is incapable of replacing his brother in a way that will help his parents overcome their grief. His guilt about Eddie is exacerbated by his belief in truth as represented through religion, evidenced through his need to pray for his brother, 'in case he was not in heaven'.[26]

This guilt pursues him into the world beyond his family, as Cormier sets up the main incident of the novel between Henry and Mr Hairston. Henry is 'filled with guilt'[27] because he is so relieved when Mr Hairston, the grocer for whom he works, refuses to employ Jackie Antonelli to fill in for him while he is on crutches. At the same time he is also aware of the racial prejudice driving Mr Hairston's decision, when he hears Hairston use terms like 'greaseball', 'kike',[28] 'polak',[29] and 'Canucks',[30] and the offensiveness of the personal comments he makes about his customers. Readers immediately wonder why Henry's ethnic sounding surname, Cassavant, is any less deserving of a racial slur. Why was he given a job by this man?

Although uncomfortable with his racist talk, Henry is also 'grateful to Mr Hairston for giving him a job'.[31] He knows something is not right when Doris, Mr Hairston's daughter, appears with a nasty bruise on her cheek, but he cannot quite work it out. He is uneasy, but simply cannot grasp Mr Hairston's dangerousness and his need for power and control over people. At 11 years old, Henry fails to recognise what is occurring. For him, the importance of his job, the security it offers, and the money he can take home to help his mother outweigh his initial qualms. Only much later does he remember the question he was asked when he applied for the job: '"Can you follow orders? Whether you like them or not?"'[32]

Mr Hairston's process of manipulation demonstrates a careful balance and finesse in its construction, as he plays an insidious cat and mouse game with Henry, before finally demanding that he perform a totally unwarranted act of destruction. Cormier's writing ensures that readers are under no illusion about the truth of the situation. Mr Hairston is psychologically abusing Henry by manipulatively and cleverly playing on his innocence, goodness, his sense of right and wrong, and the unnecessary burden of guilt that he carries within him.

Cormier's use of a limited third person narrative lets the reader see things from Henry's perspective and in so doing provides a seemingly limited view of what is happening. Cormier, however, expects his reader to look beyond Henry's often naïve and contradictory perceptions. For example, Henry does not like secrets, and 'He was disappointed that his mother had kept the doctor a secret from him'.[33] At the same time, however, he lies to her about his nightmare saying '"I can barely remember it"',[34] rather than involving her in his moral dilemma.

Cormier's ironical touch is further evidenced when, unintentionally, Henry fulfils Mr Hairston's demand to destroy old Mr Levines' model village, because he sees a rat. This incident captures the agony of an action that cannot be changed. Henry realises that he, '*didn't want to do it* ... But he had done it, after all'.[35]

Although he cannot escape the truth of his action, he still tries to believe it was unintentional, even though he was poised with the mallet when the rat appeared. Cormier's incisive use of language has already signalled to readers that while a rat appears responsible for his action, 'there is [in fact] a rat in every storeroom',[36] a statement that in many ways fits with Eco's notion of an 'unquestionable assumption' that results in a 'fictitious truth'.

It is significant that Henry finally realises the truth when he understands that 'He [Mr Hairston] didn't want me to be good anymore'.[37] This realisation empowers Henry to refuse his 'reward' for carrying out the destruction and to break the cycle of evil that had ensnared him. Through this entire subtle, insidious, and overwhelming depiction of the corruption of goodness Cormier creates a realistic and truthful text, providing the reader with a model of truth, a literary truth that works within the framework of this story.

In *We All Fall Down*, rather than using one sustained voice for the entire text, Cormier uses his cinematic narrative style to provide a broader range of viewpoints. While he remains with the third person structure, he alternates the positions from which he relates his story, to challenge and invite the reader to think about what is happening from different perspectives. At the beginning of the novel the reader becomes an intimate observer of the violent trashing of a house that underpins this whole text. This home invasion is narrated almost clinically in that times and actions are clearly stated, but the focus then flicks immediately to narration from the perspective of the Avenger, an elusive and mysterious observer of much of the action. Thus, readers are given a far more personal and emotional reaction to the scene, one that also cues them into the strangeness of someone observing the house, not just now but frequently. The Avenger considers this house and its family 'his territory',[38] and seeks revenge for the invasion of this territory. The opening raises many questions for readers before the narrative voice then moves to the perspectives of 15-year-old Jane Jerome and 16-year-old Buddy Walker, the key protagonists.

Patricia Head argues that through such methods of narration, Cormier 'subverts the assumption that literature should present a straightforward schematic view of the world'.[39] She supports this view by suggesting that his use of disrupted narratives alert the reader to a 'world that can no longer be conveyed through more ordered narratives' and that Cormier's texts 'try to articulate a world that compromises a multiplicity of interpretations'.[40] In this way he demands that his readers recognise some basic truths embedded in today's society – life is complex and we are ultimately responsible for our choices.

Cormier's constantly changing narrative perspectives, the manipulation of time frames, and the simple comments dropped into the narrative, such as the police being puzzled because there were 'no signs of forced entry',[41] set problems for readers to solve, while also providing spaces for them to integrate and work through their own ideas. Such structures help delineate the situational irony readers face when they read about Jane and Buddy's blossoming relationship. There is the despair of knowing that however important and sweet this relationship may seem, it is doomed to failure because it is built on lies. Readers have to face Buddy's delusions about his part in the trashing, his drinking, and his inability to face the truth. When Jane asks him difficult questions, 'He answer[s] guardedly, telling her the truth but shading it'.[42] Similarly, it is disturbing that the truth of Jane losing her house key at the mall becomes a lie in the hands of Harry Flowers, who picks it up, and tells the police that Jane gave it to him. To him, the important thing is 'the effect the key had on everybody at the police station',[43] in particular, Jane's father. Harry's lie has sown the seed of distrust, and the relationship between Jane and her father is irrevocably damaged.

The duplicity of Harry Flowers is evidenced by the contradictory observations made about him. At one moment Buddy sees Harry's 'meticulous', 'Spotlessly clean' appearance, with his 'handsome face unblemished, serene',[44] but in the next instant he also understands that 'Harry was Frankenstein, the doctor who created the monster'.[45] Later, Buddy begins to realise that Harry's physical persona is not quite as he had originally thought. He notices Harry's 'weird and evil smile'[46] and 'The smirk on his face, the acne always there but overlooked because of Harry's manner, the cool appraising eyes, the what-the-hell way he stood'.[47] Even so, Buddy still fails to see the obvious consequence of his complicity with Harry's whims and how this will destroy his relationship with Jane.

The end of Jane and Buddy's relationship is as powerful as it is inevitable, when Jane, accidently meeting with Buddy after she has become aware of all his evasions of truth, is faced with some hard truths about life: 'As pity moved into the hole inside her, she discovered how distant pity was from hate, how very far it was from love'.[48] Such a simple straightforward statement about an impossible relationship leaves no doubt in the reader's mind about the relationships of Cormier's literary world echoing the challenges of relationships in the real world. Both characters are forced to face the truth: relationships built on lies, fantasy, and pity simply cannot survive.

Craig Clarke recognises the authenticity of the way in which Cormier constructs this text in that although it is 'a very dark book … there is a thread of hope that runs throughout the story that lightens it towards palatability. The teenage characters feel real and Cormier is wonderful at describing the problems that affect people at that age … his writing evoke[s] old feelings through its truth.'[49]

Tenderness looks at another impossible relationship, one also built on lies and fantasy, which again cannot succeed. The truth evidenced in this text, however, is played out very differently from that in the previous text. The temptations and ironics underscoring *Tenderness*, and the way Cormier works with truth, start with his naming of characters: Lori (short for Lorelei, the siren of Clemens Brentano's and later Heinrich Heine's poems, who lured sailors to their death) and Eric Poole, who finds himself charged with murder by drowning of the only one of his victims he ever really cared for, and whom he tried to save.

Cormier alternates, mainly, between the two key narratives, using first person for Lori and limited third person for Eric, and also includes, to a lesser extent, the narrative of Jake Procter, the old cop. Readers are privileged in knowing how Lori and Eric think, but they are also aware, through Jake's narrative, that Eric is not as secure in his world as he thinks. Readers and Jake are the only ones who understand Lori's death was an accident. Cormier again captures the situational irony of Eric finally telling the truth, only to have no-one believe him. The deceit Eric perpetrated to the court – that being an abused child has led him to murder his parents – is believed. Cormier's narratives for Lori and Eric enable him to build the fictional reality and fantasy of both their worlds, as they re-interpret the truth of their lives through their own perceptions of the world. Lori, a promiscuous, precocious 15 year old, sees sexual abuse as meeting her need for tenderness, while Eric creates a self-image that grants him the ability and self delusion to believe that the murders he commits are motivated by tenderness. He is totally confident about his beauty, his cleverness, his ability to deceive.

Cormier's irony also works through a series of contradictions. Nothing is quite as it seems. Visually Lori is blonde and beautiful with many characteristics of an innocent child inside a woman's body. Although sexually precocious, and conscious of the sexual power of her body, which she uses when it is to her advantage, she clings desperately to her perception that she is still 'technically' a virgin.[50] Her belief in this is such that on her night in the motel with Eric, she further proclaims this status by dressing herself in white, like a traditional bride on her wedding night, and significantly, it is in this same outfit that she drowns.

Naïvely, as is revealed through her unreliable first-person narrative, she believes she is in control, while it is evident that she is a victim caught within a dysfunctional family situation and a web of self destruction. She attempts escape in numerous ways: by running away, lying to herself and others, living in a fantasy world, trying to slash her wrists, using her body in a search for 'tenderness', and constantly chasing her fixations in the hope of 'being fixed'. Her moral code enables her to understand that sometimes she is 'a real bitch',[51] but it does not bother her. She does what is needed to survive, from lying to stealing to aiding and abetting murder. Although she knows Eric was jailed for murdering his parents, she does not seriously consider him to be a killer. It is only later that she begins to realise that perhaps there is something about Eric that she does not understand. His tenderness puzzles her, but he also lies to her. When he knows she has caught him in a lie, he changes: 'He is like two people in one body'.[52] She is scared. Even so, when he admits that he intended to kill her she remains deluded, because, as she thinks to herself: 'in my heart, where it counts the most, I know he wouldn't have done it', 'now I know I am safe'.[53] Always convinced everything will turn out well, she is unable to face the truth about Eric or his intentions when, from the Ferris wheel, she notices him moving towards the woods with the Senorita.

Eric is a beautiful and handsome child, who grows into an equally attractive young man. However, he has the mind and behaviour of a psychopath, a fact he works hard to hide. He is an angel in appearance and a monster inside. His interior soul is also at odds with his puritanical dislike of bad language and body odours, and his fastidious views about dress. He, too, believes he is in control as demonstrated by his self-mutilating in order to appear a victim of child abuse, his manipulative use of his charm and smile, his power over his victims, and in his illusions about tenderness. Only the old cop Jake sees through his masquerade. Initially, in his dysfunctional family existence Eric was the centre of his mother's world, and he is angry when he is displaced by Harvey, his stepfather. In Eric's mind, she is to blame for his humiliation in being rejected by her and by a girl in eighth grade who refused to go to the Spring Dance with him. Although not stated directly it is evident to the reader that Eric's relationship with his mother was less than healthy as he remembers 'dark nights, her long black hair enveloping him, her lips trailing across his flesh … *my darling, Eric… my darling*',[54] actions he tries to replicate with his victims.

Eric is the only one who understands that Lori lives in a fantasy world and that very little of what she says is actually the truth about her existence. A further ironic twist is added when twice he decides he must kill her, once as a 12-year-old then later as a 15-year-old, but on both occasions he finishes up trying to rescue her. The final twist is that in trying to save her, his sole act of moral behaviour, she drowns and he is accused of her murder. Kathy Neal Headley highlights the intent of this incident by acknowledging Cormier's interest in moral questions, even though the morality involved is of a wholly different order 'than the purely personal concerns of most teen novels'.[55]

Cormier culminates this text in the darkness of Eric's jail cell when Eric has his first experience of tears. The reader learns that 'Later, in the deepest heart of the night, the monster cried'.[56] What is the truth left at the heart of this text? Is it that even monsters cry, or is that even if monsters cry they remain monsters? This is one of those spaces where Cormier demonstrates his trust in the intelligence of his readers by challenging them to fill in the gaps, determine their own final understandings, and realise that finding truth is never simple. Anne Scott Macleod accedes to this view, acknowledging that Cormier's work opens 'the complex questions of the function of literature'.[57] She also recognises that although Cormier's work is 'hard-edged' and 'unequivocally downbeat',[58] readers will find the essence of truth contained in 'aspects of contemporary reality' from which 'the young are not immune'.[59]

Perspectives of response

Teen readers' responses to Cormier's work range from simple to complex, as the following responses to *Tenderness* demonstrate. Tami Daniel's response is simple 'I didn't like this book, primarily because it scared me!'[60] For Vivian, the response is more complex, with the book coming as a complete shock:

> I went into it expecting to hate Eric, and probably Lori, too, but still interested in the 'mind of a serial killer'. I finished it ... sympathizing with Eric. However disturbing that might be ... The ending was truly tragic ... the last chapter really got me. It gave him such a human element, even dare I say it, loving, that I was almost heartbroken at the ending.[61]

Cormier knows the psychological and physical violence of his texts causes considerable angst for some readers, but he also believes he has readers who respond to the intent of his work and the ways in which he presents truth. He claims that 'In a lot of instances, young adults are living that darker side of life or are aware of it through television, movies or what they see and hear on school buses or in the school corridors' and that 'they are tired of books where everyone walks off into the sunset together'.[62] In his own mind, he has a clear understanding of how readers respond to his work, and he is unequivocal about the integrity of his writing. Responding during an interview to the question 'Is it fair to expect people to deal with the truth and honesty you display in your writing at an age in which they haven't experienced it for themselves?' he states:

> Listen, I can't afford to sit at my typewriter and worry about a 13 or 14-year-old's sensitivity. If they can't handle it, tough. On the other hand, I know that audience is out there ... My books are ... highly challenged in America. I think it's because of that truth thing you've brought up. Despite all that, my best answer to the censors is to keep writing, because I think they'd like to shut me up ... I have my own standards. *Tenderness* is a very tough book ... When you're dealing with a serial murderer, a serial killer, and a sexually precocious girl, it's easy to let the blood flow and the sex roll, the harder part is to contain it, and suggest it. So my conscience is clear ... You seldom get a censorship attempt from a 14 yr old boy. It's the adults who get upset. The letters I get are letters

of support and the line that runs through them all is 'You tell it like it is'. Some people get upset because we do humanize monsters. They think we're making monsters attractive. They'd rather keep the monster as a monster.[63]

Critics, too, express a range of responses to his work. Winifred Whitehead, for example, considers that Cormier 'deliberately panders to a taste for violence',[64] while Nancy Veglahn though less judgmental, suggests that Cormier's work shows 'no moral blandness, no picture of a world in which all will be well if everyone just tries a little harder' and that 'readers hoping for the triumph of justice and goodness [in Cormier's work] are likely to be disappointed'.[65]

This wide range of responses clearly demonstrates Rosenblatt's transactional theory in action. Each critic has explored Cormier's texts for themselves and all have engaged in transactions with the texts where they have used both the text and their own life experiences to find truths that resonate with their own understandings of the texts. The central aspect of these example responses is that while all find aspects of Cormier's work challenging, their reasons for doing so differ dramatically. None seriously argue with his portrayals of truth but focus more on his methods, and the suitability of his approach for a young readership, believing that in many cases he breaks unwritten conventions about boundaries in literature for young people. It is however, important to contextualise these comments and realise that a number of them were written up to 20 years ago. The world has changed a lot since then, but even today responses to Cormier's work remain ambivalent.

Cormier's protagonists, and in turn his readers, are faced with often unpleasant truths embedded within political and cultural dilemmas faced by society. Truths that concern: the hypocrisy of many institutions; the innate evil that exists in the world; the corrupt nature of power; the destruction of innocence; and the sleight of hand with which truth is used to justify, excuse, or explain the choices his protagonists make. Such truths will always provide challenges for readers.

Conclusion

In taking Cormier's representations of truth as a focus for this essay, it is important to acknowledge that in the larger context of society, the philosophical problem of truth has been with us for many centuries, and although there is no simple way of addressing or determining truth, an exploration of Cormier's writing through this lens enables us to consider the many responses to his work, including criticism and acclaim, from a different perspective. The truth Cormier conveys in these three texts is embedded within his multiple methods of working with irony, the complexity of his narratives, and his masterful use of language. He demonstrates his respect for readers and their integrity, not by stating the obvious, not by being didactic, not by providing a simplistic view of life in today's world, but through a complex inter-weaving of situations and relationships, which is manifest through the range of ways he uses irony, narrative, and language.

Cormier constantly explores a range of different complexities about truth through the contexts he creates and the decisions his various protagonists make about the paths they choose on their life journeys. He plays with the notion of there being no perfectly good or perfectly bad path. Protagonists consistently face moral dilemmas and the difficult, ultimately life-changing process of weighing up the consequences of their actions and what they decide to do with the 'truth' of the situation as he constructs it and they discover it. In trying to stay true to his belief that, 'the books give [young readers] a dose of reality, of what's really going on in the world out there that's waiting for them,'[66] Cormier ultimately sees his purpose as trying '"to write realistic stories about believable people reflecting the world as it is, not as we wish it to be"'.[67] His dedication to this purpose, and the way he frames truth, by leaving important spaces for astute and intelligent readers to explore their own understandings of his texts, not only contribute to the longevity of his work but also indicate why his texts are still widely read, debated, and celebrated.

Notes

1. Umberto Eco, *On Literature* [2002] (Orlando, FL: Harcourt, 2004).
2. Wolfgang Iser, 'The Reading Process: A Phenomenological Approach', 1980, in Jane P. Tompkins (ed.), *Reader-Response Criticism: From Formalism to Post-Structuralism,* (Baltimore, MD: Johns Hopkins University Press, 1988): 50–69.
3. Louise Rosenblatt, *The Reader, The Text, The Poem: The Transactional Theory of the Literary Work* [1978] (Carbondale and Edwardsville, IL: Southern Illinois University Press, 1981).
4. Jane P. Tompkins, 'An Introduction to Reader-Response Criticism' [1980], in Jane P. Tompkins (ed.), *Reader-Response Criticism: From Formalism to Post-Structuralism,* (Baltimore, MD: Johns Hopkins University Press, 1988): ix–xxvi.
5. Raman Selden, *A Reader's Guide to Contemporary Literary Theory,* 2nd edn (New York: Harvester Wheatsheaf, 1989).

6. Eco: 7.
7. Wolfgang Iser cited in Tompkins, 'An Introduction to Reader-Response Criticism': xv.
8. Rosenblatt: x.
9. John Rowe Townsend, 'Standards of Criticism for Children's Literature' [1971], in Peter Hunt (ed.), *Literature for Children: The Development of Criticism*, ed. by (London: Routledge, 1990): 57–70.
10. Rosenblatt: xii.
11. Herbert N. Foerstel, *Banned in the U.S.A.: A Reference Guide to Book Censorship in Schools and Public Libraries* (Westport, CT: Greenwood Press, 1994): 122.
12. Robert Cormier, *Teenreads,* Interview (21 April 2000): www.teenreads. com/authors/au-cormier-robert.asp (accessed 9 May 2012).
13. Foerstel: 115.
14. Foerstel: 118.
15. Cormier, (21 April 2000).
16. Robert Cormier, *Robert Cormier Meets Melvin Burgess Part 2* (undated, a): www.achuka.co.uk/special/cormburg2.htm (accessed 9 May 2012).
17. M. H. Abrams, *A Glossary of Literary Terms*, 7th edn (Boston, MA: Heinle & Heinle, 1999): 135.
18. Sylvia Patterson Iskander, 'Readers, Realism, and Robert Cormier', *Children's Literature*, 15 (1987): 7–18, at 8.
19. Ibid.: 9.
20. Ibid.: 9 10.
21. Cormier, (undated, a).
22. Robert Cormier, *Tenderness* [1997] (London: Puffin Books, 1998): 14.
23. Anne Scott MacLeod, 'Robert Cormier and the Adolescent Novel', *Children's Literature in Education,* 41 (1981): 74–81, at 75.
24. Robert Cormier, *Tunes for Bears to Dance to* [1992] (London: Lions, 1994): 8.
25. Ibid.
26. Ibid.: 22.
27. Ibid.: 10.
28. Ibid.
29. Ibid.: 11.
30. Ibid.: 68.
31. Ibid.: 11.
32. Ibid.: 75.
33. Ibid.: 32.
34. Ibid.: 75.
35. Ibid.: 85.
36. Ibid.: 83.
37. Ibid.: 88.
38. Robert Cormier, *We All Fall Down* [1991] (London: Puffin Books, 2001): 3.

39. Patricia Head, 'Robert Cormier and the Postmodernist Possibilities of Young Adult Fiction', *Children's Literature Association Quarterly,* 21 (1996): 28–33, at 29.
40. Ibid.: 29.
41. *We All Fall Down*: 21.
42. Ibid.: 146.
43. Ibid.: 107.
44. Ibid.: 14.
45. Ibid.: 15.
46. Ibid.: 136.
47. Ibid.: 140.
48. Ibid.: 194.
49. Craig Clarke, *Craig's Book Club: Book Reviews* (2009): http://geocities. ws/craigsbookclub/cormier.html#fall (accessed 9 May 2012).
50. *Tenderness*: 17.
51. Ibid.: 25.
52. Ibid.: 143.
53. Ibid.: 157.
54. Ibid.: 162.
55. Kathy Neal Headley, 'Duel at High Noon: A Replay of Cormier's Works', *The ALAN Review*, 21(2) (1994): 75. http://scholar.lib.vt.edu/ ejournals/ALAN/winter94/Headley.html (accessed 9 May 2012).
56. *Tenderness*: 189.
57. MacLeod: 80.
58. Ibid: 74.
59. Ibid.: 80.
60. Tami, *Goodreads* (21 February 2011): www.goodreads.com/book/show/ 51944.Tenderness (accessed 9 May 2012).
61. Vivian, *Goodreads* (28 June 2010): www.goodreads.com/book/show/ 51944.Tenderness (accessed 9 May 2012).
62. Quoted in Foerstal: 117.
63. Robert Cormier, *Robert Cormier Meets Melvin Burgess Part 1* (undated, b): www.achuka.co.uk/special/cormburg.htm (accessed 9 May 2012).
64. Winifred Whitehead, *Old Lies Revisited: Young Readers and the Literature of War and Violence* (London: Pluto Press, 1991): 5.
65. Nancy Veglahn, 'The Bland Face of Evil in the Novels of Robert Cormier', *The Lion and the Unicorn,* 12:1 (1988): 12–18, at 12.
66. Cormier, (21 April 2000).
67. Quoted in Foerstal: 123.

9

Interactive Texts and Active Readers: Robert Cormier's 'Adolescent Poetics' in the Light of Wolfgang Iser's Theory of Aesthetic Response

Dimitrios Politis

> I admit freely I'm an arrested adolescent ... I think a lot of us carry around the baggage of adolescence in our lives, so I don't have to sit there and take a big leap into how a 14 year old boy or girl feels, because I know how they felt, they felt exactly how I felt. Those feelings are universal and timeless. ... When I start to write, frankly what I do is write for an intelligent reader. ... I'm not one of these people who write for themselves, I write to be read, and I'm very conscious of my reader. I write to upset the reader, and to provoke the reader, and I feel I can go to my full capacity for that intelligent reader, who often turns out to be 14 years old.[1]

Two pivotal observations derive from Robert Cormier's statements above: the first is his retained sense of adolescence and aptitude for understanding young adults; the second is his conscious intention to be 'provocative' in writing for teenagers, necessitating 'intelligent' readers' active participation in the reading process he inaugurates with his fictions. Although both observations highlight Cormier's 'adolescent poetics', the latter one represents it most.

Robert Cormier's poetics: novels of departure

Cormier first addressed an adolescent readership in 1974 with his young adult novel *The Chocolate War*, and found the contact this entailed with teenagers fascinating. It was mainly his correspondence with young adults that gave impulse and continuity to his writing for adolescents, and the 14 novels that followed, including *I Am the Cheese* (1977), *After the First Death* (1979), *The Bumblebee Flies Anyway* (1983), *Beyond The Chocolate War* (1985), *Fade* (1988), *We All Fall Down* (1991), *Tunes for Bears to Dance to* (1992), *Tenderness* (1997), and the posthumously published *The Rag and Bone Shop* (2001), were all written for this readership.

In these 'adolescent novels of ideas',[2] almost all of which reflect his 'adolescent poetics', the axes of his bold thematics – including uneasy puberty, corrupted power, betrayal, guilt, self-alienation and psychological alienation, paranoia, fear, intimidation, and psychoses – are clearly discernible. However, the signature features of his writing for adolescents also include a partial distancing of his heroes from other people or their personal quests, an insistent fictional focus on the influence of external circumstances and forces that constrain and control these heroes,[3] adolescent heroes' (innate) tendency towards independence and rebellion against the adults who wield power, and a recognition of the dark side of life that infuses his novels with a sense of 'gloom'.[4] It is these components, in conjunction with his sensitivity, realism, complex narratives, and emphasis on cinematic dialogue practices,[5] that constitute Cormier's 'adolescent poetics'. Two main coefficients are discernible in his 'poetics': first, the intersection of his heroes' quests and power structures; second, the intense involvement of his readers in actualising his writing. If the former endows an interactive intention on his novels, the latter requires his readers to become active. Both these coefficients could perhaps best be understood in the light of an equally interactive view of the relationship between a literary text and its reader of the sort proposed by the German proponent of the 'Aesthetic Response' (*Theorie Ästhetischer Wirkung*), Wolfgang Iser.

Wolfgang Iser's aesthetics: points of theory

Iser's examination of the reading process and the aesthetic response the literary text provokes leads him to combine the text as an objective entity with the subjective disposition of the reader. As he declares, such a realisation requires the reader actively to make meaning, while he stresses that 'the literary work is an effect to be experienced' not 'an object to be defined'.[6] Denominating this relationship between text and reader as 'interaction',[7] Iser identifies it with the praxis relating the two. He describes this interaction by defining his approach to notions such as the 'implied reader', (literary) 'repertoire', and (literary) 'strategies'.

The 'implied reader' is mainly a 'role offered by the text', which is to say is 'rather the conditioning force behind a particular kind of tension produced by the real reader when he accepts the role'.[8] This reader is also a 'model which makes it possible for the structured effects of literary texts to be described', or a 'standpoint' from which the real reader 'can assemble the meaning toward which the perspectives of the text have guided him'.[9] Taken together, the various aspects of the notion thus fully indicate the relationship the author establishes with his readers.

The 'repertoire', which is taken to be the 'content' of the literary work, consists of social assumptions and cultural norms along with literary references or allusions incorporated into the text,[10] namely, as Iser describes it, 'the whole culture from which the text has emerged'.[11] All these elements promote interplay between the text and the reader by providing the latter with the 'guidelines that are essential in view of the overall function of the text'.[12] The reader has then to reorganise all these textual indications in order to develop his or her account of the text, since the text tends to defamiliarise his or her assumptions while it causes indeterminacies between text and reader as well as between text and reality. The reader is thus forced into an 'intertextual' or into an 'extra-textual' dimension, as 'the literary text has no concrete situation to refer to'.[13]

The reader's activity is made possible by virtue of the 'strategies', which serve as the 'form' of a literary work. Iser lends these strategies a significant dual function: 'to organise both the material of the text and the conditions under which that material is to be communicated'.[14] 'Strategies', which are not regarded as simple techniques or devices located in the text,[15] tend to utilise the 'repertoire' as a referential context.[16] As examples of these 'strategies', Iser cites the 'background–foreground' relationship ('primary code–secondary code')[17] and the 'theme-horizon' structure. Comparing the 'primary' code with the 'schematised aspects' of the text, and the 'secondary' with the aesthetic object itself, he describes a procedure through which the reader is directed by the 'primary' code to decipher the 'secondary' one, as 'the chosen element evokes its original setting'.[18] The reader has also to combine the elements that he or she selected, directed by the principle of 'theme and horizon'. Due to the continuous and interactive relationship between text and reader, the reader is able to assimilate all the multiple textual perspectives gradually. For the reader, every moment constitutes a 'theme', while many 'themes' constitute the 'horizon' of his or her comprehensive procedure.[19]

During the reading process, the reader has to modify expectations and to transform memories by means of a 'wandering viewpoint', in order to inform the reading procedure.[20] Travelling continually between his or her temporary expectations and their refutation, the reader tries to achieve 'consistency-building', by organising the information offered by the text and transforming the textual signs into 'mental images'. Perceiving what is present in the text, the reader has to 'ideate' what is absent or implied according to the 'schematised aspects' indicated by the text. However, having set up the reading process, the text punctuates it by interpolating 'blanks' or 'points of suspended connectability',[21] meaning empty spaces between the segments (e.g., characters, plot) of the text. The reader is then required to fill in the 'blanks' that appear along the syntagmatic axis of reading, in the light of the knowledge accumulated during the preceding stages of his or her reading. In this way, the reader is allowed to create multiple combinations or new associations based on the textual elements and to adopt a standpoint from where his or her older views/perspectives appear outdated or are negated, meaning that a 'dynamic blank' appears on the paradigmatic axis of reading. Together with the 'blanks', these 'negations' imbue the text with a 'negativity' and formulate 'a kind of unformulated double' text,[22] which demands a retroactive reading stance from the reader. In this case, the reader may be regarded as active, since he or she is producing the meaning, and as passive, since his or her involvement is determined by the textual structures. Eventually, Iser claims, 'blanks and 'negations' play an essential part in the success of the reciprocal communication between text and reader, so long as they instruct the reader to complete the meaning of the text.[23]

Iser's main concern is to construct an interactive theoretical model that could provide a reliable framework for studying a reader's potential response. In the light of this model we can describe and elucidate Cormier's 'adolescent poetics' – necessarily briefly and with reference to only a few of his novels for young adults given the space limitations of the essay.

Readers in the making: the development of active participants

The notion of the 'implied reader' may help us understand the relationship Cormier establishes with his real readers, as well as the meanings and expectations he negotiates with them.[24] Cormier does, in fact, employ a fictitious reader who 'designates a network of response-inviting structures, which impel the [real] reader to grasp the text'.[25] Grasping his adolescent readers' need to understand their emotions and the motives of the people who frame their lives, he depicts his heroes struggling to structure their identities and to define themselves, usually dramatically. A selection of representative characters from his novels who act this way include: Jerry Renault in *The Chocolate War* and *Beyond the Chocolate War*, who dares to 'disturb the universe'[26] in which he feels trapped by challenging a school tradition, and who, ultimately, tries to escape the power of a devious authority influence and survive; Adam Farmer in *I Am the Cheese*, who is struggling to discover his identity, distrusts his 'protectors', and challenges their intentions, as he becomes aware of the threats to his fragile fate; Kate Forrester, who tries to escape from terrorists, and Miro Shantas who tries to escape from himself by implementing the plans of the terrorist group to which he belongs in *After the First Death*; Barney Snow in *The Bumblebee Flies Anyway*, who tries to piece together his past, but discovers things that may jeopardise his future; Buddy Walker in *We All Fall Down*, who struggles to find comfort and support from the people around him; Henry Cassavant in *Tunes for Bears to Dance to*, who learns about trusting people and struggles to survive in a cruelly diverse world; Paul Moreaux in *Fade*, who learns that his ability to become invisible brings knowledge of others and himself; Lori Cranston and Eric Poole in *Tenderness*, whose paths cross as they both search for 'tenderness'. According to Sylvia Patterson Iskander, all these characters 'are plausible in the context of our social experience and expectations' and behave as real teenagers while they engage thoughts and 'systems of values that readers can accept as plausible'.[27] In fact, though quite different in comparison to other typical heroes of young adult literature who represent more positive role models and who conform more closely to grown-up values, Cormier's rebellious protagonists can effectively motivate real readers to adopt the 'implied' role offered to them.

Cormier also seems to recognise his readers' need to realise the literary experience offered through his heroes as analogous to their own lives. Therefore, as Brian McHale puts it, he creates 'the reader who must be or become to optimize the reading of the text'.[28] This 'implied reader' is thus a textual structure, which constitutes the possible image or presence of a real recipient, as well as a standpoint that activates the role of the real reader when he or she accepts that role in order to complete the realisation of the literary text. Thus, the teenage readers of *The Chocolate War*, *I Am the Cheese*, *The Bumblebee Flies Anyway*, *We all Fall Down* or *Tunes for Bears to Dance to*, progress hand in hand with the teenage protagonists in the struggle to structure their respective identities through a procedure of identification. However, it is possible that, during this identification process, readers could be affected by a sense of betrayal and disorientation as they identify themselves with protagonists who have been 'crushed' or 'beaten' by power structures. Like Jerry, Adam, Barney, Buddy or Henry, who cannot plead indifference or ignorance for the conditions that regulate their lives, so, too, Cormier's readers 'cannot count on fictional escapes from the hard choices of life'.[29] They have to recognise the various levels of reality presented in these novels,[30] in which case the identification process may become an encounter between subjectivity and consciousness, a 'maturation process',[31] which fits rather well with an unconventional adolescent reader. In fact, the readers' relationship with the fictionally-represented social or real worlds may reinforce their sense of relationship with the contemporary ones.[32] Cormier is thus requiring his real readers to participate actively in his texts via the implicit readers and to experience their meanings in order to communicate with him.[33] This is why he creates his 'implied' readers in the same way he constructs his second self – the 'implied author'.[34] Although he places both his protagonists and his implied readers in a hard, bleak world, he offers them hope; above all, however, he gives them the chance to recognise their deficiencies as well as suggesting ways of balancing them out. This means that he does not give his heroes[35] what he gives his readers: a second chance to 'move beyond the close of the novels to a new sense of personal responsibility'.[36] In other words, he offers them an interpretative standpoint to which they are led by the textual indications his characters formulate and implied readers activate.[37] Just as Jerry, Adam, Barney, Buddy or Henry comprehend the systems via which they find themselves through a process of inner searching, his real readers grasp the textual parameters and live them as if they were real. In Cormier's case, we can therefore assert that the term 'implied reader' refers specifically to a transferral process in which the text is perceived by the consciousness of the real reader and transubstantiated into experience by the latter's continual participation in it.[38]

Readership in progress: journeying with adolescents

As 'a meeting point between text and reader',[39] the 'repertoire' in Cormier's young adult novels mainly consists of the elements Iser's term entails: elements of reality and elements of the literary tradition. Though it is not reproduced but represented, this reality serves as a reasonable fictional context in which 'contingencies and complexities' are reduced to – and are retained as – 'a meaningful structure'.[40] In this case, the 'repertoire' may 'project the real',[41] while it also 'represents a reaction to the thought systems'[42] or functions as a 'literary reaction to historical problems'.[43] In many of Cormier's novels, where there are indications of 'extra-textual' connections, the 'repertoire' focuses on re-defining reality via the protagonists' relationship with it. *The Chocolate War*, for example, places Jerry in a tough school context, which teenagers will be familiar with from their day-to-day experiences. His reaction to a school tradition and challenging of dominant thought and power systems, seeks to change this reality and then overcome his individuality, while his actions have political implications.[44] Similar implications are projected in *I Am the Cheese, After the First Death, The Bumblebee Flies Anyway, We All Fall Down*, and *Tunes for Bears to Dance to*. In *I Am the Cheese*, Cormier represents the political and historical dimensions of a government practice ('The Witness Relocation Program') more emphatically as it was seen around the 'Watergate' era, while in *After the First Death*, he 'examine[s] patriotism as a force of potential evil'.[45] He comments on intimidation practices in both *The Bumblebee Flies Anyway* and *I Am the Cheese*, while he remarks on patriotism and terrorism in *We All Fall Down* and criticises racism in *Tunes for Bears to Dance to*.

Most of Cormier's adolescent novels are populated by realistic characters who convey their own 'repertoire' and experience many aspects of a real world: fear, love, death, power, violence, terrorism, betrayal, sacrifice, innocence, illness, suicide. By making his readers share his heroes' desperate lives, for example Adam's 'horrifying discovery' in *I Am the Cheese*, Cormier 'encourages our acceptance of the ambiguous boredom and glory of normal life'.[46]

However, there are instances of these plausible characters trying to overcome reality through procedures by which they challenge their fictional entity. A good example is Ben Marchand, the general's son in *After the First Death*. Ben is used to writing down his experiences in order to feel better, and his writing serves as 'a story within a story'. Nevertheless, because these stories are interpolated into the main narrative, they not only challenge Ben's fictionality, or the fictionality of the novel as a whole, they also interrupt the coherence of the reading process. In addition to such characters, the literary modes Cormier employs, in many cases, can be seen as a kind of 're-codification', a challenge to, or even a subversion of, reality both 'real' and fictional. The prime subversion of real objects (the wheelchair, the fake car) in *The Bumblebee Flies Anyway*, for example, questions reality as well as fiction, and not only affords readers' insights into ordinary life, but also the opportunity to deal with alternative or distorted aspects of reality. Eventually, such narrative arrangements tend to defamiliarise readers' familiar experiences with literary modes or life. Functioning as 'blanks', in Iser's sense of punctuating textual coherence, they attract the readers' attention and provoke their active embroilment in the reading process.

The whole setting in *Fade* extends the story's realistic potential to question the boundaries between fiction and reality. Here, Cormier uncovers the construction of fictional reality and 'alerts his readers to the unreliability of a notion of reality', directing them to discern the process by which the meaning is constructed.[47] The assumptions made by the readers in the novel (such as Susan, Meredith or Jules) about the intentions underlying Paul's manuscript deconstruct and challenge its fictionality, since they function as fictions about fiction. By exposing the author's and reader's roles, Cormier is thus lending a meta-fictional flavour to the reading procedure, challenging the activity of the real readers, but also the conceptualisation or construction of the 'implied author' and 'implied reader'.[48] Again, the narrative modes employed in this novel bring about 'empty spaces' between the segments of fiction, because each chapter stands as a separate narrative dedicated to one of the novel's character-readers. 'Constituting a field of vision for wandering viewpoint', these 'blanks' force the readers to ideate what is absent, and to join any extant segments together to enable a complete comprehension of the textual or fictional sequence.[49]

In all the examples above, Cormier projects the possibilities of his worlds in a postmodernist way, exposing his fictions as a 'liberated' space for writing and reading activities. Moreover, by using complex and multifocused narratives in his novels, or by defamiliarising usual literary conventions like happy endings, victorious protagonists, and so forth, he transcends usual reading procedures and expectations. As a result, the reading process becomes retroactive to reveal the ways in which the fiction is structured and perceived.[50] His real readers, trying to recognise his 'repertoire' and reshape their own, find themselves close to and detached from the text at one and the same time; they become conscious of the deceptive mechanisms at work in Cormier's fictions and remove themselves from the conventional limits of storylines.

In most of the novels mentioned above, literary allusions also seem to govern Cormier's imaginative worlds. For example: Jerry's key-phrase in *The Chocolate War*, 'Do I dare disturb the universe',[51] is associated with the poem 'The Love Song of J. Alfred Prufrock' (1915) by T. S. Eliot[52]; the song[53] Adam sings in *I Am the Cheese* as well as his father's reference to a 'mystery novel'[54] stand as literary allusions, while the book is connected, albeit indirectly, with *The Catcher in the Rye* (1951) by J. D. Salinger;[55] and his last novel, *The Rag and Bone Shop*, draws its title from the last line of a poem by W. B. Yeats.[56] In all these cases, where a text directly or indirectly reveals its interdependence on other texts,[57] readers form the substance of their response by seeking guidance in the verbal clues the text offers them. Although an intertextual interpolation should not always be regarded as a 'blank' on the syntagmatic axis of reading, which is to say a 'severance of connection with context', it does entail the readers' active involvement. In that case, they must seek significance in the text in order to achieve a 'consistency-building' of the meanings the text transfer. Eventually, all these allusions serve as helpful intertextual references and provide readers with 'an organization of signifiers which ... designate instructions for the production of the signified'.[58] The allusions may allow readers to view the operation of the textual dynamics in their totality.

In Cormier's young adult novels, the 'strategies' employed activate readers' participation intensively, offering them the possibility to organise their comprehension of these texts. In fact, 'strategies' establish the rules that must be common in the communication between text and reader in order for such interplay to be 'successful'.[59] The reader first perceives the 'schematised aspects' − the 'referential context' of the fiction − through the 'background–foreground' relationship, then organises his or her comprehension on the basis of this.

The death of Jerry's mother and the new place in which he lives with his father in *The Chocolate War*, the absence/search for Adam's parents and his relationship with Doctor/Agent Brint in *I Am the Cheese*, the students taken hostage in *After the First Death*, Barney's illness in *The Bumblebee Flies Anyway*, and Henry's family situation in *Tunes for Bears to Dance to*, can all be regarded as Cormier's novels' 'background'. Taking this as a foundation, as 'schematised aspects', readers 'foreground' the actions of the heroes and the present-day incidents of their narrative/fictional lives. This is how readers decode and understand heroes' behaviour and evaluate their reactions and motives, as well as the consequences of their lives: Jerry's reaction, Adam's behaviour, Kate's actions and Miro's practices, Barney's fantasies, Henry's betrayal/compromise. This allows readers access to the world of the text, and permits them to grasp and combine every textual indication they can. Through selecting among the latter, the readers allow their viewpoint to fill in any 'blanks' that have appeared, moving back and forth through the text, using the chosen indications to evoke their original context. In this case, they come across four perspectives: the narrator's voice, the characters' views, the plot process, and their own potential response to textual signs.[60] This brings readers' creative abilities to the fore, as they have to decide on which of the four perspectives to focus each time.[61] However, in addition to selecting these perspectives and in order to comprehend the text, the readers also have to combine and assimilate them piecemeal ultimately to form their own perspective. Readers are interested for the moment in the way a hero operates, and this is the 'theme' of the moment, while the hero's general behaviour forms a behaviour 'horizon' for the hero and understanding for the readers based on the perspective of the narrator, the other characters or the plot. The readers cannot immediately understand Adam's or Barney's reaction to their protectors because, despite being central figures, they do not reproduce dominant norms of thought and behaviour.[62] Their respective behaviours create 'blanks', which the readers cannot easily fill in. Gradually, however, during their 'wandering viewpoint', the readers grasp the different perspectives in the narrative and begin to suspect its polyphony. At this point, readers understand that they have to combine these perspectives if they are to understand how they function and utilise their dynamic. There follow some illustrative examples.

The opening phrase of *The Chocolate War* – 'They murdered him'[63] – shocks readers and gets their immediate attention. However, the description of football that follows replaces the fear of a murder with the intensity of a competitive game played by adolescents. Throughout the novel, readers have to fill in 'blanks' that are foregrounded by numerous 'themes' of a similar ilk and different perspectives (of the heroes: Brother Leon, Obie, Archie, et al., or of the plot), in order to construct the 'horizon' and achieve a 'consistency-building' of their comprehension, so as to form their own perspective. The readers thus become aware that their ability to mould their own perspective is postponed along with the construction of meaning, and that this can go on until the end of the novel. In addition, comments such as: 'Cities fell. Earth opened. Planets tilted. Stars plummeted. And the awful silence',[64] following Jerry's continual refusal to sell chocolate in *The Chocolate War*, form a perspective that can abrogate other perspectives and affect the plot. Functioning as 'blanks', these comments direct readers to experience a 'negation' with regard to the perspective they may determine or adopt.

The first chapter of *I Am the Cheese* depicts a boy riding his bicycle through peaceful, plausible scenery. The 'theme' of this chapter is completely different from that of the next one, in which the contents of a cassette recording a meeting are transcribed. This interchanging of 'themes' will continue throughout the book, using deceptive narratives, until readers manage to understand what is really going on. In this novel, the 'blanks' between narratives function literally as 'points of suspended connectability',[65] since they form completely different perspectives on characters and plot. Even Adam's memory gaps function as textual 'blanks' that postpone the making of meaning and force readers to become detached and involved at the same time.[66] As they experience 'negation' after 'negation', readers progressively realise that they will always miss something and the resulting frustration is ultimately meant to activate them. Just as his heroes appear simultaneously energetic in their effort to comprehend the situations that surround them and passive due to the (power) structures that dominate them, so his readers are both potentially active in the making of meaning and passive in the imposition of textual signs that direct their reading activity. Although the two novels begin differently, their narrative perspectives drive readers to take almost similar stances.

Readers may derive a similar feeling as they read *The Bumblebee Flies Anyway* or *After the First Death*. In the first, along with the protagonist, they are trying to uncover a seemingly terrible secret; in the second, they have to continually wander their viewpoint through first-person and third-person narratives, and through present and past tenses.[67] In every case, Cormier's readers are not entirely free to lean only on what is 'implicit' in the texts; they also need to identify 'explicit' elements and amend their initial expectations by completing the 'blanks' and dealing with the text's 'negations' in order to achieve the same complete contact with it[68] as the novelistic heroes have with their lives.

Thus, during the reading process, Cormier's readers accept the role aspects of an 'implied reader' and experience textuality through the provocative 'repertoire' he employs and the complex 'strategies' he uses. He does not present his adolescent readers with 'a schematic view' of the fictional worlds in which he involves them; rather, the literary work is a vivid and challenging experience for them. Moving beyond the requirements of simple realistic fictions for adolescents and inaugurating more demanding reading procedures, Cormier forces his readers to adopt a 'wandering viewpoint', so as to inform the reading process, to achieve a 'consistency-building' of the meaning and, finally, to fill in any 'blanks' that have appeared and overcome any 'negations' that have emerged. As a consequence, in an effort to grasp all the textual indications, his readers move beyond the conventional limits of the storyline into other dimensions as they strive to assimilate literary modes and, ultimately, to actualise meanings. Forever carrying out his own 'numbers',[69] Cormier plagues his protagonists as well as his readers, impelling them to treat their relationship with his fictional worlds as a reciprocal praxis, as an 'interaction'. Indeed, it is such an interactive relationship that it may offer them multiple interpretations and lived experiences, which could lead them to another view of the literary experience as well as of their own lives.

In conclusion

Studying Cormier's novels for young people through Iser's theory and in the light of literary criticism on them, it was not this essay's intention to interpret Cormier's novels, but rather to reveal the conditions that could call forth their various possible impacts on potential readers. In the course of this essay, the view that Cormier's novels belong to that genre of young adult novels which can lend probability to a theory, has been confirmed. This study has thus confirmed two of Iser's hypotheses in the best possible way: first, that the literary text is richer than any of its individual realisations,[70] and second that good literature transcends familiar conventions and dares to establish another reading regime.[71]

That the main factor that has ensured Cormier's standing as a pioneer in the field of literature for adolescents is chiefly the interactive relationship he seems to establish with his readers, has been also suggested. It is now apparent that this relationship, being the process of readers' activation via his interactive texts, ought to be the yardstick by which his novels are evaluated and appraised, capturing as they do the essence of his 'adolescent poetics'.

Notes

1. Taken from the last interview Robert Cormier gave, along with Melvin Burgess, to Jonathan Douglas in 2000: www.achuka.co.uk/special/cormburg.htm (accessed 9 May 2012).
2. Peter Hollindale, 'The Adolescent Novel of Ideas', *Children's Literature in Education*, 26(1) (March 1995): 83–95.
3. This specific feature connects Cormier directly with an American neorealistic, rather naturalistic, movement in the realm of young adult literature that manifested itself in the 1960s. See also Anne Scott

MacLeod, 'Robert Cormier and the Adolescent Novel', *Children's Literature in Education*, 12(2) (June 1981), 74–81, at 74-5; Sylvia Patterson Iskander, 'Readers, Realism, and Robert Cormier', *Children's Literature*, 15 (1987), 7–18, at 7–8.

4. See Iskander: 7. See also Kimberley Reynolds, *Radical Children's Literature: Future Visions and Aesthetic Transformations in Juvenile Fiction* (New York: Palgrave Macmillan, 2007): 81–2.

5. Aidan Chambers, 'An Interview with Robert Cormier', *Signal*, 30 (1979), 119-32 (at 125-26, 132). See also Jonathan Douglas, 'Robert Cormier Meets Melvin Burgess': www.achuka.co.uk/special/cormburg2.htm [accessed 7 January 2011].

6. Wolfgang Iser, *The Act of Reading: A Theory of Aesthetic Response* (Baltimore: Johns Hopkins University Press, 1978): 10.

7. Ibid.: 20.

8. Ibid.: 36.

9. Ibid.: 38.

10. Ibid.: 125.

11. Ibid.: 69.

12. Ibid.: 80–1.

13. Ibid.: 66.

14. Ibid.: 86.

15. Ibid.: 87.

16. Ibid.: 86.

17. Ibid.: 92.

18. Ibid.: 93.

19. Ibid.: 96–9.

20. Ibid.: 108–18.

21. Ibid.: 198.

22. Ibid.: 225–6.

23. Ibid.: 167–8.

24. Aidan Chambers, 'The Reader in the Book' [1977], in Peter Hunt (ed.), *Children's Literature: The Development of Criticism* (London: Routledge, 1990): 91–114, at 93–4) (first published in *Signal*, 23 (1977), 64–87).

25. Iser (1978): 34.

26. Robert Cormier, *The Chocolate War*, 1974 (New York: Alfred A. Knopf, 2004): 123.

27. Iskander: 11.

28. Brian McHale, *Postmodernist Fiction*, 4th edn (London: Routledge, 1993): 84.

29. Iskander: 12.

30. Ibid.: 7.

31. Roberta Seelinger Trites, *Disturbing the Universe: Power and Repression in Adolescent Literature* (Iowa: Iowa University Press, 2000): 9.

32. Iskander: 10.

33. Wolfgang Iser, *The Implied Reader: Patterns of Communication in Prose Fiction from Bunyan to Beckett* (Baltimore: Johns Hopkins University Press, 1974): 30.

34. Ibid.: 30.
35. Jerry may be an exception, since he has his 'second chance' in *Beyond the Chocolate War* (New York: Dell Laurel-Leaf, 1985), the sequel to *The Chocolate War*.
36. Iskander: 17.
37. Iser (1978): 36–8.
38. Ibid.: 67.
39. Ibid.: 69.
40. Ibid.: 70, 125.
41. Ibid.: 69.
42. Ibid.: 72.
43. Ibid.: 82.
44. See: MacLeod 75; Robyn McCallum, *Ideologies of Identity in Adolescent Fiction: The Dialogic Construction of Subjectivity* (New York/London: Garland Publishing, Inc., 1999): 44–5.
45. Chambers (1979): 128–9.
46. Perry Nodelman, 'Robert Cormier Does a Number', *Children's Literature in Education*, 14(2) (June 1983): 94–103, at 103.
47. Patricia Head, 'Robert Cormier and the Postmodernist Possibilities of Young Adult Fiction', *Children's Literature Association Quarterly*, 21(1) (Spring 1996): 28–33: at 30).
48. Ibid.: 31.
49. Iser (1978): 197.
50. Head: 30–1.
51. *The Chocolate War*: 123.
52. T. S. Eliot 'The Love Song of J. Alfred Prufrock', [1915] *Prufrock and Other Observations* (London: The Egoist Ltd, 1917).
53. The song, 'The Farmer in the Dell', retains the overtones and freshness of an oral nursery rhyme, which would normally offer someone familiar and enjoyable territory. See P. F. Anderson, 'The Mother Goose Pages', *The Mother Goose Pages*, 21 (2001): www-personal.umich.edu/~pfa/dreamhouse/nursery/rhymes/dell.html (accessed 9 May 2012).
54. Robert Cormier, *I Am the Cheese* [1977] (New York: Alfred A. Knopf, 2007): 38.
55. In Salinger's book, the hero, Holden Caulfield, says he would like to be able to phone the author of a book he's read whenever he feels like it. By including his telephone number in *I Am the Cheese* to permit more direct contact with his readers, Cormier seems to have responded to Holden's wish. See ACHUKA, 'Robert Cormier London, July 2000': www.achuka.co.uk/special/cormier01.htm (accessed 9 May 2012). On Cormier's relationship with Salinger, see also Reynolds: 70.
56. W. B. Yeats, 'The Circus Animals' Desertion' published in *Last Poems and Two Plays* (Dublin: Cuala Press, 1939).
57. J. A. Cuddon, *The Penguin Dictionary of Literary Terms and Literary Theory*, 3rd edn (London: Penguin Books, 1992): 454.
58. Iser (1978): 65.

59. Ibid.: 86, 87.
60. Ibid.: 96, 100.
61. Ibid.: 103, 111–12.
62. Ibid.: 100.
63. *The Chocolate War*. 3.
64. Ibid.: 112.
65. Iser (1978): 198.
66. Nodelman: 95.
67. Frank Myszor, 'The See-Saw and the Bridge in Robert Cormier's *After the First Death*', *Children's Literature*, 16 (1988): 77–90.
68. Iser (1978): 168–9, 230.
69. Cormier uses the term 'numbers', for the practical jokes his characters play in *I Am the Cheese*: 52–8.
70. Iser (1978): 62–8.
71. Ibid.: 219–25.

Bibliography of Robert Cormier's Works and Further Reading

This selected bibliography focuses primarily on Cormier's young adult novels and literary analysis of those works. Annotations have been added to some entries where these may be helpful. For a listing of Cormier's shorter works (primarily for adults), including short stories and nonfiction, and for book reviews, awards and film adaptations (for film adaptations also see note 40 to the Introduction of this volume), see Patty Campbell, *Robert Cormier: Daring to Disturb the Universe* (New York: Delacorte, 2006): 249–81.

Books by Robert Cormier

Listed chronologically. Unless noted in brackets all are novels for young adults.

Now and At the Hour (1960) (adult).
A Little Raw on Monday Mornings (1963) (adult).
Take Me Where the Good Times Are (1965) (adult).
The Chocolate War (1974).
I Am the Cheese (1977).
After the First Death (1979).
Eight Plus One (1980) A collection of short stories previously published in magazines for adults, several featuring young characters. The stories are prefaced by introductions by Cormier.
The Bumblebee Flies Anyway (1983).
Beyond the Chocolate War (1985).
Fade (1988).
Other Bells for Us to Ring (1990), published as *Darcy* (1991) in the UK.
We All Fall Down (1991).
I Have Words to Spend: Reflections of a Small-Town Editor (1991) Essays for adult readers originally published as newspaper columns, edited and with a Preface by Cormier's wife, Constance Senay Cormier.
Tunes for Bears to Dance to (1992).
In the Middle of the Night (1995).
Tenderness (1997).
Heroes (1998).
Frenchtown Summer (1999) An autobiographically influenced verse narrative; the 2000 Listening Library audiobook edition includes an interview with Cormier.
The Rag and Bone Shop (2001).

Archives

Robert Cormier Collection, University Archives and Special Collections, Amelia V. Gallucci-Cirio Library, Fitchburg State College, Fitchburg, Massachusetts, USA.

Selected essays and speeches by, and interviews with, Robert Cormier

Judith Bugniazet, 'A Telephone Interview with Robert Cormier', *The ALAN Review*, 12:2 (Winter 1985): 14-18.

Aidan Chambers, 'An Interview with Robert Cormier', *Signal*, 30 (1979): 119–32.

Robert Cormier, 'The Pleasure and Perils of Writing Young Adult Novels', in Peter Kennerley (ed.), *Teenage Reading* (London: Ward Lock Educational, 1979): 55–61.

Robert Cormier, 'Forever Pedaling on the Road to Realism', in Betsy Hearne and Marilyn Kaye (eds) *Celebrating Children's Books: Essays on Children's Literature in Honor of Zena Sutherland* (New York: Lothrop, Lee & Shepard, 1981): 45–53. Cormier discusses the realism of his work, mentioning *The Chocolate War*, *I Am the Cheese* and *After the First Death*.

Robert Cormier, with questions from Bruce Clements, 'A Rattlin' Good Story', in Barbara Harrison and Gregory Maguire (eds.) *Innocence & Experience: Essays & Conversations on Children's Literature* (New York: Lothrop, Lee and Shepard, 1987): 234–42.

Robert Cormier, 'Creating *Fade*', *The Horn Book Magazine*, (March–April 1989): 166–73.

Robert Cormier, 'Robert Cormier', in Donald R. Gallo (ed. and compiler) Speaking for Ourselves: Autobiographical Sketches by Notable Authors of Books for Young Adults (Urbana, IL: National Council of Teachers of English, 1990): 57–8.

Robert Cormier, 'A Book is not a House: The Human Side of Censorship', in Donald R. Gallo (ed.), *Authors' Insights: Turning Teenagers into Readers and Writers* (Portsmouth, NH: Boynton/Cook-Heinemann, 1992): 65–74. Cormier discusses censorship.

Robert Cormier, 'Probing the Dark Cellars of a Young Adult Writer's Heart', Frances Clarke Sayers Lecture, 17 May 1998, University of California, Los Angeles: UCLA Department of Library and Information Science, 1999. Cormier discusses elements in his life that may have influenced the darkness of his work.

Robert Cormier, 'A Character by Any Other Name…', *English Journal*, 90(3) (2001): 31–2. Cormier discusses naming his characters, including Eugene in *Frenchtown Summer*.

Robert Cormier, 'Looking Back While Going Forward', in Alethea Helbig and Agnes Perkins (eds), *The Phoenix Award of the Children's Literature*

Association, 1995–1999 (Lanham, MD: Scarecrow Press, 2001): 93–105. Speech in 1997 accepting the Phoenix Award for *I am the Cheese*. Includes, slightly edited, the Introduction Cormier wrote for the Knopf twentieth-anniversary edition of the novel.

Geraldine DeLuca and Roni Natov, 'An Interview with Robert Cormier', *Lion and the Unicorn* 2:2 (1978): 109–35. Useful early interview with Cormier.

Interview with Robert Cormier, London, 11 July, 2000, Part One: www. achuka.co.uk/special/cormier01.htm (accessed 9 May 2012). Achuka interview with Cormier (continued in Part Two) before his evening discussion with Melvin Burgess (see 'Robert Cormier Meets Melvin Burgess' below).

Interview with Robert Cormier, London, 11 July, 2000, Part Two: www. achuka.co.uk/special/cormier02.htm (accessed 9 May 2012).

Paul Janeczko, 'In their own words: An Interview with Robert Cormier', *English Journal* 66.6 (1977): 10–11.

Mitzi Myers, '"No Safe Place to Run To": An Interview with Robert Cormier', *The Lion and the Unicorn* 24:3 (2000): 445–64. A useful, widely quoted interview with Cormier.

'Robert Cormier' Internet Public Library (1996): www.ipl.org/div/askauthor/Cormier.html (accessed 10 May 2012). Aimed at young readers but contains some useful interview responses by Cormier.

'Robert Cormier Meets Melvin Burgess: Part 1', chaired by Jonathan Douglas, London, 11 July 2000: www.achuka.co.uk/special/cormburg. htm (accessed 10 May 2012). Interview with Robert Cormier and British young adult author Melvin Burgess, conducted four months before Cormier's death. Continued in Part 2.

'Robert Cormier Meets Melvin Burgess: Part 2', chaired by Jonathan Douglas, London, 11 July 2000: www.achuka.co.uk/special/cormburg2. htm (accessed 10 May 2012).

See also: Sieruta in 'General Criticism' below.

General criticism on Cormier's work

Book-length works

Wendy Hart Beckman, *Robert Cormier: Banned, Challenged, and Censored* (Berkeley Heights, NJ: Enslow, 2008). Discusses Cormier in relation to censorship. Includes chapters on *The Chocolate War*, *I Am the Cheese*, *After the First Death*. Primarily useful for a pre-university readership.

Patricia J. Campbell, *Presenting Robert Cormier*, updated edition (Boston: G. K. Hall, 1989). Extended version of original book on Cormier published in 1985. Covers his work up to and including *Fade*. Contains a chapter on Cormier's adult novels and short stories, photographs, chronology and family tree of the characters in *Fade* that are not included in her later *Robert Cormier: Daring to Disturb the Universe*.

Patty Campbell, *Robert Cormier: Daring to Disturb the Universe* (New York: Delacorte, 2006). Biographical study of Cormier discussing all his young adult fiction. It includes a bibliography of Cormier's works, awards, book reviews, and film versions of his novels, and material which Campbell obtained directly from Cormier. It adds new material to and revises Campbell's earlier *Presenting Robert Cormier*.

Kathy Neal Headley, 'Duel at High Noon: A Replay of Cormier's Works', *The ALAN Review* 21:2 (Winter 1994): 1–5. Discusses cinematic influences, hope and morality in Cormier's young adult fiction up to *Fade*.

Margaret O. Hyde, *Robert Cormier* (Philadelphia: Chelsea House, 2005). Discusses Cormier and his work. For a pre-university readership.

Jennifer Keeley, *Understanding I Am the Cheese* (San Diego, CA: Lucent, 2001). Primarily for a pre-university readership but contains useful material.

Robert LeBlanc, *Postmodernist Elements in the Work of Robert Cormier* (Saarbrücken, Germany: VDM Verlag, 2009). Based on MA thesis from Fitchburg State College, Fitchburg, MA, 2005.

Virginia R. Monseau, *Teaching the Selected Works of Robert Cormier* (Portsmouth, NH: Heinemann, 2007). Guide to teaching Cormier to High School students. Chapters on *After the First Death, Heroes, Tunes for Bears to Dance to, The Rag and Bone Shop, Frenchtown Summer*.

Fu-Yuan Shen, *Narrative Strategies in Robert Cormier's Young Adult Novels*, PhD dissertation, Ohio State University, 2006. Available at http://etd.ohiolink.edu/view.cgi?acc_num=osu1135277215 (accessed 10 May 2012). Uses narrative theory to examine connections between Cormier's narrative methods and controversial themes. Discusses all his young adult novels but does not discuss *Frenchtown Summer*.

Sharon A. Stringer, 'The Psychological Changes of Adolescence: A Test of Character', *The ALAN Review* 22:1 (Fall 1994): 27–9. Uses psychological concepts to discuss Cormier's work. Includes brief discussion of *The Chocolate War, I Am the Cheese, After the First Death, The Bumblebee Flies Anyway*.

Sarah L. Thomson, *Robert Cormier* (New York: Rosen Central, 2003). Discusses Cormier and his work. For a pre-university readership.

Other general criticism

Patty Campbell, 'A Loving Farewell to Robert Cormier', *Horn Book Magazine*, 77(2) (March–April 2001): 245–8. Reprinted in Patty Campbell, *Campbell's Scoop: Reflections on Young Adult Literature* (Lanham, MD: Scarecrow, 2010): 85–8. Reflections on the death of Robert Cormier.

Laurie Collier and Joyce Nakamura, *Major Authors and Illustrators for Children and Young Adults*. London: Gale, 1993. Entry on Cormier outlining his life and work up to 1991.

Stefan R. Dziemianowicz, 'Robert Cormier', in R. Baird Shuman (ed.) *Great American Writers: Twentieth Century* (New York: Marshall Cavendish, 2002): 293–310.

W. Geiger Ellis, 'Cormier and the Pessimistic View', *The ALAN Review*, 12(2) (Winter 1985): 10–12, 52–3.

Herbert N. Foerstel, *Banned in the USA: A Reference Guide to Book Censorship in Schools and Public Libraries*, revised and expanded edition (Westport, CT: Greenwood, 2002). Includes sections discussing banning of *I Am the Cheese*, *The Chocolate War* and *We All Fall Down* and on Cormier's views on censorship challenges to his books.

Donald R. Gallo, 'Reality and Responsibility: The Continuing Controversy Over Robert Cormier's Books for Young Adults', in Dorothy M. Broderick (ed.) *The VOYA Reader* (Metuchen, NJ: Scarecrow, 1990): 153–60. [First published in *Voice of Youth Advocates* (December 1984): 245ff]. Discusses controversy over *The Chocolate War*, *After the First Death* and *I Am the Cheese*.

Lyn Gardner, 'Robert Cormier', *The Guardian,* 6 November 2000: www. guardian.co.uk/news/2000/nov/06/guardianobituaries.books/print (accessed 10 May 2012). Obituary of Cormier.

Patricia Head, 'Robert Cormier and the Postmodernist Possibilities of Young Adult Fiction', *Children's Literature Association Quarterly*, 21(1) (1996): 28–33.

Alethea Helbig and Agnes Perkins, *The Phoenix Award of the Children's Literature Association, 1995–1999* (Lanham, MD: Scarecrow Press, 2001): 89–144. Contains five essays on Cormier's work, a speech and essay by Cormier, a biographical sketch and list of his books.

Sarah K. Herz and Donald R. Gallo, *From Hinton to Hamlet: Building Bridges Between Young Adult Literature and the Classics,* 2nd edition (Wesport, CT: Greenwood, 2005). Contains brief discussions linking themes of *Tunes for Bears to Dance to* with *The Adventures of Huckleberry Finn*, of *The Chocolate War* to *Hamlet* and *We All Fall Down* to *Julius Caesar*.

Peter Hollindale, 'The Adolescent Novel of Ideas' *Children's Literature in Education*, 26(1) (1995): 83–95. Reprinted in Sheila Egoff et al (eds), *Only Connect: Readings on Children's Literature*, 3rd ed. (Toronto: Oxford University Press, 1996): 315–26. Discusses *The Chocolate War* (briefly), *I Am the Cheese* and *After the First Death*.

Peter Hunt, 'Robert Cormier (1925–)', *Children's Literature* (Oxford; Blackwell, 2001): 51–3.

Sylvia Patterson Iskander, 'Robert Cormier', in *Concise Dictionary of American Literary Biography: Broadening Views, 1968–1988* (Farmington Hills, MI: Gale Group, 1989): 34–51.

Sylvia Patterson Iskander, 'Readers, Realism, and Robert Cormier', *Children's Literature*, 15 (1987): 7–18. Discusses *The Chocolate War*, *I Am the Cheese*, *After the First Death*, *The Bumblebee Flies Anyway* and *Beyond the Chocolate War*.

Rebecca Lukens, 'From Salinger to Cormier: Disillusionment to Despair in Thirty Years', in Joseph O'Beirne Milner and Lucy Floyd Morcock Milner (eds), *Webs and Wardrobes: Humanist and Religious World Views in Children's Literature* (Lanham, MD: University Press of America, 1987):

7–13. Compares J. D. Salinger's *Catcher in the Rye* as 'realistic yet hopeful' with Cormier's *The Chocolate War, I Am the Cheese* and *After the First Death* in which 'Hope vanishes. Despair wins'.

Anne Scott MacLeod, 'Ice Axes: Robert Cormier and the Adolescent Novel', in Anne Scott MacLeod *American Childhood: Essays on Children's Literature of the Nineteenth and Twentieth Centuries* (Athens, GA: University of Georgia Press, 1994): 189–97. [Essay originally published as 'Robert Cormier and the Adolescent Novel' in *Children's Literature in Education*, 12.2 (Summer 1981): 74–81.] Discusses *The Chocolate War, I Am the Cheese* and *After the First Death* as political novels.

Robyn McCallum, *Ideologies of Identity in Adolescent Fiction: The Dialogic Construction of Subjectivity* (New York: Garland, 1999). Contains some discussion of *The Chocolate War, I am the Cheese* and *Fade*.

Virginia R. Monseau, 'Studying Cormier's Protagonists: Achieving Power through Young Adult Literature', *The ALAN Review* 22:1 (Fall 1994): 31–3: http://scholar.lib.vt.edu/ejournals/ALAN/fall94/Monseau.html (accessed 10 May 2012). Discusses *The Chocolate War, I Am the Cheese, After the First Death*.

Ciara Ní Bhroin, 'Cynical or Compassionate? The Young Adult Novels of Robert Cormier', *Journal of Children's Literature Studies*, 1(2) (July 2004): 23–32.

Alleen Pace Nilsen and Don L. F. Nilsen, 'Names to Establish Tone and Mode: Robert Cormier and Francesca Lia Block', in Alleen Pace Nilsen and Don L. F. Nilsen, *Names and Naming in Young Adult Literature* (Lanham, Maryland: The Scarecrow Press, 2007): 23–46. Examines names in *The Chocolate War, I Am the Cheese, After the First Death* and *Heroes*.

Mike Peters, '*The Chocolate War* and After: The Novels of Robert Cormier', *The School Librarian* (August 1992): 85–7.

David Rees, 'The Sadness of Compromise: Robert Cormier and Jill Chaney', in David Rees, *The Marble in the Water: Essays on Contemporary Writers of Fiction for Children and Young Adults* (Boston: Horn Book, 1980): 155–72. Discusses *The Chocolate War, I Am the Cheese,* and *After the First Death*.

Tony Schwartz, 'Teen-Agers' Laureate', *Newsweek* (16 July 1979): 87–8, 92.

Peter D. Sieruta, 'Cormier, Robert', in Anita Silvey (ed.) *Children's Books and Their Creators* (Boston, MA: Houghton Mifflin, 1996): 170–2. Overview of Cormier and his work. Includes an essay by Cormier.

John S. Simmons, 'You Dared, Bob: Thank God You Dared', *ALAN Review* (Winter 2001): 8: http://scholar.lib.vt.edu/ejournals/ALAN/v28n2/simmons.html (accessed 10 May 2012).

Joe Stines, 'Robert Cormier', in Glenn E. Estes (ed.), *American Writers for Children since 1960: Fiction, Dictionary of Literary Biography* vol. 52 (Detroit, MI: Gale, 1986): 107–14. Discusses Cormier's work up to and including *Beyond the Chocolate War*. Includes a draft page from *Beyond the Chocolate War*.

C. Anita Tarr, 'The Absence of Moral Agency in Robert Cormier's *The Chocolate War*', *Children's Literature* 30 (2002): 96–124. Focuses primarily on *The Chocolate War*, but also argues that Cormier's fiction generally depicts characters who lack moral agency and objectify women.

Susan Thompson, 'Images of Adolescence: Part II', *Signal* 35 (May 1981): 108–25. Includes discussion of Cormier.

Nancy Veglahn, 'The Bland Face of Evil in the Novels of Robert Cormier', *The Lion and the Unicorn*, 12(1) (1988): 12–18. Examines the evil of older male authority figures against protagonists in *The Chocolate War, Beyond the Chocolate War, I Am The Cheese, After the First Death* and *The Bumblebee Flies Anyway*.

Martha Westwater, *Giant Despair Meets Hopeful: Kristevan Readings in Adolescent Fiction* (Edmonton, Alberta: University of Alberta Press, 2000). The chapter 'Robert Cormier and Monumental Time' (111–33) discusses *The Chocolate War, Beyond the Chocolate War, I am the Cheese, The Bumblebee Flies Anyway* and *Fade* in relation to Julia Kristeva's concept of monumental time and the need for forgiveness.

Deanna Zitterkopf, 'Robert Cormier', *Children's Literature Association Quarterly*, 11(1) (1986): 42–3. General description of Cormier's first five young adult novels.

Criticism of individual texts

The Chocolate War and Beyond the Chocolate War

Thomas A. Atwood and Wade M. Lee, 'The Price of Deviance: Schoolhouse Gothic in Prep School Literature', *Children's Literature* 35 (2007): 102–26. Includes analysis of *The Chocolate War* as Schoolhouse Gothic fiction.

Norma Bagnell, 'Realism: How Realistic Is It? A Look at *The Chocolate War*', *Top of the News* 36 (Winter, 1980): 214–17.

Dedria Bryfonsk (ed.), *Peer Pressure in Robert Cormier's the Chocolate War* (Farmington Hills, MI: Greenhaven Press, 2009).

Kay Parks Bushman and John H. Bushman, 'Dealing with the Abuse of Power in *1984* and *The Chocolate War*', in Joan F. Kaywell, *Adolescent Literature as a Complement to the Classics* (Norwood, MA: Christopher-Gordon, 1993): 215–22. Discusses teaching *1984* and *The Chocolate War* to high school students.

Mike Cadden, 'The Irony of Narration in the Young Adult Novel', *Children's Literature Association Quarterly*, 25(3) (2000): 146–54. Includes discussion of *The Chocolate War*.

Patty Campbell, *Robert Cormier: Daring to Disturb the Universe* (New York: Delacorte, 2006). Includes chapters on *The Chocolate War*, on controversy over *The Chocolate War* and on *Beyond The Chocolate War*.

Betty Carter and Karen Harris, 'Realism in Adolescent Fiction: In Defense of *The Chocolate War*', *Top of the News* 36 (Winter 1980): 283–5.

Bruce Clements, 'A Second Look: *The Chocolate War*', *Horn Book Magazine* 55 (April 1979): 217–18. Draws brief comparisons with Shakespeare's characters.

Karen Coats, 'Abjection and Adolescent Fiction', *JPCS: Journal for the Psychoanalysis of Culture & Society* 5(2) (Fall 2000): 290–300. Psychoanalytical reading of *The Chocolate War*.

Fiona Hartley-Kroeger, 'Silent Speech: Narration, Gender and Intersubjectivity in Two Young Adult Novels', *Children's Literature in Education* 42(4) (Dec 2011): 276–88. Examines male and female subjectivity in *The Chocolate War* by Robert Cormier and *The House on Mango Street* by Sandra Cisneros.

Betsy Hearne, 'Whammo, You Lose', *Booklist* 1 July 1974: 1199. Early negative review of *The Chocolate War*.

Ted Hipple and Jennifer L. Claiborne, 'The Best Young Adult Novels of All Time, or *The Chocolate War* One More Time', *The English Journal*, 94(3) (January 2005): 99–102. Discusses polls of best young adult literature.

Yoshida Junko, 'The Quest for Masculinity in *The Chocolate War*: Changing Conceptions of Masculinity in the 1970s', *Children's Literature* 26 (1998): 105–22. Considers masculinity in *The Chocolate War* suggesting that it is 'a powerful indictment of conventional manhood'.

Kara Keeling, '"The Misfortune of a Man Like Ourselves": Robert Cormier's *The Chocolate War* as Aristotelian Tragedy', *ALAN Review* 26(2) (Winter 1999): 9–12. Reads *The Chocolate War* as tragedy rather than realism.

Murray Knowles and Kirsten Malmkjær, *Language and Control in Children's Literature* (London: Routledge, 1996): 14–50. Analyses language in relation to violence and sex in *The Chocolate War*.

Bettina Kümmerling-Meibauer, 'The Status of Sequels in Children's Literature: *The Long Secret* and *Beyond the Chocolate War*', in Sandra L. Beckett (ed.) *Reflections of Change: Children's Literature Since 1945* (Westport, CT: Greenwood, 1997): 65–73.

Lourdes Lopez-Ropero, '"You are a Flaw in the Pattern": Difference, Autonomy and Bullying in YA Fiction', *Children's Literature in Education* 43(2) (2012): 145–57. Includes discussion of *The Chocolate War* as a precursor of a new post-Columbine subgenre of young adult fiction that focuses on bullying.

Anne Lundin, 'A Stranger in a World Unmade: Landscape in Robert Cormier's Chocolate War Novels', in Alethea Helbig and Agnes Perkins (ed.), *The Phoenix Award of the Children's Literature Association, 1995–1999* (Lanham, MD: Scarecrow Press, 2001): 127–31.

Robbie March-Penny, 'From Hardback to Paperback: *The Chocolate War*, by Robert Cormier', *Children's Literature in Education* 9(2) (Summer 1978): 78–84. Discusses *The Chocolate War* when it had recently been issued in paperback, promoting it for use in high school classes.

Jen Menzel, 'Intimidation in Cormier's *Tunes for Bears to Dance To*, *We All Fall Down*, and *The Chocolate War*', *The ALAN Review*, 31(1) (Fall 2003): 21–3: http://scholar.lib.vt.edu/ejournals/ALAN/v31n1/menzel.html (accessed 10 May 2012).

Perry Nodelman, 'Robert Cormier's *The Chocolate War*: Paranoia and Paradox', in Dennis Butts (ed.), *Stories and Society: Children's Literature in its Social Context*, (Basingstoke: Macmillan, 1992): 22–36.

Zibby Oneal, '"They tell you to do your own thing, but they don't mean it": Censorship and *The Chocolate War*', in Nicholas J. Karolides, Lee Burress, and John M. Kean (eds), *Censored Books: Critical Viewpoints* (Lanham, MD: Scarecrow, 1993): 179–84.

Elizabeth Ann Poe, 'Alienation from Society in *The Scarlet Letter* and *The Chocolate War*', in Joan F. Kaywell (ed.), *Adolescent Literature as a Complement to the Classics* (Norwood, MA: Christopher-Gordon, 1993): 185–94. Discusses teaching *The Scarlet Letter* and *The Chocolate War* to high school students.

Barbara G. Samuels, 'The Beast Within: Using and Abusing Power in *Lord of the Flies*, *The Chocolate War*, and Other Readings', in Joan F. Kaywell (ed.), *Adolescent Literature as a Complement to the Classics* (Norwood, MA: Christopher-Gordon, 1993): 195–214. Discusses teaching *Lord of the Flies* and *The Chocolate War* to high school students.

Jan Susina, '*The Chocolate War* and "The Sweet Science"', *Children's Literature in Education* 22(3) (Sept. 1991): 169–77. Discusses boxing (and football) in *The Chocolate War*.

C. Anita Tarr, 'The Absence of Moral Agency in Robert Cormier's *The Chocolate War*', *Children's Literature* 30 (2002): 96–124. Feminist reading which argues that the novel is misogynistic and that its characters lack moral agency.

Roberta Seelinger Trites, *Disturbing the Universe: Power and Repression in Adolescent Literature* (Iowa: Iowa University Press, 2000). Discusses *The Chocolate War* and very briefly *I Am the Cheese*. A Foucauldian approach.

See also in 'General Criticism' above: Beckman; Campbell, *Presenting Robert Cormier*; Foerstel; Gallo; Headley; Herz and Gallo; Hollindale (brief discussion); Iskander, 'Readers'; Lukens; MacLeod; McCallum; Monseau, 'Studying'; Nilsen and Nilsen; Rees; Shen; Stines; Stringer; Veglahn; Westwater.

I Am the Cheese

Phyllis Bixler, 'I Am the Cheese and Reader-Response Criticism in the Adolescent Literature Classroom', *Children's Literature Association Quarterly*, 10(1) (Spring 1985): 13–16. Reader–response approach to *I Am the Cheese* describing an assignment inspired by Perry Nodelman's article 'Robert Cormier Does a Number' in which students recorded responses to a first and second reading of the novel.

Kristine M. Bjerk, 'Journey to Understanding: Defending *I Am the Cheese*', in Nicholas J. Karolides (ed. and Introduction), *Censored Books, II: Critical Viewpoints, 1985–2000*, Foreword by Nat Hentoff (Lanham, MD: Scarecrow, 2002): 243–9. Provides a rationale defending *I Am the Cheese* against censorship challenges.

Patty Campbell, *Robert Cormier: Daring to Disturb the Universe* (New York: Delacorte, 2006). Includes a chapter on *I Am the Cheese*.

Robert Cormier, 'Looking Back While Going Forward', in Alethea Helbig and Agnes Perkins (eds), *The Phoenix Award of the Children's Literature Association, 1995–1999*, (Lanham, MD: Scarecrow Press, 2001): 93–105. Speech in 1997 accepting the Phoenix Award for *I am the Cheese*. Includes, slightly edited, the Introduction Cormier wrote for the Knopf twentieth-anniversary edition of the novel.

Lisa Rowe Fraustino, 'The Age of Cheese: Readers Respond to Cormier', in Alethea Helbig and Agnes Perkins (eds), *The Phoenix Award of the Children's Literature Association, 1995–1999* (Lanham, MD: Scarecrow Press, 2001): 111–17.

Jennifer Keeley, *Understanding I Am the Cheese* (San Diego, CA: Lucent, 2001).

ReLeah Lent and Gloria Pipkin, 'We Keep Pedaling', *ALAN Review* (Winter 2001): 9–11. Memories of the Panama City, Florida 1980s censorship case against *I Am the Cheese* by the teachers who sought to teach Cormier's novel. Also mentions *The Chocolate War*.

Maia Pank Mertz, 'Enhancing Literary Understandings through Young Adult Fiction', *Publishing Research Quarterly*, 8(1) (Spring 1992): 23–33. Discusses the teaching of style and structure through *I Am the Cheese* and Paul Zindel's *The Pigman*.

Perry Nodelman, 'Robert Cormier Does a Number', *Children's Literature in Education*, 14(2) (1983): 94–103. Recreates a first reading of the novel and explores the puzzles and tricks Cormier plays on readers.

See also in 'General Criticism' above: Beckman; Campbell, *Presenting Robert Cormier*; Foerstel; Gallo; Headley; Hollindale; Iskander, 'Readers'; Lukens; MacLeod; McCallum; Monseau, 'Studying'; Nilsen and Nilsen; Rees; Shen; Stines; Stringer; Veglahn; Westwater.

After the First Death

Amelia M. Bell, 'Adolescent Initiation in Cormier's *After the First Death*', *ALAN Review* (Winter 1985): 19, 37–8.

Patty Campbell, *Robert Cormier: Daring to Disturb the Universe* (New York: Delacorte, 2006). Includes a chapter on *After the First Death*.

Geraldine De Luca, 'Taking True Risks: Controversial Issues in New Young Adult Novels', *The Lion and the Unicorn* 3(2) (Winter 1979–80): 125–48. Includes discussion of *After the First Death*.

Alethea Helbig, 'Peace, Justice, and Liberation Theology in *After the First Death*', in Alethea Helbig and Agnes Perkins (eds), *The Phoenix Award of the Children's Literature Association, 1995–1999*, (Lanham, MD: Scarecrow Press, 2001): 139–44.

Millicent Lenz, 'A Romantic Ironist's Vision of Evil: Robert Cormier's *After the First Death*', in Priscilla A. Ord (ed.), *Proceedings of the Eighth Annual Conference of the Children's Literature Association, University of Minnesota, March, 1981*, (Boston: Children's Literature Assoc, 1982): 50–6.

Gregory Maguire, 'Belling the Cat: Heroism and the Little Hero', *The Lion and the Unicorn* 13(1) (June 1989): 102–19. Discussion of the heroism of the young in fiction including *After the First Death*.

Virginia R. Monseau, 'Cormier's Heroines: Strength Overlooked', *The ALAN Review* 19:1 (1991): 40–1, 43. Discusses female characters in *The Bumblebee Flies Anyway* and *After the First Death*.

Virginia R. Monseau, *Responding to Young Adult Literature* (Portsmouth, NH: Boynton/Cook Heinemann, 1996). Some discussion of the novel from a High School teaching perspective.

Frank Myszor, 'The See-Saw and the Bridge in Robert Cormier's *After the First Death*', *Children's Literature* 16 (1988): 77–90. Examines, and includes a diagrammatic chart of, the novel's narrative structure.

Judith Plotz, 'The Disappearance of Childhood: Parent-Child Role Reversals in *After the First Death* and *A Solitary Blue*', *Children's Literature in Education* 19(2) [69] (1988): 67–9. Discusses the 'assault on childhood by adults' in *After the First Death* and Cynthia Voight's *A Solitary Blue*.

See also in 'General Criticism' above: Beckman; Campbell, *Presenting Robert Cormier*; Gallo; Headley; Hollindale; Iskander, 'Readers'; Lukens; MacLeod; Monseau, 'Studying'; Monseau, *Teaching*; Nilsen and Nilsen; Rees; Shen; Stines; Stringer; Tarr (brief discussion); Veglahn.

The Bumblebee Flies Anyway

Patty Campbell, *Robert Cormier: Daring to Disturb the Universe* (New York: Delacorte, 2006). Includes a chapter on *The Bumblebee Flies Anyway*.

Linnea Hendrickson, 'Truth, Fiction, and the Impossible in Robert Cormier's *The Bumblebee Flies Anyway* and *Fade*', in Alethea Helbig and Agnes Perkins (eds), *The Phoenix Award of the Children's Literature Association, 1995–-1999* (Lanham, MD: Scarecrow Press, 2001): 119–25.

Virginia R. Monseau, 'Cormier's Heroines: Strength Overlooked', *The ALAN Review* 19(1) (1991): 40–41, 43. Discusses female characters in *The Bumblebee Flies Anyway* and *After the First Death*.

See also in 'General Criticism' above: Campbell, *Presenting Robert Cormier*; Headley; Iskander, 'Readers'; Shen; Stines; Stringer; Veglahn; Westwater.

Fade

Patty Campbell, *Robert Cormier: Daring to Disturb the Universe* (New York: Delacorte, 2006). Includes a chapter on *Fade*.

Robert Cormier, 'Creating *Fade*', *The Horn Book Magazine*, (March–April 1989): 166–73.

Patricia Head, 'Robert Cormier and the Postmodernist Possibilities of Young Adult Fiction', *Children's Literature Association Quarterly*, 21(1) (1996): 28–33.

Linnea Hendrickson, 'Truth, Fiction, and the Impossible in Robert Cormier's *The Bumblebee Flies Anyway* and *Fade*', in Alethea Helbig and Agnes Perkins (eds), *The Phoenix Award of the Children's Literature Association, 1995–1999* (Lanham, MD: Scarecrow Press, 2001): 119–25.

Maria Nikolajeva, *Children's Literature Comes of Age: Toward a New Aesthetic* (New York: Garland, 1996). A few pages on metafiction in *Fade*: 199–201.

Susan Louise Stewart, 'In the Ellison Tradition: In/Visible Bodies of Adolescent and YA Fiction', *Children's Literature in Education* 40(3) (Sept. 2009): 180–96. Discusses invisibility and whiteness in *Fade*, Sapphire's *Push* and Virginia Hamilton's *The Planet of Junior Brown*.

Joyce Sweeney, 'The Invisible Adolescent: Robert Cormier's *Fade*', in Nicholas J. Karolides (ed.), *Censored Books II: Critical Viewpoints 1985–2000* (Lanham, MD: Scarecrow, 2002): 163–6. Provides a rationale defending *Fade* against censorship challenges.

See also in 'General Criticism' above: Campbell, *Presenting Robert Cormier*; Headley; McCallum; Shen; Westwater.

Other Bells for Us to Ring (Darcy)

Patty Campbell, *Robert Cormier: Daring to Disturb the Universe* (New York: Delacorte, 2006). Includes a chapter on *Other Bells for Us to Ring (Darcy)*, *Tunes for Bears to Dance to* and *Heroes*.

See also in 'General Criticism' above: Shen.

We All Fall Down

Patty Campbell, *Robert Cormier: Daring to Disturb the Universe* (New York: Delacorte, 2006). Includes a chapter on *We All Fall Down* and *In the Middle of the Night*.

Michael Cart, *From Romance to Realism: 50 years of Growth and Change in Young Adult Literature* (New York: HarperCollins, 1996). Mentions Cormier several times. Discussion of *We All Fall Down*: 178–87.

Michael A. Grimm, 'Unfortunate Reality: Fictional Portrayals of Children and Violence', in Harry Eiss (ed.), *Images of the Child* (Bowling Green, OH: Bowling Green State University Popular Press, 1994): 115–41.

Jen Menzel, 'Intimidation in Cormier's *Tunes for Bears to Dance to*, *We All Fall Down*, and *The Chocolate War*', *The ALAN Review*, 31(1) (Fall 2003): 21–3: http://scholar.lib.vt.edu/ejournals/ALAN/v31n1/menzel.html (accessed 10 May 2012).

John S. Simmons, 'The Avenger Strikes Again: *We All Fall Down*', in Nicholas J. Karolides (ed.), *Censored Books II: Critical Viewpoints 1985–2000* (Lanham, MD: Scarecrow, 2002): 427–35.

See also in 'General Criticism' above: Foerstel; Herz and Gallo; Shen; Tarr (brief discussion).

Tunes for Bears to Dance to

Patty Campbell, *Robert Cormier: Daring to Disturb the Universe* (New York: Delacorte, 2006). Includes a chapter on *Other Bells for Us to Ring (Darcy)*, *Tunes for Bears to Dance to* and *Heroes*.

Janet E. Kaufman and Lynn Kaufman, 'Identity from Destructive Behavior: Robert Cormier's *Tunes for Bears to Dance to*', in Jeffrey S. Kaplan (ed.) *Using Literature to Help Troubled Teenagers Cope with Identity Issues* (Westport, CT: Greenwood Press, 1999): 167–86.

Adrienne Kertzer, '*Tunes for Bears to Dance To*: Prayers and Silence', in Alethea Helbig and Agnes Perkins (eds), *The Phoenix Award of the Children's Literature Association, 1995–1999* (Lanham, MD: Scarecrow Press, 2001): 133–7.

Jen Menzel, 'Intimidation in Cormier's *Tunes for Bears to Dance To*, *We All Fall Down*, and *The Chocolate War*', *The ALAN Review*, 31(1) (Fall 2003): 21–3: http://scholar.lib.vt.edu/ejournals/ALAN/v31n1/menzel.html (accessed 10 May 2012).

See also in 'General Criticism' above: Herz and Gallo; Monseau, *Teaching*; Shen.

In the Middle of the Night

Patty Campbell, *Robert Cormier: Daring to Disturb the Universe* (New York: Delacorte, 2006). Includes a chapter on *We All Fall Down* and *In the Middle of the Night*.

See also in 'General Criticism' above: Shen.

Tenderness

Patty Campbell, *Robert Cormier: Daring to Disturb the Universe* (New York: Delacorte, 2006). Includes a chapter on *Tenderness*.

See also in 'General Criticism' above: Shen; Tarr (brief discussion).

Heroes

Patty Campbell, *Robert Cormier: Daring to Disturb the Universe* (New York: Delacorte, 2006). Includes a chapter on *Other Bells for Us to Ring (Darcy)*, *Tunes for Bears to Dance to* and *Heroes*.

Kerry Mallan, 'Challenging the Phallic Fantasy in Young Adult Fiction', in John Stephens (ed.), *Ways of Being Male: Representing Masculinities in Children's Literature and Film* (New York: Routledge, 2002): 150–63. Includes discussion of masculinity in *Heroes*.

See also in 'General Criticism' above: Nilsen and Nilsen; Shen.

Frenchtown Summer

Patty Campbell, *Robert Cormier: Daring to Disturb the Universe* (New York: Delacorte, 2006). Includes a chapter on *Frenchtown Summer* and *The Rag and Bone Shop*.

Robert Cormier, 'A Character by Any Other Name...', *English Journal*, 90(3) (2001): 31–2. Cormier discusses naming his characters, including Eugene in *Frenchtown Summer.*

Lyn Gardner, 'Dead Bodies in Suburbia', *Guardian Review* 19 August 2000: www.guardian.co.uk/books/2000/aug/19/booksforchildrenandteenagers (accessed 10 May 2012). Briefly but usefully discusses Cormier's work especially *Frenchtown Summer.*

See also in 'General Criticism' above: Monseau, *Teaching.*

The Rag and Bone Shop

Patty Campbell, 'The Last Cormier', *Horn Book* 77(5) (September/October 2001): 623–6. Reprinted in Patty Campbell, *Campbell's Scoop: Reflections on Young Adult Literature* (Lanham, MD: Scarecrow, 2010): 106–11. Discusses *The Rag and Bone Shop.*

Patty Campbell, *Robert Cormier: Daring to Disturb the Universe* (New York: Delacorte, 2006). Includes a chapter on *Frenchtown Summer* and *The Rag and Bone Shop.*

See also in 'General Criticism' above: Shen; Monseau, *Teaching.*

Index